EtymologyRules

#wordsmatter
#wordmatters
#etymologyrules
#cultivateyourmind

ISBN: 978-0-578-35341-8 (Paperback)
ISBN: 978-0-578-35341-8 (Hardcover)

Design & Photography ℅ Sustain Branding (www.sustainbranding.com)

Printed by EtymologyRules, LLC., in the United States of America.

First printing edition 2021.

EtymologyRules Publishing
5230 Georgia Ave NW #305
Washington, DC 20011

www.EtymologyRules.com

Acknowledgements

To my mother and father, Ida and Prentis Lee:
Thank you for instilling in me a love of language and literacy at a young age. You planted the seeds of EtymologyRules long before it was even a thought. I dedicate this first book to you.

To my favorite English teacher, Victoria Merriweather:
I appreciate your love of words and passion for passing this on to others. Thank you for your insight and encouragement; for being a fellow visionary and seeing the bigger picture; and for your commitment to cultivate the minds of the youth.

To my design editor, David Son Dey:
From day one, you saw the essence of EtymologyRules. Your innovation and originality brought polish and refinement to this project. Looking forward to the next one!

To my teacher and friend, Abdullah EL Talib Mosi Bey:
I am forever grateful for your guidance and wisdom. Thank you for all the tutoring sessions, books, articles, phone calls, emails, lecture opportunities, networking, examples, ideas, knowledge, the list goes on...Thank you for helping me bring EtymologyRules to life.

Table of Contents

Pre-Test

Directions: Select the best answer to the following questions about words and their basic components and structure.

1) What is a **phoneme**?
   a. an utterance of sound conveying complete meaning on its own
   b. the smallest unit of sound in a given language
   c. the smallest unit of writing in a given language
   d. the smallest unit of meaning in a word that cannot be further divided

2) What is a **grapheme**?
   a. an utterance of sound conveying complete meaning on its own
   b. the smallest unit of sound in a given language
   c. the smallest unit of writing in a given language
   d. the smallest unit of meaning in a word that cannot be further divided

3) What is a **morpheme**?
   a. an utterance of sound conveying complete meaning on its own
   b. the smallest unit of sound in a given language
   c. the smallest unit of writing in a given language
   d. the smallest unit of meaning in a word that cannot be further divided

4) What is a **syllable**?
   a. a unit of pronunciation in a word that contains a vowel sound
   b. the smallest unit of sound in a given language
   c. a letter
   d. the smallest unit of meaning in a word that cannot be further divided

5) What is a **word**?
   a. an utterance of sound conveying complete meaning on its own
   b. the smallest unit of sound in a given language
   c. the smallest unit of writing in a given language
   d. the smallest unit of meaning in a word that cannot be further divided

6) Sort the following lexeme and lexical units into their respective groups; write the lexemes in the circles and the lexical units in the spaces below the circles.

do   penned   does   doesn't   penknife   trace

tracing   redo   did   pen name   pen pal   pen

( )   ( )

_____   _____

_____   _____

_____   _____

_____   _____

_____   _____

7) Circle the free morphemes and put a box around the bound morphemes.

class   rupt   gener   un   flip   try   fid

mount   recent   pro

8) True or False: the word reformer has a derivational ending. _____

9) How many *vowels, consonants, phonemes, graphemes, morphemes, and syllables* are in each of the listed words?

Word	Vowels	Consonants	Phonemes	Graphemes	Morphemes	Syllables
mislead						
scale						
graphic						

10) What type of vowel sound is in the word *jail*?
a.   long
b.   short
c.   r-influenced
d.   diphthong

11) What type of vowel sound is in the word *foil?*

a. long

b. short

c. r-influenced

d. diphthong

12) What type of consonant sound is in the word *be?*

a. labial

b. dental

c. guttural

d. semi-vowel

13) What type of consonant sound is underlined in the word <u>k</u>eep?

a. labial

b. dental

c. guttural

d. semi-vowel

14) List the **vibrating** or **voiced consonants** in each of these words:

a. diaper _____

b. gargle _____

c. chop _____

15) List the **plosives consonants** in each of these words:

a. vapor _____

b. teach _____

c. shake _____

16) What type of syllable is underlined in the following words (*choose from the following: closed, open, silent e, vowel team, consonant + le, or r-influenced*)?

a. <u>ti</u>ger _____

b. <u>bishop</u> _____

c. lit<u>tle</u> _____

17) What is the origin of each of the following words?

a. wife _____

b. solar _____

c. psychopath _____

18) Complete the prefix/root/suffix chart below. Be sure to give the meaning of the prefix and root, and the part of speech of the suffix.

Word	Prefix + meaning	Root + meaning	Suffix + POS
interdict			
retract			
malefactor			
verify			
asteroid			

Welcome to *EtymologyRules*. This is the first in a series of texts about words—their origins and components, their forms, their usages and their meanings, how they change over time, their relations to one another and how they affect our lives on a micro- and macrocosmic level. Etymology is the study of the true meaning of words, as *-ology* is "the study of" or, literally, "words pertaining to a given field or subject," and *etym-* comes from the Greek word *etymon*, meaning "truest" or "truth." So this book and overall series is about the truth behind words and are designed to give you guidelines behind analyzing and using words to effectively communicate your ideas- knowing word origins gives us a basis to learn about their presence in today's society. Learning about how words operate can ultimately help us strengthen our literacy skills, both reading and writing.

Imagine language was a meal—each word a dish and you a master chef parsing out its ingredients. Etymology becomes an imperative science to sharpen your senses. *Etymology* is the study of the "true sense of words," namely their lexical origins and evolutions. The term derives from the Greek words *etymon* meaning "truth" and *logia* meaning "words about." Thus, etymology is a treatise on the truth about words. And since words are symbols for knowledge, etymology is a discourse on the truth about ideas. After you read *EtymologyRules*, truths will begin to emerge as you boil words down into bite-sized parts and critically taste them, developing your palate to become word connoisseurs.

Book 1 of *EtymologyRules* is a workbook, so plan to interact with it. Take your time and let the concepts sink in. See the exercises as mental weightlifting and etymology as a barbell loaded with lexical weight. *EtymologyRules* is your linguistic workout program that strengthens your word usage, critical reading and writing skills, and it makes you a more effective communicator.

EtymologyRules: Back to Basics can teach you to dissect a word, revealing basic spelling patterns and the grammatical structure of the English tongue. Each chapter teaches you about phonemes, graphemes and morphemes; roots and affixes; parts of speech; the history of English; and word origins. These are the basics of vocabulary acquisition. Knowing about words improves how we interpret language. Words are capsules filled with meaning; when words combine, they share the masterpieces that swell throughout humans' minds.

— So, without further ado, I present
EtymologyRules: The Basics

Rule 1: <u>Struggles with reading and illiteracy have become a global epidemic, primarily affecting those indigenous to Africa and the American continents.</u>

North America: The United States of America

Illiteracy is a global affliction that impedes social progress throughout both first- and third-world nations. Surprisingly, the United States suffers this plight despite its economic stability and high standards of living (both of which sociologists often correlate with high literacy rates).

In 2019, the National Institute of Literacy reported that 43 million Americans possess low literacy skills, 8.2 million of whom are functionally literate. Forty to sixty percent of post-secondary students were required to take remedial reading classes in their first year of college (Jimenez et. al, 2016). The National Assessment of Educational Progress (also known as the Nation's Report Card) reported that in 2019, over 60% of fourth- and eighth-grade students scored below proficient in reading (proficiency meaning demonstrating an ability to "interpret and recall basic information" and "make inferences when reading a text"). The following are fourth-grade proficiency reading scores, as reported by Nation's Report Card:

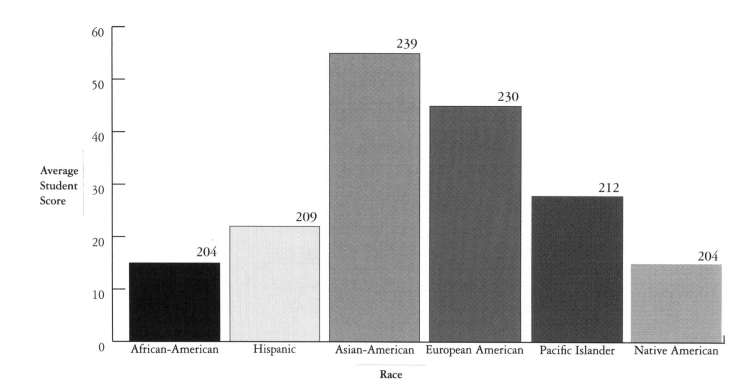

These statistics confirm that there is an achievement gap in America between people of varying races. Indeed, the achievement gap is not an indication of cognitive abilities; it exists because of lack of resources. Wealthier, often white, communities have access to test prep, extracurricular learning opportunities and private tutors. The achievement gap reflects far-reaching racist policies created to support the notion of white superiority. This is important to note. Many psychologists in past years sought to use statistics on reading and race to purport that Blacks were inherently less intelligent than whites; many scholars have artfully refuted this claim. In *The Mismeasure of Man*, Stephen Jay Gould contends that intelligence cannot be quantified into an intelligence test's single number. Ranking people based on this artificial measure is an effort to justify the disparities among races worldwide by claiming that superior intelligence is inherently a white trait.

Nonetheless, it is quite alarming that reading levels vary based on race even today, as noted in US News & World Report:

> [T]he achievement gap between white students and Black students has barely narrowed over the last 50 years, despite nearly a half century of supposed progress in race relations and an increased emphasis on closing such academic discrepancies between groups of students (2015, p. 1).

The NAEP has analyzed the results of reading assessments nationwide since 1992 and found that the average fourth grader scored below proficient. Current educational practices and systems are not meeting students' needs, and communities that have historically been denied access to quality education are most in need of effective literacy instruction by knowledgeable and experienced teachers.

In addition to race and ethnicity, there is an achievement gap between children from high-income versus low-income communities. In 2019, students eligible for the National School Lunch Program (NSLP) scored below proficient. Again, the results of this assessment do not speak to intelligence but to one's access to quality education. In the early grades, low-income students perform on par with middle-class students; however, low-income students sustain small losses during the summer whereas middle-class students experience small gains (Gunning, 2013, p. 44). This is often due to middle-class families' access to academic enrichment programs to mitigate regression and ensure children continue to strengthen their literacy skills. Low-income families and communities tend to have fewer resources allocated for enrichment opportunities through camps and tutors.

Exposure also plays a role in the academic achievement gap; educated parents expose their children to texts and establish a culture of literacy in the home. As children have access to quality reading materials and see their parents read for pleasure, they are more inclined to engage in reading during free time, contributing to their literacy development. In addition, children of educated parents acquire academic vocabulary through family discussions during which parents use higher-level language. Thus, children of educated parents in high-income households tend to have strong comprehension because of their exposure to texts and vocabulary. With such disparities, a gap in achievement between the rich and the poor is inevitable and bound to grow without remedy or intervention.

The literacy epidemic requires immediate attention as illiteracy is one of the strongest common factors among incarcerated individuals (Kidder, 1990). Individuals with poor academic achievement are more likely to join gangs (O'Cummings, Bardack and Gonsoulin, 2010), and juveniles with low literacy are more likely to engage in criminal behavior (EDJJ, 2015), both of which lead to incarceration. In his book *Retarding America: The Imprisonment of Potential*, National Institute of Justice researcher Michael Brunner states "[r]eviews of the research literature provide ample evidence of the link between academic failure and delinquency...this link is welded to reading failure" (p. v). Causation is certainly understandable if not expected. In modern society, people write to keep records of everything—textbooks and manuals contain records of information and ideas. Contracts are records of agreements between two or more parties. In law, constitutions and case law are written records of legal understandings that dictate established precedents and principles to govern a policy. Literacy is a survival skill in the 21st century, the lack of which inhibits access. As the strain theory notes, the likelihood of crime increases with an uptick in life stressors (such as a lack of resources), and poor literacy skills limit one's access to resources.

Additionally, illiteracy limits access to keys that illuminate the mind, leaving humanity in the dark. This is why thesauri state that *illiteracy* is synonymous with *blindness*. The erudite man is one who has "been brought out of darkness into marvelous light." Literacy is a method of communicating thought and evidences a progressive, enlightened society, allowing one to freely consider, express and access information and ideas.

Countries in Crisis: South Asia and sub-Saharan Africa

UNESCO (2016) reports that there are 758 million illiterate adults worldwide and that two-thirds are women. Countries in South Asia and sub-Saharan Africa yield the lowest literacy rates; less than 50 percent of the population read and write proficiently while in Central and Eastern Asia, Europe and the Americas, the average literacy rate is higher than 90 percent. Literacy often becomes a focal point in developing nations implementing plans for modernization. Correlation studies show that literate societies are wealthier than those with pervasive illiteracy and those that improve their literacy rates decrease the percentage of people living in poverty. Bangladesh, Brazil, China, Egypt, India, Indonesia, Mexico, Nigeria and Pakistan serve as examples of this phenomenon.

The ability to read is the ability to make meaning of a series of written statements just as people do when listening to someone speak. Statements contain words, which are symbols of thoughts and ideas. One's knowledge and breadth of words, then, represents the body of their ideas and the quality of their thinking. Moreover, the ability to make meaning with said words is the ability to construct and share concepts that shape perspectives and influence identities. Nations with highly literate populations can record and transmit culture. Literate societies spread ideas to a significant number of people who, in turn, can read about and create new ideas. Literacy is fundamental to cultural development and progressive thinking among people and societies worldwide.

Rule 2: <u>Reading instruction involves five components and all must be present for children to develop literacy skills.</u>

The *EtymologyRules* book series also serves to inform the reader of the basic components of reading instruction. In an effort to help teachers, caregivers, administrators and policymakers, each book will provide insight into various aspects to reading. Strong schools and learning centers require effective reading programs. There is much debate about what methods and techniques yield the best results. The National Reading Panel (2000), a commission of the National Institute of Child Health and Human Development, identifies five components of reading instruction developing readers need to be strong readers:

• phonemic awareness • phonics • fluency • vocabulary • text comprehension

This book addresses the first three components while the entire series helps readers strengthen their vocabulary, fluency and comprehension. Phonemic awareness and phonics can both be categorized under "alphabetics" and are necessary for readers to develop decoding and word recognition skills[1] while vocabulary and text comprehension are under the comprehension umbrella. Both are essential to make meaning of the text.

Alphabetics

Phonemic awareness is the ability to distinguish between phonemes or individual sounds in a word. The NRP defines phonemes as "the smallest units constituting spoken language." The English language consists of about 44 phonemes. Phonemic awareness is a branch of **phonological awareness**, which University of Virginia professor Marcia Invernizzi (2017) defines as the "conscious ability to tend to and manipulate the sounds within words, including syllables, onset and rime and phonemes" (Reading Foundations lecture). Phonemes, or sounds in a word, are important because words are a compilation of

[1]"Word recognition is the ability of a reader to recognize written words correctly and virtually effortlessly" (Bruce and Davidson, 2002).

sounds and recognizing sound distinctions helps one distinguish between words. For example, lock contains three sounds: /l/, /ŏ/, and /k/. Changing the initial consonant sound to /s/ creates the word *sock* with a different semantic representation. Thus, phonemic awareness is a foundational skill for emergent readers and writers. Phonemic awareness tasks ask students to isolate, identify, categorize, blend, segment and delete phonemes in words.

Exercise	Description	Example
Isolation	recognizing the individual sound in a word	"What is the first sound in mat?" (/m/)
Identification	recognizing the common sound in different words	"What sound is the same in bat, beg, and bell?" (/b/)
Categorization	recognizing the word with the odd sound given three or four words	"Which word does not belong: bat, beg, map?" (map)
Blending	listening to a sequence of separately spoken sounds and combining them to form a known word	"What word is /r/ /u/ /n/?" (run)
Segmentation	breaking a word into its sounds by tapping out or counting the sounds or by pronouncing or pointing out each sound	"How many phonemes are in the word bush?" (three: /b/ /u/ /sh/)
Deletion	recognizing what remains when a specific phoneme is removed	"What is stop without the /s/?" (top)

Early readers must develop phonemic awareness to recognize letter-sound relationships and begin to decode words. "Correlation studies have identified phonemic awareness and letter knowledge as the two best school-entry predictors of how well children will learn to read during their first two years in school" (NRP, 1999, p. 2-1). Phoneme manipulation helps students improve their word reading and spelling skills. Additionally, at-risk and disabled readers benefit from both informal and explicit phonemic awareness instruction.

Next, early readers must understand that written words contain letters that represent the 44 phonemes of the English language. These letters or **graphemes** are symbols, and readers must have knowledge of and use sound-symbol relationships to "come up with an approximate pronunciation of a word and then check it against his or her oral vocabulary" (Blevins, 1998, p. 8). Thus, students benefit from phonics instruction, which teaches students to map sounds into spellings and enables readers to decode words. Decoding words is a strategy that helps readers develop word recognition. To **decode** a word involves analyzing its letters to determine the sounds they represent and blending the sounds together to produce a word. As beginning readers build their sight word knowledge and recognize more words automatically, they begin to read more fluently. Fluent reading allows readers to focus mental energy on discerning the meaning of text. Many older students with reading difficulties have poor word attack and fluency skills because of a lack of a foundation in phonics, which subsequently impacts their comprehension (Flanigan, Hayes, Templeton, Bear, & Invernizzi, 2010). As text complexity increases, students require a sound method of decoding multisyllabic words quickly and efficiently. Fluent reading allows them to spend more mental energy on making meaning of the text. Many older students with reading difficulty are found to have poor word attack and fluency skills because of a lack of foundation in phonics which subsequently impacts their comprehension (Flanigan, Hayes, Templeton, Bear & Invernizzi, 2010).

Phonics is taught a variety of ways as indicated in the chart below:

Method	Description
Synthetic	Looking at letters which indicate phonemes present in the word, students learn to convert letters into sounds and blend them into words.
Analytic	Learning phonemes and spelling patterns by analyzing a set of words with a common phoneme; students recognize spelling features through inductive reasoning.
Embedded	This is phonics taught in context; students only learn to decode a word they encounter in text.
Analogy-based	Learning to use parts of word families that students know to identify unknown words that have similar parts.
Onset-rime	Learning to identify the sound of the letter or letters before the first vowel (onset) and the sounds remaining in a word (rime) for example, students learn the word family *ack*: *black, stack, shack, sack, rack*.
Phonics through Spelling	Learning to segment words into phonemes and make words by writing letters for phonemes.

A high number of scholars and researchers support the claim that African-American children and children living in poverty benefit from systematic, direct phonics instruction (Kunjufu, 2009; Ladson-Billings, 1994; Baumann, 1998; Perkins and Cooter, 2006; Strickland, 1994). Direct instruction refers to the implementation of straightforward and explicit instructional techniques used to teach a specific skill. Systematic phonics teaches the letter-sound correspondences in a methodical manner. As students learn to read words, their fluency and comprehension improve. Thus, an effective foundational or remedial reading program requires systematic phonics instruction for students to develop strong word attack and word acquisition skills.

The NRP found that the synthetic method is the most effective way to teach phonics; however, several studies also indicate that an analytic approach is also beneficial to students as they can employ inductive reasoning and critical thinking skills rather than rote memorization. Regardless of the method, research indicates that phonics instruction is key to developing fluent readers. Despite this, many teachers do not teach phonics, contributing to the reading epidemic America faces today.

Most researchers agree that teachers should expose all students to some form of phonics instruction in early education; this gives them the tools to decode words using their knowledge of sound-symbol relationships. Additionally, effective reading programs include **syllabic analysis**, teaching students to use sub-units or word parts and syllabication rules to decode multisyllabic words. Phonics instruction teaches students to read single-syllable one-syllable words, while syllabic analysis instruction teaches students to read monosyllabic words. Researchers have found remediation that includes phonics and syllabic analysis instruction benefits three types of students: kindergarten and first graders identified as "at-risk" readers; students with learning disabilities; and second through sixth graders who are low achieving in subject areas that rely heavily on reading and writing (NRP, 2000). While adolescent struggling readers can benefit from phonics instruction to build word attack skills, it is ideal for students to build these skills as beginning readers. Thus, alphabetics instruction overall is a good preventative measure that builds fluent readers who can comprehend a text.

Fluency

Fluency comes from the Latin word *fluentia*, meaning "to flow." Thus, speaking fluently means to be able to speak using words freely and with ease; it is as if thoughts flow smoothly like a stream. **Reading fluency** is the ability to read a text free from word identification problems that impede text comprehension in both silent and oral reading (Gunning, 2013). Fluency then frees readers from using their mental energy to decode a text; instead, they use their mental energy to make meaning of a text (comprehension). As mentioned, fluency is both an oral and silent reading skill. While most people equate fluency to reading rate alone, oral reading fluency also measures accuracy, automaticity and prosody.

Tim Rasinski, Professor of Education in the Department of Teaching, Leadership and Curriculum Studies at Kent State University, defines fluency as the "ability to develop and have control over surface-level text processing so that [the reader] can focus on understanding the deeper levels of meaning embedded in the text" (Rasinski, 2004, p. 46).

Fluent readers can read text with accuracy at a consistent pace or with automaticity and proper expression or *prosody*.

Automaticity is the ability to read and decode words accurately, effortlessly and without delay (Rasinski & Samuels, 2011). Systematic phonics instruction builds the word attack skills necessary for readers to pronounce the word, but students must develop automaticity so they can utilize their mental faculties to comprehend text rather than decode it. Repeated exposure to these words helps students build word recognition, thus increasing their ability to read a text fluently. As readers automatically recognize words, they begin to increase the number of words they can read in a minute, or their **reading rate**, which is critical in determining a reader's level. (See Grade Levels + Reading Rate chart in the Appendix.) Slow and choppy reading is considered dysfluent and, in most cases, is evidence that the reader does not understand the text.

As students develop automaticity at an appropriate rate, they began to read text with melodic inflection, developing **prosodic reading**. Reading with prosody means to use pitch, stress and timing to convey meaning when reading aloud. Prosody in reading is an indication that readers are making sense of the text and, thus, can be said to aid in developing comprehension as it builds a bridge between automaticity and comprehension (Rasinski & Samuels, 2011). Therefore, reading rate, automaticity and prosody are essential aspects of fluency, which in turn is necessary to comprehend text—the ultimate goal of reading.

Thus, it can be said that:

- Strong, fluent readers: read with expression, read in phrases and clauses, use intonation[2] and pauses based on punctuation

- Weak, dysfluent readers: lack expression, read word by word, and read with improper intonation and pauses (punctuation is a miscue or not a cue at all)

---

[2] Intonation: changes in tone and pitch based on the meaning of the text

Many teachers do not think that fluency is important. Cassidy and Cassidy publish "What's Hot in Reading" annually, and for years teachers have rated fluency both not hot and not a significant component of reading instruction (2010–2017). However, research and experience show that fluency instruction is key for emergent, beginning and transitional readers to start to build independence and begin truly enjoying and learning from the texts they read.

Comprehension

The term *comprehension* is most often used synonymously with the word *understand*. Teachers often think asking students "did you understand what you read?" is the same as asking "did you comprehend?" However, reading comprehension comprises more than simply understanding the text; it requires the reader to make meaning using words present in a text and the reader's prior knowledge.

Most importantly, reading **comprehension** requires thought and cognition, and the reader makes meaning given his or her knowledge of graphemes and phonemes, morphemes, syntax (how words and phrases are organized to create well-formed sentences), semantics (what words mean or represent) and context, all while recognizing and in some cases, decoding, words. The word *comprehend* comes from the Latin word *comprehendere*, meaning 'to take together, unite, or include' (*com* 'together' + *prehendere* 'grasp'); during comprehension the mind uses information presented to *seize* or *grasp* the author's overall message. Reading comprehension happens when the reader analyzes the author's words so that the mind can take hold of an idea; it is a magical moment, as the reader allows the text to activate their thinking and engages the author's message rather than passively receiving information. There are two types of comprehension: (1) vocabulary or word comprehension, and (2) passage or text comprehension.

Vocabulary comprehension is the ability to understand the idea(s) that a word represents. A word is a symbol of thoughts or ideas, and the more words a student knows, the more discriminating they can be with their thoughts. With regard to reading, the importance of vocabulary has long been recognized by educators. In 1925, the *Yearbook of the National Society for the Study of Education* (Hiebert and Kamil, 2005, p.1) noted: "growth in reading power means, therefore, continuous enriching and enlarging of the reading vocabulary and increasing clarity of discernment in the appreciation of word values."

Academic achievement is closely tied to vocabulary and reading comprehension. At all levels of instruction, students read text to learn information, gain new perspectives and evaluate others' propositions. Learning words is directly connected to learning new concepts, particularly in the history, social studies, and science classrooms. For example, subject-specific words such as *tyranny*, *microeconomics*, *photosynthesis*, and *cognition* are fundamental to learning in history, economics, biology and psychology classes. Additionally, one must use their knowledge of vocabulary to label new ideas in science and technology (i.e. *internet*, *gigabyte*, and *emoticon*). Thus, vocabulary can impact a person's success in their academic and professional career.

It is crucial to include robust vocabulary instruction when teaching a student to read. A student's vocabulary grows from wide reading or reading text from a range of genres and for a variety of purposes (Cooper, Furry and Van Vleck, 2008). However, students reading below their grade level often have an aversion to reading independently due to a) poor reading experiences in school; or b) lack of exposure to text at their appropriate level (leading to dysfluent reading and poor text comprehension). As teachers expose students to difficult text with little support, they struggle to read and begin to avoid reading.

Good writers and readers must develop a sophisticated use of and understanding of language. Language abilities are categorized as both *expressive* and *receptive*. **Expressive language** describes how a person communicates their wants and needs. It refers to the use of words, sentences, gestures and writing to convey meaning and messages to others and includes the vocabulary one uses during written and spoken communication. Expressive language skills are essential for writers to create simple and complex sentences. **Receptive language** is a person's ability to understand the gestures and words they see, read and hear. Both expressive and receptive language skills are required for students to develop strong vocabulary skills. They must be able to use words accurately during writing activities and understand word meanings while reading. Students must specifically develop their expressive and receptive vocabulary to be effective writers and readers, respectively. Also, writers and readers must use active vocabulary (words that a person both uses and understands) and their passive vocabulary (words that a person understands but does not actively use). Lastly, students require academic vocabulary to be successful readers, writers and learners overall. Academic vocabulary can be categorized into the following tiers (Beck, McKeown, & Kucan, 2002):

Tier 1 or *Basic General Vocabulary*: high-frequency words that often appear in oral language; they are most often learned by listening to and engaging in everyday speech. Examples include *dog*, *book*, *that*, *it*, etc.

Tier 2 or *Descriptive Vocabulary*: high-frequency words that appear in a variety of contexts and domains. These words often have multiple meanings. Examples include *measure*, *inverse*, *liberal*, *equation*, etc.

Tier 3 or *Precision Vocabulary*: low-frequency and subject-specific words and phrases. Examples include *sovereignty, permafrost, isotope, economics,* etc.

Poor vocabulary negatively impacts comprehension when students read text that has too many difficult words. Educational researcher William Nagy notes that "[t]he proportion of difficult words in a text is the single most powerful predictor of text difficulty and a reader's general vocabulary knowledge is the single best predictor of how well the person will understand [a] text" (2003, p. 1). Thus, students require both direct and indirect instruction to learn new words as well as strategies to understand words' meanings both in and out of context.

Students should learn to use morphemic analysis and context clues to understand unknown words. They must also learn to use a dictionary effectively. **Morphemic analysis** refers to the ability to identify word meanings based on affixes and roots as well as word derivations. For example, if a reader knows the prefix re means 'back, again,' they have insight into the meaning of words like *revision, reinstitute* and *reignite*. Knowing that the root vert means 'to turn' provides a clue to the meanings of words like *introvert, inverted* and *revert*.

Intermediate and advanced readers and writers use morphemic analysis to read all types and genres of text; thus, morphemic analysis is key to literacy development. Using **context clues** is a strategy in which the reader defines unknown words in a sentence by closely studying its surrounding words. Writers often give clues, such as the definition or a synonym, an antonym or situations and explanations that give readers hints at a word's meaning. Readers must learn how to use these clues to understand an author's usage of a word. Lastly, readers should become familiar with how lexicographers organize dictionaries and how they define words; advanced readers begin to distinguish between denotations, connotations, word usages and shifts in word meanings. A good dictionary is a resourceful tool for a reader, especially one who reads a wide variety of texts.

While it is crucial for readers to decode words, read fluently, and learn word meanings, students must have opportunity to develop their text or passage comprehension. Comprehension is more than simply "understanding the text"; it involves the reader actively engaging in making connections between the text and their thinking in order to make meaning. Reading comprehension is an interactive process "involving the reader, the text, and the context in which the text is read" (Gunning, 2016, p. 309). To strengthen comprehension skills, students must develop prior knowledge, learn strategies and understand their purpose for reading.

Linguists and psychologists explain text comprehension through the schema and situational model theories. The **schema theory** espouses that readers rely on *schemata*, units of organized knowledge, to comprehend the text. As readers read, they use what they already know or *background knowledge* to make predictions, ask questions and make inferences about the text. The **situational model** views comprehension as a process of building mental models of the information, situations and events depicted in the text. Words and syntax convey a surface-level meaning called a *textbase*. Readers use the textbase to develop a running summary of a text, which ultimately builds a mental model of said text. The main difference between the schema and situational model theories is that the schema theory views the reader as bringing knowledge and interacting with the text, whereas the situational model views the reader as gaining information from the text. One could say that the "schema theory describes how familiar situations are understood; situation model theory describes how new situations are comprehended" (Gunning, 2016, p. 310). Both models of comprehension indicate that good readers think intentionally about the text and utilize specific strategies to interact with the text.

Readers employ comprehension strategies before reading (*preparational*); during reading (*organizational* and *elaboration*); and after reading (*metacognitive*).

Preparational strategies:
- previewing or scanning the text
- activating prior knowledge about the topic of the text
- predicting events or the information to be learned through the text
- setting the purpose of reading the text

Organizational strategies:
- understanding the central idea of a passage or the main idea of a paragraph
- identifying and distinguishing important details
- sequencing and organizing details
- paraphrasing and summarizing

Elaboration:
- making inferences
- visualizing the text
- producing questions about the text
- evaluating the author's message

Metacognitive:
- monitoring and regulating one's comprehension
- reviewing and evaluating one's reading performance

• repairing or correcting comprehension struggles

Classroom teachers and researchers have found that these strategies enhance one's comprehension of the text (Keene & Zimmerman, 1997). Initially, these strategies require a considerable amount of mental input, but with practice readers learn to generalize each strategy during authentic, real-world reading.

Thus, reading is not a passive act but, rather, an interactive mental process. Readers bring their reasoning skills, attention and prior knowledge to construct meaning. Also, readers must utilize surface features, such as word choice and sentence structure. Those with inadequate vocabulary or who have difficulty with syntax will struggle to understand more complex passages. Thus, students need to develop word recognition through phonics, fluency and adequate language skills (including vocabulary) to comprehend text.

Struggling readers often have a significant gap in one or more of the five components of reading and understandably so. A reader who lacks strong word attack and word reading skills will likely struggle with **text** or **passage comprehension**. Comprehension is more than merely "understanding the text"; it involves the reader actively engaging in making connections between the text and their thinking to make meaning. Reading comprehension then is "intentional thinking" to construction meaning; it is an interactive process "involving the reader, the text and the context in which the text is read" (Gunning, 2016, p. 309).

Rule 3: <u>School instructional leaders should place more emphasis on teachers providing word study instruction to help students develop phonemic awareness, decoding and vocabulary skills, which ultimately improves their fluency and text comprehension.</u>

One particular rule specifically addresses phonemic awareness and phonics because educators and policymakers hold varying views on best practices for developing early readers' skills. Over the past 20 years, an increasing number of teachers have adopted the *whole language* or *meaning-centered* approach to reading instruction. Whole language is a teaching philosophy in which emerging and early readers are exposed to whole text and are encouraged to make meaning by analyzing graphophonic, semantic and syntactic aspects of language. The whole language approach encourages students to memorize words as whole units as opposed to using sound-symbol relationships and word attack skills. Instead of learning decoding skills in isolation, whole language instruction teaches students various literacy skills (including decoding and word attack) through minilessons and conferences.

Thus, teachers provide phonics instruction through discussion and activities from texts that children have read and reread with their teacher and by writing letters to represent the sounds that they hear in words. Invented spelling is encouraged and students learn spelling and grammar rules by editing their own writing. Proponents of whole language, such as Constance Weaver, believe this method is more effective than teaching systematic phonics, as "forming concepts about language—oral or written—is easier when learners are presented with whole, natural language, not unnatural language patterns…not the vastly simplified language of some primers in basal reading programs and not bits and pieces of language found in many workbook exercises and skills programs" (1996).

The problem with whole language instruction is that students do not receive the phonics foundation necessary to decode unfamiliar words. Research shows that good readers can use phonics to break down newly encountered words. Once students can attack and identify words, they can begin to develop reading fluency—that is, the ability to read text smoothly, accurately, clearly and with expression. This is how students become independent readers who focus on comprehending the text.

In addition to phonics and phonemic awareness, this first text in the series teaches beginning vocabulary skills. Learning about morphemes and word parts helps students understand how words and word meanings are formed. Additionally, students must learn about denotation and connotation to better understand why words have multiple meanings. An etymological instructional approach to vocabulary teaches students how to analyze morphemes and word origins as opposed to solely using context clues. Many teachers question whether students need to learn word parts and morphemic analysis. Some believe that students only need exposure to vocabulary in context, not direct instruction on word study and building vocabulary skills.

Direct vocabulary instruction is extremely important for developing readers and a strong word study curriculum is rooted in etymology. Etymological instruction teaches students to analyze morphemes (prefixes, root and suffixes in a word) to define unknown words while reading a text. Ninety percent of multisyllabic words in the English lexicon are of Latin origin, and most other words are Greek-based (What Percentage of English Words are Derived From Latin, Dictionary.com, n.d.). Literacy expert Tim Rasinski states that through morphology, students can learn 1,000-4,000 new words each year, as one root word can expose students to 20 different words (2008). Thus, when students study word origins, morphemes and Latin and Greek derivatives, they can find success in language arts, science, social studies and mathematics classes—for isn't vocabulary critical to all areas of learning?

Is vocabulary instruction necessary for students to improve their literacy? According to Graves and Fitzgerald (2006), school reading material contains more than 180,000 words. As stated earlier, students develop their vocabularies through wide reading. There is a direct correlation between time spent reading independently and the number of words read per year. Students who are reading text that is too difficult or who only read for one minute a day read 106,000 words a year, while students who read texts at their instructional or independent level for at least 20 minutes a day read over 1.8 million words a year (Anderson, Wilson and Fielding, 1988). Students must learn to use morphemic analysis and contextual clues while reading to comprehend unknown words.

One of the best ways to develop phonics, phonemic awareness and vocabulary is through word study. Word study is an instructional approach developed by researchers and professors of literacy education (Bear, Invernizzi, Templeton & Johnston, 2004). The premise of the approach is that students' spelling attempts give insight into their reading, particularly how they decode words and comprehend word meanings. Contrary to popular belief, most English words follow a predictable spelling pattern based on orthographic generalizations and etymological principles. Emergent readers develop phonemic awareness while beginning and transitional readers learn phonics and syllabic analysis for decoding purposes. Intermediate and advanced readers learn to use morphemic analysis as well as dictionary usage skills to determine the meaning of academic vocabulary. Most importantly, students categorize words based on common features rather than engage in rote memorization. For example, beginning readers may sort the words *back, bake, smack, stack, lake, Jake, black* and *rake* into two categories based on the sounds in the word (long versus short a) and spelling patterns (*-ck* versus the *-ke*) and discover generalizations or rules of the English language. Research has shown that students become effective decoders and spellers via word study, which ultimately helps students improve their reading fluency and overall comprehension.

Overall, good literacy instruction should teach orthographic aspects of language (for decoding and spelling), fluency, vocabulary by way of morphology and semantics, mental models and strategies for comprehension and, most importantly, provide the opportunity to practice and utilize word knowledge and reading strategies through authentic reading experiences (Bear, 1991; Bear, Invernizzi, Templeton and Johnston, 2004; Moats, 2000).

Rule 4: <u>Concepts of Words in Text (COW-T), prosody, syntax and leveled reading are critical aspects of reading instruction.</u>

Phonemic awareness and COW-T

While late elementary, middle and high school teachers are primarily responsible for strengthening students' vocabulary and comprehension skills, our early childhood and early elementary school teachers lay literacy foundations, allowing students to decode and fluently read text. But how does this process take place? How does a child go from being a pretend reader to being able to read and eventually comprehend a text? It begins with students being able to identify words in print, developing as a child's "concept of word in text (COW-T)" (Morris, 1993). An analysis of a child's sight word knowledge, finger-pointing reading and invented spelling shows that a child has phonological awareness (and, in the case of late beginning readers, phonemic awareness), which aids them in the development of COW-T and, ultimately, the ability to begin to read.

Prosody and expression in fluency

Prosody is a critical part of fluency; expression and intonation indicate that a reader is comprehending the text. However, many teachers do not include this in their instruction. Beginning and transition readers benefit from modeled reading, reader's theatre, paired reading and reading chants, poetry and songs to improve their prosody.

Syntax and grammar—phrasal fluency

Many readers struggle with fluency because of the various types of phrases in sentences. Some are confused by the commas and the syntax of language; these students' require both modeled reading and explicit instruction in reading and grammar. **Grammar** is the study of how the sentences are constructed in a given language; emphasis is placed on rules designating the placement of phrases, clauses and words to create sentences. Grammar is an often overlooked but important component of effective literacy instruction as it explains how words in a given language function. Additionally, teachers can teach transitional readers common phrases through explicit phrasal fluency activities. This, combined with grammar instruction, exposes students to English syntax.

Stages of Reading Development

The Stages of Reading Development is a continuum of literacy skills that readers develop over time. Rather than simply reporting a student's reading level, which is often nondescript, identifying a reader's stage informs parents and teachers of the student's instructional needs, allowing for instruction to specifically meet the learner's needs.

Literacy researchers Chall, Ehri, Frith and Juel have independently identified a similar progression through the stages of reading (Bear, Invernizzi, Templeton and Johnston, 1996, p. 21). The five stages of reading and writing are as follows:

Pre-literate/Emergent Reader and Writer

Learning to read begins at birth. Oral language is a necessary foundational skill that parents naturally impart when they talk to and around their infant children. During this time, children should engage in wordplay, and parents should model good reading for their child. In addition, emergent readers should learn rhymes and engage in wordplay to develop oral language skills. Parents should read to their children and, as they build oral language skills, have discussions about the text they read together. Children often engage in pretend reading, which leads to word recognition and beginning word decoding. As emergent readers, they are learning how to segment speech into words, syllables and sounds. In addition, they are considered pre-alphabetic, as they are building their ability to identify, recognize and write letters. Their ultimate goal is to develop COW-T, phonemic awareness and alphabet knowledge. As emergent writers, children often begin by making illegible markings and eventually make efforts to write letters they see most often in the texts they read.

Beginning Reader and Writer

These learners have developed basic COW-T and phonemic awareness skills and are thus able to attend to sounds in a word for decoding purposes. These skills allow students to build sight word knowledge and read decodable text. At this level, learners both read and write word by word; they spell using letter names and vowel sounds as they are now alphabetic and understand the sound-symbol relationship. Their oral reading is choppy as they focus on decoding words and word recognition versus reading for meaning. The goal of a beginning reader and writer is to become a fluent reader by building decoding skills and automatic word reading. Word study is key; students should learn medial short vowels, beginning and ending consonants, and consonant blends and digraphs. In addition, repeated readings of decodable text help students build reading stamina and fluency, a key to progress through the stages of reading and writing.

Transitional Reader and Writer

As beginning readers read, they build decoding skills and harvest more sight words. Knowing how to read more words allows students to read fluently and attend more to the meaning of a text rather than on word decoding and recognition. A transitional reader is one that has built a sustainable amount of reading fluency; there is less finger-point reading and word-by-word reading. This allows students to read silently and engage in more independent reading. They are able to write fluently due to the fact that they can spell more words with automaticity. They have great speed and spend less attention on spelling so they can concentrate on their ideas. They also have a greater sophistication in their written expression, especially as they develop their vocabularies. In spelling, students develop knowledge of long vowel spelling patterns, diphthongs, complex consonants and homophones. Parents can help readers at this stage by encouraging children to read at home for at least 20 minutes daily.

Intermediate Reader and Writer

At the intermediate stage, readers are expanding their interests and beginning to integrate and sharpen their use of reading strategies. Reading fluency and rate has significantly increased, and students read with greater prosody and expression. As writers, they are confident. They are developing a clear voice and can attend to their audience and their purpose. In word study, they learn about syllable junctures and how to identify affixes to read multisyllabic words. They can work on longer pieces and revise and edit their works. Instructional focus should be on content area and disciplinary reading; in particular, students should be able to recognize the various text structures and text features most commonly found in content-area text. Vocabulary should be a significant focal area of literacy instruction, as it is key to improving comprehension, particularly academic vocabulary. Students should also be exposed to new topics and genres to develop their background knowledge.

Advanced Reader

Advanced readers have a substantial amount of word knowledge and are learning to use the generative process to read unknown words. The generative process refers to segmenting words into morphemic chunks (Greek and Latin word elements and affixes) to identify the meaning of the word. Critical reading instruction should also be a primary focus for the advanced reader. Writers can produce different forms for a variety of purposes and functions; they can distinguish between different structures based on the writing genre. Additionally, an expanding vocabulary improves their word choice and ultimately strengthens individual style and voice. A strong vocabulary allows advanced writers to revise and edit their works more effectively and use the language with greater precision.

Reading Level

While those who fill the seats of government stress the importance of high-stakes standardized tests (state tests such as SOLs in Virginia and PARCC in Washington, D.C. and Maryland), teachers use reading diagnostics to determine a student's reading level. Reading specialists use a variety of diagnostic tools, including reading inventories, interviews and surveys; writing samples and spelling assessments. Reading inventories consist of two activities: reading *words in isolation and reading words in context.*

Students first read words in isolation to demonstrate their word attack and word recognition skills. Next, they read leveled passages and answer questions about a series of passages while the teacher records students responses. The teacher also takes a record of students' oral and silent reading to determine fluency. Assessors calculate the percentage of words read correctly in the context of the passage and the number of words read per minute. All of these factors combined indicate students' independent, instructional and frustration level of reading. Developing readers should include students reading text at their independent level on their own and at their instructional level with a teacher. Reading text at their frustration level should be avoided as much as possible, for readers then struggle to fluently read and comprehend the text.

A Note on Word Study

Word study is a philosophical framework based on the developmental spelling theory. The premise is that teachers gain insight into a student's orthographic knowledge of words based on their spelling. Orthography refers to "straight writing" (ortho 'straight, correct' and graph 'write, writing') and focuses on sounds in words and spelling patterns used to represent sounds. As students' orthographic knowledge develops, they strengthen their ability to read, comprehend, spell and use words astutely. Word study progresses as well through five phases that correlate to the five stages of reading and writing development. However, the five stages exist within three overarching layers of English spelling: alphabetic, pattern and meaning (Henderson, 1990).

The Alphabetic Layer

At this level, beginning writers rely on sound-symbol relationships to spell words. That is, they use single letters to represent individual sounds. This layer of English orthography correlates to Old English spoken by Anglo-Saxons in England from the sixth century until the Norman invasion in 1066 AD. Old English speakers spelled words using sound-symbol correspondences, much like our beginning readers and writers do today.

Emergent Stage (pre-alphabetic): Readers begin this stage lacking knowledge of the alphabet and letter-sound correspondences. The goals at this stage are to build alphabetic knowledge (identification and production), phonemic awareness and an emerging reader's concept of a word in text (COW-T).

Letter Name-Alphabetic (LN) Stage: Readers begin to spell with beginning and ending sounds; they use letter names to invent spelling but confuse short vowel sounds. The goal of this stage is for students to master spelling of short vowel words with consonant blends and digraphs as well as preconsonantal nasals.

The Pattern Layer

All words do not have a direct letter-to-sound relationship as some spellings already belong to certain words. For example, one could not spell *fight* as FIT, for this is how the word *fit* is spelled. For a remedy, earlier spellers of the Middle English period (1066-1400s) developed patterns to represent the phonemes in both single and multisyllabic words. Readers initially rely on sound-symbol relationships but progress to using several orthographic patterns to aid in both reading and spelling.

Within Word Pattern (WWP) Stage*: Readers enter this stage using short-vowel patterns and letter-sound correspondences to aid in reading and spelling words. Thus, they often use but confuse long vowel and ambiguous vowel patterns, complex consonants, and homophones. The goal of this stage is for students to use both sound and pattern cues when reading monosyllabic words.

Syllables and Affixes (SA) Stage*: Readers and writers at the SA stage spell most monosyllabic words correctly but struggle with two-syllable words. One primary goal of the SA stage is for students to recognize and use syllabic patterns, helping them identify syllable juncture and understand how to attach inflectional suffixes (-ing, -ed) to monosyllabic words.

The Meaning Layer

At the meaning layer of orthography, readers and writers understand that groups of letters not only represent sounds but also meaning; thus, patterns aid in building vocabulary acquisition as well as decoding skills. Semantic units or morphemes and word histories are keys to comprehension and give explanations behind the "inconsistencies" and "complexities" of the English language (refuting the claim that English is hard to learn because there are too many exceptions to the rules). The meaning layer developed from the exponential growth in intellectual and scientific discourse during the Renaissance and Scientific Revolution, bringing a profusion of Greek- and Latin-based words into the English lexicon.

Within Word Pattern (WWP) Stage*: When studying homophones, readers and writers at the WWP stage also utilize the meaning layer of orthography.

Syllables and Affixes (SA) Stage*: An additional goal of this stage is for students to recognize and analyze morphemes (affixes and root or base words) to both decode and define words.

Derivational Relations (DR) Stage: Readers and writers at the DR stage spell most words correctly but lack solid knowledge about derivations. This lack of knowledge impacts their ability to spell final suffixes, assimilated prefixes, unstressed vowels and various Greek- and Latin-based elements.

All About Phonemes, Graphemes and Morphemes

"The spoken word, and that alone, is the word itself. The written form is only its picture or representation to the eye, and frequently represents it imperfectly." — PRIMER OF ENGLISH ETYMOLOGY

"Language has a number of interacting components: phonology, morphology, syntax, semantics, prosody, and pragmatics." — NATIONAL INSTITUTE ON DEAFNESS AND OTHER COMMUNICATION DISORDERS, 2003

"Words are the elementary and constituent parts of every language, made use of by every nation on the face of the globe…to express their various ideas to each other, and give names and appellations to the different objects around them." — GEORGE LEMON, AUTHOR OF ENGLISH ETYMOLOGY, OR A DERIVATIVE DICTIONARY OF THE ENGLISH LANGUAGE: IN TWO ALPHABETS

"Words are verbal symbols of ideas, and the more ideas you are familiar with, the more words you know." — NORMAN LEWIS, AUTHOR OF WORD POWER MADE EASY

Rule 1: A word is the smallest element in language that is able to convey complete meaning on its own.

"Word" is of Germanic origin, relating to *Wort* (German) and *woord* (Dutch). It literally refers to "an utterance of sound." Words are labels for concepts and ideas; thus, a word is able to convey meaning, even in isolation. For example, *chair* verbally refers to a 'piece of furniture with four legs that individuals use for sitting.' This is a complete word, as it conveys the

A word may serve one of the following functions, mentioned below:
• name person, place, thing or idea (**noun**, *n.*);
• replace a noun (**pronoun**, *pron.*);
• identify an action or state of being/existing (**verb**, *v.* **often times followed by** *intr.* **or** *tr.*);
• modify other words (**adjective**, *adj.* and **adverb**, *adv.*);
• show excitement (**interjection**, *interj.*); or
• express the relationship between other words (**conjunction**, *conj.* and **preposition**, *prep.*).

Figure A.

meaning of a *specific object*. Another example would be *dance,* which means to 'move rhythmically, usually to music, in either prescribed or improvised steps and gestures.' In this case, the meaning refers to a *specific action*.

The categories mentioned in Figure A are collectively called **parts of speech**; parts of speech are used to classify a word based on its meaning, function and form. All words must fall into one of these categories or else it is **NOT** a word.

What IS and is NOT a Word

Words do not require additions for the meaning to be completely expressed; this differs from phonemes, morphemes and graphemes as you will see momentarily. However, a brief example is below:

> *Joy* is a word, as it is a **noun** that conveys the idea of intense and exultant happiness. "**The *joy* I have in my heart cannot be expressed with words.**"

> *Joyful* is also a word (**adjective**), describing people, place, things or ideas that are filled with joy. "**This *joyful* occasion is a cause for celebration.**"

> Joyful is simply the word "joy" combined with the morpheme "-ful" indicating a noun is "full of joy." While joy is typically used on its own, -ful is not and, thus, is NOT a word.

Remember: A word a) conveys complete meaning, b) does not require affixes or additional morphemes, and c) must be classified as having a part of speech.

Rule 1 Practice — Circle the words in the following list. Refer to a dictionary for assistance. It will be evident that the entry is a word versus a grapheme or morpheme because there will be abbreviations to indicate the part of speech. An example and nonexample are provided.

Example "real"

re·al (rē′əl, rēl)
adj.
  1.

    a. Being or occurring in fact or actuality; having verifiable existence: *real objects; a real illness.*

    b. True and actual; not imaginary, alleged, or ideal: *real people, not ghosts; a film based on real life.*

    c. Of or founded on practical matters and concerns: *a recent graduate experiencing the real world for the first time.*

As indicated via the dictionary entry, real is an adjective (adj); it *IS* a word.[1]

Nonexample (not a word) "pre"

pre- (prī)
pref.
  1.

    a. Earlier; before; prior to: *prehistoric.*

    b. Preparatory: preliminary: *premedical.*

    c. In advance: *prepay.*

  2. Anterior; in front of: *preaxial*

As indicated via the dictionary entry, pre is a prefix; it *IS NOT* a word.

---

[1] You may use any generic dictionary for this activity. The dictionary used above is the American Heritage Dictionary of Indo-European Roots (www.ahdictionary.com)

1) un   2) re

3) phonology   4) f

5) in   6) renew

7) of   8) ism

9) schism   10) less

Rule 1 Practice 2 — For numbers 1–6, identify the part of speech for the words above (write responses in the space provided). For numbers 6–11, identify each word's part of speech. Two examples are provided.

<u>Example</u>
Word: real   Part of Speech: adjective
Word: swim   Part of Speech: verb

1) Word: _____   Part of Speech: _____

2) Word: _____   Part of Speech: _____

3) Word: _____   Part of Speech: _____

4) Word: _____   Part of Speech: _____

5) Word: _____   Part of Speech: _____

6) Word: spa   Part of Speech: _____

7) Word: relax   Part of Speech: _____

8) Word: enjoyable   Part of Speech: _____

9) Word: energize   Part of Speech: _____

10) Word: with   Part of Speech: _____

Words combined create phrases and clauses, which produce sentences or verses when combined. A collection of sentences or verses is a paragraph or stanza. A combination of paragraphs can be a chapter in a book, a short story, an article, etc. and a combination of stanzas results in poems or prose.

Overall, it is difficult to define words, and thus, linguists conceptualize words as <u>lexemes</u>.

However, what are the components of words? What would a wordsmith put together to construct a word? Phonemes, graphemes, syllables and morphemes are the building blocks of words and, subsequently, of all language.

It is easier to distinguish between words in print than in speech. That is because the distinction between different words in speech is an abstraction. In print, readers can distinguish one word from another because the visual space that exists between two words serves as linguistic boundaries. For example:

   Thissentencehasfivewords.   vs.   *This sentence has five words.*

The example on the left shows a sentence without spaces between words, so the reader's eyes do not naturally know where one word ends and another begins.

The example on the right contains spaces between the words, making it possible to determine the beginning and ending point of each word.

Hearing words in speech is more akin to reading the example on the left because readers cannot necessarily hear where a word begins or ends. Most adult native English speakers take this for granted as their exposure to the language allows them to distinguish between words in speech with ease. Seeing a word in print aids in building word knowledge. Some linguists define a word as "a single semantic unit without spaces between its letters" (although sometimes they can have hyphens, such as *mother-in-law* and *good-hearted*). Overall, it is difficult to define words, and thus, linguists conceptualize words as **lexemes**.

On Lexemes and Words

A **lexeme** is a unit of meaning in a language; it is akin to a word but includes the set of inflected forms of the word. For example, jump is a lexeme that is a verb. Jumps, jumping and jumped are inflections of jump and, thus, are also part of the lexeme. Jump is considered to be a **lemma**, the citation form of the lexeme. The lexeme includes including *jump, jumps, jumping*, and *jumped*.

Inflections on a lexeme do not change a lexeme's part of speech. Adding *-s*, *-ed* or *-ing* to the end of *jump* does not change its part of speech; those lexical units are still verbs. Adding inflectional suffixes to a lemma does not create a new mental representation and, thus, does not create a new lexeme.

Derivations on a lexeme either change a word's part of speech or create a new meaning and a new entry in one's mental lexicon. A *jumper* is the noun form of *jump*, created by adding *-er* to the original lexeme. Adding *un-* to the lexeme *happy* changes the meaning of the original lemma entirely. Both *jumper* and *unhappy* are new lexemes created, but are related to the lexemes *jump* and *happy,* respectively.

As previously mentioned, a lexeme can be a single word or, more specifically, a simple lexeme. However, it can also be a phrase, such as *hot dog*. A phrasal lexeme consists of at least two words that when combined have a distinct meaning. For example, apart from one another, *hot* describes temperature and *dog* is a four-legged mammal. Combined, *hot dog* refers to a cooked sausage served on a partially sliced bun. *Hot dog* is a lexeme because it is a unit of meaning in English that stands on its own (similar to a word). However, *hot dog* is not a word but, rather, a two-word lexeme.

It is most important to note that the concept of a word is rather ambiguous; instead, linguists view words as lexemes. This text will use the term "word" to refer to a lexeme and the lexical units apart of that lexeme word family.

Rule 1 Practice 3 — Determine whether each of the following is a lemma (the lexeme without an inflectional ending). An example is provided below:

<u>Ex</u>: blast   lemma
    blasted   not a lemma

1)   spray _____   2)   spraying _____

3)   undo _____   4)   state _____

5)   stated _____

Rule 1 Practice 4 — Given the lemma of a lexeme, list words that are inflections and derivations of the lemma. An example is provided below:

Lemma	Inflections	Derivations
care	caring, cared, cares	careful, carefully, careless, carelessness, uncared, carer
respect (v.)		
sign (n.)		
round (adj.)		
will (v.)		
apply		

Words combine to create a sentence, which conveys a statement, question, exclamation or command. Sentences then combine to create paragraphs or stanzas.

Sentences are structured based on a language's grammar, which consists of morphology and syntax.

Rule 2: <u>All words contain phonemes, which are the smallest units of sound in a word.</u>

A **phoneme** is a single sound found in a given language but does not convey complete meaning on its own. It is the smallest unit of speech sound that distinguishes one word from another. Phonemes are assembled to form words. For example, the word *cat* has three sounds that when blended cause people to visualize a four-legged, carnivorous mammal with soft fur, a short snout and retractable claws.

To express the individual sounds in *cat*, we write the word in the following manner: /k/, /a/ and /t/. Thus, cat is a word, but /k/ is a phoneme. It does not express any idea in particular and, thus, cannot be a word. There are a total of three phonemes in the word *cat*.

Another example is the word "rush." Take a moment to elongate each sound in the word "rush." /R/-/u/-/sh/. This word also has three phonemes (despite the fact that it has four letters, which we will discuss in the next rule). We don't say /r/-/u/-/s/-/h/. The /s/ and /h/ combined represent the sound we hear at the beginning of the word *shoe*.

The first layer of word knowledge is auditory. Learning a word begins with hearing or saying it; that is to say, word knowledge begins with analyzing sounds, or phonemes, in a word. Phonemes are created by the movement of tongues and lips. By changing the shape of the vocal tract, people can produce a desired sound; a combination of these sounds builds a word. Phonemes are the building blocks of word parts, syllables and words themselves.

> *Let's look at two more examples:*
> How many phonemes are in the word "wealthy"? Did you say two? That is incorrect. While there are two syllables (weal-thy), there are far more phonemes. Here's a hint. In each syllable, there is always one vowel sound. That means you have to have an a, e, i, o, u in every syllable.
> Answer: five! /w/-/e/-/l/-/th/-/e/
> Here is a longer word. "Competition" Take a moment to count the number of phonemes. If you said 10, you are correct.
> It breaks down as follows:
> /c/-/o/-/m/-/p/-/e/-/t/-/i/-/sh/-/o/-/n/

One must be familiar with the phonemes in the English lingua to truly know a word (precisely the goal of an etymologist). Word construction starts with **phonetics**, which is the study of how speech sounds are made, transmitted and received.[2] Phonetics differs from **phonology**,[3] which is a general science regarding the principles that govern how linguists organize sounds in languages (American Heritage Dictionary, 2016). Both phonology and phonetics derive from the Greek word *phonos* meaning "sound," but phonetics is a branch of phonology. Developing word knowledge begins with two linguistic principles pertaining to sound because words are utterances or sounds that convey ideas. Philologists systematically analyze these utterances via phonetics and phonology. Future lessons will elucidate this point further through the study of **sound changes**, which means any processes of language change that affect the pronunciation (phonetic change) or its sound system structures (phonological change).

Rule 2 Practice — Identify the number of phonemes in the following words.

1) fan _____   2) plan _____   3) chum _____

4) realize _____   5) reliable _____

Extension: Which words above have more letters than phonemes? Why do you think that is the case?

[2] American Heritage Dictionary (www.ahdictionary.com)
[3] Ibid

Rule 3: <u>Phonemes can be classified as either consonants or vowels.</u>

There are 144 different phonemes in the English language, which are either vowel or consonant sounds.

How Sounds Are Made

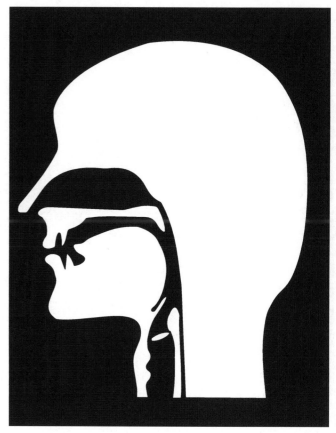

Every sound in the English language is made by moving air through the vocal tract (throat, nose and mouth). By moving the tongue and lips, the shape of the vocal tract changes to produce distinct sounds. Sounds can be classified as *consonant* and *vowel* phonemes, which are produced in two different manners.

Rule 3 Part I: <u>Vowels are phonemes produced without obstruction via the lips, teeth or throat.</u>

Vowels are sounds that have no stricture: that is, the sound is created when air freely escapes the mouth or nose. Changes in vowel sounds are based on slight movements of the tongue, throat and lips.

In written language, we represent vowel sounds with the letters *a, e, i, o, u* and sometimes *y*. *W* is considered a semi vowel, especially when it follows the letters *a* (*br<u>aw</u>l*), *e* (*n<u>ew</u>*) and *o* (*b<u>ow</u>*).

Elementary students learn to classify each of the five vowels listed above as **long** or **short**. In actuality, linguists understand vowels as a range of sounds produced by the mouth's shape. For example, opening the mouth wide creates the short *a* sound (*<u>a</u>pple*) while the long *e* (*<u>ea</u>gle*) sound is created when the mouth is a bit more closed.

What about the /aw/ sound found in *all*? This sound is produced when the jaw is dropped. It differs significantly from the /oo/ sound found in *book*, which is produced from the back of the throat when the mouth is slightly ajar. Thus, what we have discovered is that vowels are best classified as the range of sounds made based on the following criteria:

- mouth's shape
- the part of the tongue that is raised
- the height of the raised tongue
- the position of the soft palate (the back of the roof of the mouth)

Sounds are also distinguished by the position from which the sounds are created (place of articulation, such as the front of the mouth; the middle; or the back of the throat).[4] The chart below demonstrates places of articulation for given vowels in the English language:

5 Front Vowels					—	3 Middle		—	4 Back Vowels			
ee	ih	ay	eh	aa	ah	uh	er	aw	oh	ŏŏ	o͞o	
Pete	Jim	Dave	Ted	Dan	Bob	Bud	Bert	Claude	Joe	Woody	Lew	

Vowels are classified by their tenseness and length, which produce phonemic contrast. Tenseness refers to how narrow the mouth becomes during articulation. **Vowel length** is the duration of time it takes to produce a particular vowel sound. Vowels that are longer and produced with a narrower mouth are **tense**. Vowels pronounced with shorter duration and a widened mouth are **lax**.

Studying phonetics serves multiple purposes. On a basic level, phonetics is necessary to learn how to read or improve speaking skills. To help students become proficient communicators, reading teachers and speech and language pathologists should learn and employ these principles in their instructional practices. For the linguistically adept, knowledge of phonetics can help one analyze shifts in spellings and pronunciations over time, uncovering the original meaning and the truest sense of words.

The following chart contains vowel phonemes and the symbols (letters) used to represent them. The sounds are international, but the letters used to represent the sounds differ among languages. Therefore, the International Phonetic Association created symbols for universal usage (column one). These are typically used by phonologists and linguists, while the general public uses letters (column two) to represent phonemes in English words (i.e. English spelling). For example, one would use B-E-E to spell *bee*, a word referring to a flying insect known for its active role in pollination. However, a linguist might use IPA symbols /'bi:/ to reference the same thing.

[4] This is pertinent to understanding how certain vowels shifted into English over time based on a linguistic principle called The Great Vowel Shift, addressed in Book 2 of the Series.

SOUNDS	LETTERS	EXAMPLES
i:	e, ee ea ie, ei	be, eve, see, meet, sleep, meal, read, leave, sea, team, field, believe, receive
[i]	I y	it, kiss, tip, pick, dinner, system, busy, pity, sunny
[e]	e	let, tell, press, send, end
[ei]	a ai, ay ei, ey ea	late, make, race, able, stable, aim, wait, play, say, day, eight, weight, they, hey
[æ]	a	cat, apple, land, travel, mad; AmE: last, class, dance, castle, half
[a:]	ar a	army, car, party, garden, park, father, calm, palm, drama; BrE: last, class, dance, castle, half
[ai]	i, ie y, uy	ice, find, smile, tie, lie, die, my, style, apply, buy, guy
[au]	ou ow	out, about, house, mouse, now, brown, cow, owl, powder
[o]*	o	not, rock, model, bottle, copy
[o:]*	or o aw, au ought al, wa-	more, order, cord, port, long, gone, cost, coffee, law, saw, pause, because, bought, thought, caught, hall, always, water, war, want
[oi]	oi, oy	oil, voice, noise, boy, toy
[ou]	o oa, ow	go, note, open, old, most, road, boat, low, own, bowl
[yu:]	u ew eu ue, ui	use, duty, music, cute, huge, tune, few, dew, mew, new, euphemism, feud, neutral, hue, cue, due, sue, suit
[u:]	u o, oo ew ue, ui ou	rude, Lucy, June, do, move, room, tool, crew, chew, flew, jewel, blue, true, fruit, juice, group, through, route; AmE: duty, new, sue, student
[u]	oo u ou	look, book, foot, good, put, push, pull, full, sugar, would, could, should
neutral sound [ə]	u, o ou a, e o, i	gun, cut, son, money, love, tough, enough, rough, about, brutal, taken, violent, memory, reason, family
[ər]	er, ur, ir or, ar ear	serve, herb, burn, hurt, girl, sir, work, word, doctor, dollar, heard, earn, earnest, earth

Five Types of Vowel Sounds

The distinctions among vowel sounds is also measured in terms of their perceived duration—that is, the time it takes to say the vowel sound. While linguists and phonologists tend to use a more sophisticated method of classification, reading teachers and phonics tutors categorize vowels as either long, short,* diphthongs or complex, the schwa and r-controlled.

The long and short vowel classifications that reading teachers utilize are based on English orthography and, thus, aid students in word decoding and spelling.

Long vowel sounds "say their own name"; that is, a long vowel sounds the same as the name of the vowel. They are as follows:
/ā/ as in *late, aim* and *play*
/ē/ as in *be, eve* and *see*
/ī/ as in *ice, find, smile, tie* and *my*
/ō/ as in *go, note, open* and *old*
/ū/ as in *use, duty, rude* and *Lucy*

Sometimes, long vowel sounds require silent markers to indicate that a vowel represents a long sound. For example, in the word late, "e" is silent, indicating that the "a" represents a long a sound (lāt). In the word play, "y" is silent, indicating that "a" represents a long a sound (plā). In the word boat, "a" is silent, indicating the "ŏ" represents a long o sound.

Short vowels are as follows:
/ă/ as in *cat, apple* and *land*
/ĕ/ as in *let, tell* and *press*
/ĭ/ as in *it* and *kiss*
/ŏ/ as in *not, rock* and *bottle*
/ŭ/ as in *gun* and *cut*

Diphthongs[5] or ambiguous vowels are complex vowels made by gliding from one vowel sound to another within the same syllable, as in joy, joust and jaw.
/aw/ as in *saw* and *auction*
/oi/ as in *oil* and *voice*
/ou/ as in *out* and *mouse*
/oo/ as in *look, put* and *would*

The schwa is a **German** sound that is often represented as /ə/. It is not a long or short

---

[5] Diphthong comes from the Greek *di* "twice" and *phthongos* "sound, voice"; it is literally two vowel sounds that blend to be articulated as one vowel sound.

* We apply **diacritical marks** as a means of distinguishing between long and short vowel sounds in words. For example, if I see a macron (¯) above a vowel, such as /ē/, I know that I am to say the long e sound, as found in words like tree, meal and me. This differs from if I see a breve (˘) above a vowel /ĕ/, which indicates that I am to say the short e sound, as found in words like pet, felt and elf.

vowel but, rather, a mid-central vowel sound. Various letters can represent the schwa sound as in:

/ə/ represented by *a* as in *about*
/ə/ represented by *e* as in *taken*
/ə/ represented by *i* as in *pencil*
/ə/ represented by *o* as in *eloquent*
/ə/ represented by *u* as in *supply*
/ə/ represented by *y* as in *sibyl*
/ə/ represented by *i* as in *pencil*

R-influenced vowel sounds end in the /r/ sound. For example:

/ar/ as in *car* and **Arthur** and *for*
/â/ as in *care* and *bear*
/ər/ as in *washer, firm* and *fur*
/or/ as in *store, oratorical* and *floor*
/ur/ as in *occur* and *fur*
/yoor/ as in **pure** and *fury*

Every single word in the English language has a vowel sound; syllables in words are distinguishable because of vowels as each syllable contains only one vowel sound. Sound and symbol combinations help us identify whether a word has a long, short or r-influenced vowel sound, a diphthong, or is a German schwa. However, this is not all. Remember, vowels are just one of two types of phonemes found in English words.

The following exercises will only contain commonly used words that should be familiar to the reader.

Rule 3 Part I Practice 1 — Identify the type of vowel sounds in the words below. Provide both the vowel sound's classification (one of the five categories mentioned above) as well as the diacritical symbol representing the sound. Write responses in the space provided. For two-syllable words, provide the vowel's classification for the underlined syllable. An example is provided.

Example: ice   *long i, /ī/*
            joy   *diphthong, /oi/*

1)   b<u>a</u>seball _____   2)   sp<u>o</u>t _____

3)   m<u>y</u>th _____   4)   r<u>e</u>view _____

5)   j<u>u</u>mp _____   6)   sp<u>oi</u>l _____

7)   b<u>a</u>ll _____   8)   butt<u>er</u> _____

9)   P<u>au</u>l _____   10)   l<u>igh</u>t _____

Rule 3 Part I Practice 2 — Identify all the types of vowel sounds in each of the words below.

Example: tiger   *i: long*   *er: r-influenced*

1)   refresh   _____ _____

2)   bonus   _____ _____

3)   scarlet   _____ _____

4)   balloon   _____ _____

5)   circumference* _____ _____ _____

*This word has two pronunciations. Choose the pronunciation that is most natural for you.

Rule 3 Part II: <u>Consonants are phonemes produced by obstructions of air flow via the lips, teeth or throat.</u>

A consonant is a sound that the mouth produces via air coming through the vocal cords, but unlike the vowel, this speech sound is produced via the partial or complete obstruction of either the lips, teeth, or throat. This obstruction causes air to explode or blow through a narrow passage causing friction, which ultimately produces the various consonant sounds. Consonants can be classified as labials, dentals or gutturals, reflecting the methods of obstruction that produce specific sounds.

For example,
- the sound /b/, as in the initial sound in *basket*, is a **labial**; it is produced from the blocking of air via closed lips
- the sound /t/, as in the final sound in *basket*, is a **dental**; the sound is produced from the blocking of air via the teeth
- the /k/ sound, as in the initial sound in *car*, is a **guttural**; the throat blocks the air that flows through the vocal chords; the air but narrowly escapes, producing what we call the *k* or hard *c* sound

These manners of obstruction can be organized into four categories, reflected in the following chart. The chart provides a thorough classification of English consonant sounds based on the place and manner of articulation.

	NASAL	LIQUIDS	VIBRATING	NON VIBRATING	VIBRATING	NON VIBRATING	SEMI VOWELS
Labials (LIPS)	m		b	p	v	f (ph) (gh)	w (u) (wh)
Dentals (TEETH)	n	l r ..	d	t	z (s) th (soft) j (g-soft) ch	s th (soft) sh (si, ti, ch) zh (z, s, g)	
Gutterals (THROAT)	ng	..r	g (hard)	k (c-hard) (qu) (ch)		h	y (i)

Note that /f/ and /v/ are labiodentals but are considered to be part of the labial family while /j/ is a palatal in the dental family. Lastly, /ng/, /g/ and /k/ are velars and /h/ is a glottal, which are all a part of the guttural family. Additionally, r...reflects /r/ at beginning the of a word, such as *radio* while r... represents /r/ at the end of a word such as *enter*.

Another means of categorizing consonants is as either nasals, liquids, plosives, fricatives, or semi-vowels.
- A **nasal** is produced by air flowing through the nose.
- A **liquid** is produced by air flowing through a partial closure in the mouth. They are quite close to vowels in that it takes little friction to produce the sound.
- A **plosive** is a sound produced by completely stopping or blocking air flow (complete obstruction) to create a pop in sound.
- A **fricative** is a sound produced by forcing air through a narrow passage (partial obstruction) to create friction.

Thus, /p/ is a plosive labial—air flows from the lungs and is interrupted by a complete closure of the lips, which causes the air to explode from the mouth and produce a pop of sound.

On the other hand, /f/ is a fricative labial—air flows from the lungs and is interrupted by a narrow constriction, causing the air to flow turbulently and create sound.

Single consonants can also be classified as **voiced** (vibrating) or **unvoiced** (non-vibrating).
- **Voiced** consonants: vocal chords vibrate as air flows, causing the air to impart a buzzing sound
- **Unvoiced/Voiceless** consonants: vocal chords are apart; air flows freely through them

The last column in the chart is reserved for the **semi-vowel**. These are sounds that are akin to vowels in that there is little obstruction of air to produce the sound. These include /w/ as in *water* and /y/ as in *yellow*.

Rule 3 Part 2 Practice 1 — Identify the type of consonant underlined in each of the words below; tell whether the consonant is a

- labial, dental or guttural;
- a liquid, nasal, plosive or fricative; and
- voiced or unvoiced

Write your response in the space provided (see the example)

Ex: live   labial   fricative   voiced

1)	fringe	_____
2)	cons<u>t</u>ellation	_____
3)	lo<u>c</u>ate	_____
4)	legen<u>d</u>	_____
5)	<u>f</u>acilitate	_____
6)	trea<u>s</u>ure	_____
7)	<u>c</u>herish	_____
8)	<u>g</u>regarious	_____
9)	<u>r</u>elinquish	_____
10)	intege<u>r</u>	_____

Rule 3 Part II Practice 2 — Give a word that contains the type of vowel and consonant sounds requested (see example).

clip	coffee	critique	fabric	feet	flip	like
measure	south	stream				

Example: A word that contains at least one short vowel sound and two dental consonants _differ_ (d, f: labiodental consonants; i: short vowels)

1) A word that contains one long vowel with one labiodental, and one dental _____

2) A word that contains two dentals and one diphthong _____

3) A word that contains one dental, one guttural and one long vowel _____

4) A word that contains one dental, one guttural, one labial and one short vowel _____

5) A word that contains one labial, one labiodental and one short vowel _____

6) A word that contains three dentals, one nasal labials and one long vowel _____

7) A word that contains two short vowels, two labials, one liquid and three dentals _____

8) A word that contains one guttural, two labials, one short vowel and long vowel _____

9) A word that contains one dental, one guttural, one labial, one r-influenced vowel (short vowel and liquid guttural), and one short vowel _____

10) A word that contains two non-vibrating, plosive gutturals, one long vowel and one short vowel

_____

Rule 4: <u>Graphemes represent phonemes (sounds) and are the building blocks of the written word.</u>

A **grapheme** is the smallest unit in a writing system. A grapheme can represent a phoneme (or individual sound), syllable, morpheme (prefix, root or suffix), or a word in its entirety. Graphology is the study of graphemes in a language's written system.

Remember, the spoken word alone is the word itself. The written form is only a collection of symbols or visual representations of the sounds in a word. Graphemes are used to represent the phonemes, and a strong a reader uses knowledge of sound-symbol relationships to analyze and decode to properly pronounce a word.

The above images are pictures of different types of graphemes.

From left to right: Ge'ez letters (Ethiopian); Chinese Han character (men); Hebrew letter (mem); Greek letters; and Latin letter M

Types of Graphemes

Writers of English uses an alphabet (Latin alphabet) to visually represent sounds of the language. However, other languages use other types of graphemes to represent sounds in their languages. Linguists classify graphemes into the following categories (see the chart below):

Type of Grapheme	Distinguishing Features	Examples of Writing Systems	Glyph
ideograph	a glyph or an image that represents an idea or concept without indicating individual sounds in the word	Aztec, Mixtec, and other Mesoamerican writing systems (except Mayan Hieroglyphs)	𑀕 (An Aztec Glph)
logogram	a glyph or an image that represents an idea (by way of a word or morpheme)	Egyptian Hieroglyphs, Hieratic, and Demotic, script;	万 (a Han Chinese character)
syllabic	a system in which one letter represents an individual syllable	Japanese, Cree, and Cherokee	ꮆ (A Cherokee glyph)
alphabetic	a system in which letters represent consonants and vowel sounds in words	Greek, Latin	A (a letter of the Roman alphabet)

In addition are:
*   **abjad**: a writing system in which a grapheme represents a consonant only with no symbol for vowels; examples include Hebrew, Arabic and other Semitic scripts
*   **abugida**: a writing system in which a grapheme represents a consonant and vowel; examples include Ge'ez and the family Brahmic scripts (Devanagari)

In all cases, graphemes are symbols used to represent sounds in a language (including the word itself) and are the building blocks of the written word.

Graphemes of the English Language

The Latin alphabet is critical for reading and writing in English, Spanish, French, Italian, etc. In English, graphemes represent at least one phoneme, if not more (and remember, a phoneme is _____). Mapping graphemes to phonemes is a sound-symbol relationship fundamental to decoding and encoding (spelling) words. Learning about graphemes and phonemes helps beginning readers develop word attack and spelling skills, strengthening their ability to read and write.

For example, the letter B represents the /b/ sound as in **birth**, while the letter T represents the /t/ sound, as in le**ft**. The following is a comprehensive list of consonant letters that only represent one sound:

- *b* represents the /b/ phoneme as in *bat*
- *d* represents the /d/ phoneme as in *dog*
- *f* represents the /f/ phoneme as in *fish*
- *h* represents the /h/ phoneme as in *hat*
- *j* represents the /j/ phoneme as in *jam*
- *k* represents the /k/ phoneme as in *kite*
- *m* represents the /m/ phoneme as in *map*
- *n* represents the /n/ phoneme as in a *nice*
- *p* represents the /p/ phoneme as in *pull*
- *t* represents the /t/ phoneme as in *teach*
- *v* represents the /v/ phoneme as in *vet*
- *w* represents the /w/ phoneme as in *water*
- *y* represents the /y/ phoneme as in *yet* (remember, sometimes y is also a vowel)
- *z* represents the /z/ phoneme as in *zip*

Some graphemes can represent consonant or vowel sounds depending where it is in a word. For example, *w* represents a vowel sound in the words *crowd* and *saw*, while *y* represents a vowel in the words *gym*, *happy*, and *psychology*. Generally speaking, *w* and *y* are consonants when used at the beginning of a word, like in *window* and *yesterday*.

Many graphemes in the Latin alphabet can represent multiple sounds, particularly depending on their position in a word. The multiple sounds are called allophones. English allophones are as follows:

- The grapheme *c* represents both the sounds /k/ (as in *cat*) and /s/ (as in *cell*). Respectively, we call these the hard and soft c sounds.
- The grapheme g represents two sounds that we also classify as hard and soft. Hard g or /g/ is found in the word *gargle*, and soft g or /j/ is found in the word *gym*.
- The grapheme *s* can represent the sounds /s/ (*self*), the /z/ (*busy*) or the /zh/ (*treasure*).
- The grapheme *l* represents both a voiced /l/ as in *lap* and unvoiced /l/ as in *glad* and *cycle*.
- The grapheme *r* represents two different sounds based on its location; at the beginning of a word, the consonant sound is a dental liquid, as in *right* or *run*. At the end of a word, the sound is a guttural liquid, as in *ladder* or *scare*.
- The grapheme *x* represents two distinct sounds: /ks/ as in *box* and /z/ as in *xylophone*.
- The grapheme *q* represents two distinct sounds: /kw/ as in *quiet* or *quilt* and /k/ as in *plaque* or *torque*.

In some words, certain consonant letters are frequently silent, such as:
- *b*, particularly when followed by *m*, as in *lamb* or *comb*
- *h*, as in *honest* or *herb*
- *t*, as in *whistle* or *hustle*

Graphemes also represent vowel sounds. Single graphemes can represent two different vowel sounds—long or short—as noted in Rule 3 Part I of this chapter. The same letter can represent two different sounds, sometimes three (often being a source of confusion for beginning readers or English language learners). For example:

- *a* represents the /ă/ phoneme as in *cat* and the /ā/ phoneme as in *cane*
- *e* represents the /ĕ/ phoneme as in *bed* and the /ē/ phoneme as in *green*
- *i* represents the /ĭ/ phoneme as in *kid* and the /ī/ phoneme as in *bride*
- *o* represents the /ŏ/ phoneme as in *pot* and the /ō/ phoneme as in *boat*
- *u* represents the /ŭ/ phoneme as in *cut* and the /ū/ phoneme as in *flute*
- *y* represents the /ĭ/ phoneme as in *gym*, the /ī/ phoneme as in *psychic* and the /e/ phoneme as in *happy*

All of the vowels above can also represent the schwa sound, especially as an unstressed final syllable (see Rule 6).

Rule 4 Practice 1 — Provide a word that contains the grapheme requested. Then write it using diacritical marks.

Example: *c*: cat /căt/

b: _____	*d*: _____
f: _____	*h*: _____
j: _____	*k*: _____
m: _____	*n*: _____
p: _____	*t*: _____
v: _____	*w*: _____
y: _____	*z*: _____

The following graphemes represent two sounds; give an example of a word that contains each sound.

c:	_____ (hard)	_____ (soft)
g:	_____ (hard)	_____ (soft)
l:	_____ (voiced)	_____ (unvoiced)
q:	_____ (/kw/)	_____ (/k/)
g:	_____ (/ks/)	_____ (/z/)
a:	_____ (long)	_____ (short)
e:	_____ (hard)	_____ (soft)
i:	_____ (/ĭ/)	_____ (/lə/)
o:	_____ (/kw/)	_____ (/k/)
u:	_____ (/ks/)	_____ (/z/)
g:	_____ (/g/)	_____ (/j/)
s:	_____ (/s/)	_____ (/z/)

Rule 4 Practice 2 — Determine whether the underlined grapheme represents a hard or soft *c* or a hard or soft *g*.

Example: gym   soft

1) census	_____	2) civilian	_____
3) comedy	_____	4) cycle (4a 4b)	_____ _____
5) cleric (5a 5b)	_____ _____	6) gel	_____
7) gamble	_____	8) gigantic (8a 8b)	_____ _____
9) garage (9a 9b)	_____ _____	10) cogent (9a 9b)	_____ _____

Rule 4 Practice 3 — Determine whether the underlined x grapheme represents the phoneme /ks/ or /z/.

Example: axe   /ks/

1) hexagon (1a)	_____	2) xenophopia (2a)	_____
3) index (3a)	_____	4) maximum (4a)	_____
5) Xerox (5a 5b)	_____ _____		

Rule 4 Practice 4 — Determine whether the *q* grapheme represents the phoneme /kw/ or /k/.

Example: quell   /kw/

1) antique   _____   2)   question   _____

3) Baroque   _____   4)   croquet   _____

5) relinquish   _____

Graphemes alone cannot indicate which sounds are to be produced when decoding words. Readers also must consider letter combinations and a grapheme's placement in a word.

Most words follow common spelling patterns that help readers pronounce words based on location of consonants and vowels in a given word. A word like *beg* is a CVC word as it contains a consonant (*b*), a vowel grapheme (*e*), and a consonant (*g*). A word such as *tail* is a CVVC word as it contains the consonant *t*, the vowel graphemes *ai*, and the final consonant *l*. The spelling patterns indicate the consonant or vowel sound to be uttered upon seeing a word in print.

The following are typical phonetic patterns found in a majority of English words. These are not "rules" in that they do not apply to all the words in the English lexicon. Many English words have global origins and reflect non-English spelling patterns. For example, the letter *j* represents the sound heard at the beginning of *jump* in words of English or Germanic origin while the letter *j* represents the /zh/ sound in French words (*j'en appelle*) and the /h/ sound in Spanish words (*jalapeño*). The letter *i* can either denote the long *i* /ī/ sound found in *bite* or the short vowel sound /ĭ/ found in *bit*, but in words of Italian origins, *i* represents the long *e* /ē/ sound found at the end of spaghetti.

Pattern 1: When *c* or *g* is followed by *e, i* or *y*, it represents the soft sounds. For example, *ceiling*, *city*, *gym* and *geology* are all soft sounds; *camera*, *fact*, *game* and *green* are all followed by graphemes other than *e, i* or *y* and, thus, are hard sounds.

Pattern 2: When a syllable or a monosyllabic word ends in a silent *e*, the e signals that the vowel phonemes are typically long. For example, *bite*, *snake* and *flute* all contain a silent e, making the underlined vowel a long vowel phoneme. The e grapheme is silent when it follows a vowel and consonant; the associated spelling pattern is CVCe. The pattern is defined as having a consonant-vowel-consonant-silent e.

Pattern 3: When a syllable or monosyllabic word contains one vowel grapheme, it is typically a short vowel sound. These are CVC words because they follow the consonant-vowel-consonant pattern (although many contain more than one consonant in the beginning or end of the word, making it a CCVC, CVCC, CCVCC, CCCVCC, etc.). For example, words such as *chip*, *cost*, *trash* and *strict*.

Pattern 4: When a syllable or a word contains two vowel graphemes next to each other (CVVC), the vowel phoneme represented is typically the long sound of the first letter, while the second grapheme is silent. The silent letter is called a silent vowel marker. For example, *tail* (/ā/), *meat* (/ē/), *boat* (/ō/), *lane* (/ā/), *clue* (/ū/) and *sneak* (/ē/).

Pattern 5: Sometimes the CVVC spelling pattern represents diphthong or ambiguous vowel sounds (see Rule 3 Part I on Vowels). The two vowel sounds blend together to create one. Some examples include *boil* (/oy/), *about* (/ow/), *brawl* (/aw/), *book* (/o͝o/), *loose* (/o͞o/) and *brown* (/ow/).

Pattern 6: Three or more letters that represent one sound is called a **trigraph.**[6] For example, grapheme combination *igh* represents the long *i* phoneme (/ī/) as in **light**, **high** or *sight*. A list of common trigraph is found below:
- *igh* sounds like /ī/ as in **light**
- *ore* sounds like /or/ as in *bore*
- *sch* sounds like /sh/ as in *school* or /sh/ Schnitzel[7]

Pattern 7: Consonant letters that come in pairs are either consonant blends or digraphs. A **consonant blend** is two consonants that combined make two distinct phonemes. In the word blue, the consonants *b* and *l* are pairs that can be distinctly heard in the pronunciation of the word, /b/-/l/-/ū/. There are two- and three-letter blends, and there are consonants blends that are found at the beginning and end of words. The spelling patterns are typically CCVVC, CVVCC, CCVVCC, CCCVVC, etc.

2-letter Blends: Beginning consonant blends are classified as
-       l-blends (*blue*, *clean*, *flower*, *glass*, *sleep* and *play*);
-       r-blends (*brown*, *cross*, *drink*, *free*, *green*, *pray* and *tree*)
-       s-blends (*score*, *skill*, *smile*, *snow*, *squash*, *spot*, *stair* and *sweep*)

[6] Trigraph comes from the Greek *tri* meaning "three" and *graphe* meaning "something written.".
[7] In words of German origin, sch represents the /sh/ sound. In words of Greek origin, *sch* represents the /sk/ consonant blend.

2-letter Blends: Ending consonant blends include
- /ct/: *fact*, *rectangle*   -   /ft/: *gift*, *left*
- /ld/: *gold*, *wild*   -   /lf/: *shelf*, *gulf*
- /lp/: *pulp*, *scalp*   -   /lt/: *salt*, *melt*
- /mp/: *stamp*, *limp*   -   /nd/: *band*, *find*
- /nk/: *thank*, *drink*   -   /nt/: *plant*, *student*
- /pt/: *adopt*, *slept*   -   /rd/: *yard*, *bird*
- /rk/: *ark*, *mark*   -   /rm/: *firm*, *worm*
- /rn/: *born*, *fern*   -   /sp/: *clasp*, *grasp*
- /st/: *trust*, *best*   -   /sk/: *ask*, *disk*

3-letter Blends: Beginning consonant blends with three letters are typically s-blends
- /scr/: **script**, **screen**
- /spl/: **splash**, **splendid**
- /spr/: **spring**, **spray**
- /str/: **street**, **strawberry**

- A consonant digraph[8] is two consonants that when paired together represent one phoneme. The digraphs are as follows:
  o /ch/: **chair**, **such**
  o /gh/[9]: **ghost**, **rough**
  o /sh/[10] represented by *sh* and *ch*: **bush**, **shape**, **shipmate**, **champagne**
  o /th/: **bath**, **tooth**, **athlete**
  o /hw/ sound represented by *wh*: **where**, **why**
  o /f/ sound represented by *ph* and *gh*: **phonetics**, **paragraph**, **rough**
  o /k/[11] sound represented by *ch* and *ck*: **character**, **duck**, **rocking**
  o /n/ sound represented by *gn* and *kn*: **gnome**, **know**
  o /r/ sound represented by *wr*: **write**, **wretched**
  o double consonants at the end of words produce one sound (for example, *cliff*, *wall*, *glass* and *buzz*)
- Three-letter consonant combinations: Often times, words have combinations of blends and digraphs.
  o Beginning blends include /sch/ (**school**), /shr/ (**shrimp**) and /thr/ (**throw**)
  o Ending blends include /nch/ (**lunch**) and /tch/ (**witch**), /rch/ (**birch**)

Pattern 8: The grapheme combination *ti*, *si* or *ci* can represent the /sh/ sound, particularly when followed by on (tion, sion and cion) as in introduc**ti**on, ses**si**on or conscien**ti**ous.

---

[8] Digraph comes from the Greek *di* meaning "twice" and *graphe* meaning "something written."
[9] *ph* at the end of a word produces the /f/ sound, while *gh*- at the beginning of a word produces the /g/ sound.
[10] The digraph *ch* (italicized) is pronounced as /sh/ in words of French origin.
[11] *ck* is always found at the end of a word or syllable.

Pattern 9: The open vowel pattern CV, CVV is one in which the word or syllable ends with a vowel. Examples include *tea*, *too*, *baby* (ba-by; both syllables are an open vowel pattern). This pattern typically indicates that the vowel sound will be long, ambiguous or the German schwa.

Rule 4 Practice 5 — The list that follows contains nonsense words. A nonsense word is a made-up word used to help beginning readers practice their decoding. Determine whether the words below contain long, short or ambiguous vowels by analyzing spelling patterns, graphemes and the phonemes they represent.

Example: mite   *long i* or /ī/

1) fleech	_____	2) vawl	_____
3) prit	_____	4) shomp	_____
5) hute	_____	6) shoil	_____
7) kroap	_____	8) brack	_____
9) flep	_____	10) sloat	_____
11) crout	_____	12) splight	_____
13) klum	_____	14) sprail	_____
15) pliem	_____		

Rule 4 Practice 6 — The list that follows contains nonsense words. Determine whether the words below include hard or soft *c* or hard or soft *g* phonemes by analyzing spelling patterns, graphemes and the phonemes they represent.

1) blag	_____	2) cith	_____
3) flice	_____	4) gaf	_____
5) gyl	_____		

Rule 4 Practice 7 — Give an example of one of the following types of consonant clusters. Circle the cluster in your examples.

1) s-blend _____

2) l-blend _____

3) r-blend _____

4) diagraph _____

5) three-letter blend _____

Rule 4 Practice 8 — Identify whether the two underlined letters represent a consonant blend or digraph; write your response in the space provided.

Example: <u>pl</u>ay   <u>blend</u>

1) <u>sh</u>ambles _____

2) <u>st</u>ich _____

3) fla<u>nk</u> _____

4) tru<u>ck</u> _____

5) shri<u>mp</u> _____

Rule 4 Practice 9 — Identify the consonant blend(s) or digraph(s) in each word below; write your response in the space provided.

Example: crash   <u>cr: blend; sh;_____</u>

1) scuffle _____

2) thought _____

3) trout _____

4) distract _____

5) flesh _____

The above are basic rules in phonics, traditionally[12] "oddballs" or "irregular" spelling patterns that students are told to memorize. As many say, there are exceptions to every rule. For example, according to the rules, the graphemes -*ost* indicate that the vowel phoneme should be short (/ŏ/), as in c*ost* and l*ost*, but can also represent a long vowel sound /ō/, like in m*ost*, p*ost* and h*ost*. According to spelling pattern 3, the graphemes -*old* should represent short vowel phonemes but typically indicates long vowel sounds, such as the words b*old*, sc*old* and g*old*.

---

[12] I say *traditionally* because many elementary school teachers are no longer explicitly teaching phonics, which includes decoding and encoding (spelling) skills and fluency building. This is a significant reason for many reading issues we see today in America. Word attack skills are the foundation of good readers.

Many people lament about the "irregularities" of the English language, as they believe it makes English difficult to learn; in fact, it has been deemed one of the hardest language to read worldwide as people believe that English lacks rules and form. However, many modern-day English words come from other languages and, thus, have spelling patterns that reflect their linguistic origins. For example, words with *ch* representing the /sh/ phoneme are of French origin, like in **charade** and **machine**. Words of Greek origin like *phoneme* represent the /f/ phoneme with the *ph* digraph, like **phenomenon** and **metaphor**. English is a highly systematic language, but it is difficult to see the common spelling patterns among words of various origins without a thorough understanding of etymology. Learning etymology allows one to become a lexical connoisseur and better learn and use words.

Rule 5: <u>Words can be divided into syllables, a part of a word that contains one vowel sound.</u>

Thus far, Chapter 1 has covered two fundamentals: a) words comprise phonemes, and b) graphemes provide a written representation of those phonemes. Words can also be broken down into syllables. A **syllable** is a unit of pronunciation having one vowel sound with or without surrounding consonants, forming the whole or part of a word. It is larger than a single phoneme and smaller than a word. Syllables deal with the organization of the phonemes in a word. In English, it does not carry any meaning on its own.

For example:
The word *water* contains two syllables, /wa/ and /ter/.
The word *banana* contains three syllables, /ba/, /nan/ and /a/.
The word *independent* contains three syllables, in, /e/, /pend/ and /ent/

Notice that in *water*, the two syllables each contain a vowel phoneme /ə/ and /er/.
Similarly, *banana* contains three vowel phonemes /ə/, /ă/ and /ə/.
Independent contains four vowel phonemes /ĭ/, /ē/, /ĕ/ and /ĕ/.

Single-syllable words, such as *track*, *bed* and *goat*, all contain one vowel sound. However, one can use their phonemic awareness to distinguish between and manipulate initial and final sounds as well as vowel sounds in words. Initial consonant sounds are called onset while the medial vowel and final consonant sounds are called rime. For example, the onset of track is *tr-* (/tr/), while the rime is *–ack* (/ăk/). Words can be organized or classified by their onset and rime. The word **trap** shares a common onset with the word **track**. However, **back** shares a common rime with the word **track**. Track and back are considered to be a part of the same word family. Other word family examples include.

-and
band, **sand**, **bland**, **strand**, *mandate*

-eet
meet, sleet, sweet, fleet, sheet

-oil
boil, soil, coil, broil, foil

Onset and rime as well as word families are an aspect of phonemic awareness that are necessary for emerging readers to learn decoding and spelling skills.

The division of words into syllables is called **syllabification**; there are sub-rules that help us analyze, decode and spell (encode) multisyllabic words:

Rule 5.1: There are seven syllable types:

Syllable Type	Explained	Example
closed (CVC)	A syllable in which a single vowel is followed by a consonant. The vowel is usually short.	• **răb/bĭt** (cvc-cvc; both syllables contain short vowel phonemes) • **năp-kĭn** (cvc-cvc; both syllables contain short vowel phonemes)
open (CV)	A syllable ending with a single vowel. The vowel is usually long.	• **tī/ger** (cv-cvc; first syllable contains a long vowel phoneme) • **ba/by** (cv-cv; both syllables contain long vowel phonemes)
silent e (CVCe)	A syllable with the long vowel consonant- silent e pattern. The syllable is usually long.	• bāke • pīne • bōne All of these words contain long vowel sounds.
vowel team (VV)	A syllable containing two graphemes that together represent one vowel phoneme; often times, this one vowel phoneme is long.	• bōat • retrēat • rāin All contain one syllable with a long phoneme vowel sound.
r-controlled vowel (Vr)	A syllable in which the vowel(s) is followed by the single grapheme r. The vowel phoneme is "controlled by the r."	• car • mar/ket • re/port/er
diphthong (VV)	A syllable containing two vowel phonemes in which a new vowel phoneme is formed by the combination of both vowel phonemes.	• boil • cloud • look
consonant –le (Cle)	An unaccented final syllable containing a consonant and –le.	• bub/ble • spar/kle • sad/dle

Rule 5.2: *A one syllable word is NEVER divided.*
- Examples: *stop, feet, bell*

Rule 5.3: *A compound word is divided between the two words that make the word compound.*
- Examples: *rainbow* (rain-bow); *football* (foot-ball); *toothbrush* (tooth-brush)

Rule 5.4: VC/CV- *When two consonant phonemes come between two vowel phonemes, divide syllables between the consonants.*

- Examples: coffee (c<u>o</u>f-f<u>ee</u>); members (m<u>e</u>m-b<u>er</u>s); symbol (s<u>y</u>m-b<u>o</u>l)

Rule 5.5: VCC/VC- *When there are more than two consonants together in a word, divide the syllables keeping the blends together.*

- Examples: instant (in-**st**ant, not ins-tant); blanket (bla**nk**-et); replacement (re-**pl**ace-ment)

Rule 5.6: VC/CV- *When there is one consonant between two vowels in a word, divide the syllables after the first vowel.*

- Examples: bonus (bo-**n**us); tiger (ti-**g**er); review (**re**-**v**iew)

Rule 5.7: V/CV- *If following the previous rule does not make a recognizable word, divide the syllables after the consonant that comes between the vowels.*

- Examples: dozen (do**z**-en); method (met**h**-od); cabin (ca**b**-in)

Rule 5.8: VC/V- *When there are two vowels together that don't represent a long vowel or diphthong phoneme, divide the syllables between the vowels.*

- Examples: reality (**re**-al-it-y); client (cli-ent); lion (li-on)

Rule 5.9: P/R/S- *When there are prefixes or suffixes in a word, divide after the prefix and in front of the suffix (we will cover affixes in depth in chapters that follow).*

- Examples: revive (**re**-vive); succession (**suc**-cess-**sion**); reinstatement (**re**-in-state-**ment**)

Rule 5.10: *Consonant –le- When a word or syllable ends in –le, divide before the consonant in front of the –le.*

- Examples: circle (cir-**cle**); little (lit-**tle**); staple (sta-**ple**)

Rule 5.11: *When a word contains an x or a ck, divide after the ck or x.*

- Example: nickel (ni**ck**-el); boxes (box-es); duckling (du**ck**-ling)

When one comes upon an unfamiliar word, readers must analyze its spelling pattern to determine the *syllable juncture*. A syllable juncture refers to the place(s) of division in a multisyllabic word. This information is critical for developing readers; as they begin to encounter more complex and complicated words, readers must master syllabic analysis to solidify word attack skills and become fluent, comprehending readers.

Rule 5 Practice 1 — Identify the type of syllable underlined in the words below; write each response in the space provided. See the example below.

Ex: sim<u>ple</u> consonant + le (Cle)

1) <u>ma</u>gnet	_____	2) de<u>bate</u>	_____
3) flag<u>ship</u>	_____	4) <u>bri</u>dle	_____
5) in<u>ter</u>nal	_____	6) <u>cei</u>ling	_____
7) <u>stir</u>rups	_____	8) cy<u>cle</u>	_____
9) ty<u>phoid</u>	_____	10) <u>fi</u>nally	_____

Rule 5 Practice 2 — Identify the number of syllables in the words below; write each response in the space provided.

Ex. rabbit   2 (rab-bit)

1) dream	_____	2) penny	_____
3) fire	_____	4) digest	_____
5) mapped	_____	6) knitted	_____
7) authoritarian	_____	8) meander	_____
9) lavender	_____	10) intellectualization	_____

Rule 5 Practice 3 — Identify the number of syllables in the words below and find the syllable juncture; write each response in the space provided.

Ex: mascot   2 (mas-cot)

1) awestruck	_____	2) retractable	_____
3) goalie	_____	4) distract	_____
5) streak	_____	6) divide	_____
7) trivial	_____	8) racketeer	_____
9) contemplative	_____	10) disingenuous	_____

Rule 6: <u>Multisyllabic words contain primary, secondary and tertiary stress.</u>

In most multisyllabic words, one syllable is stressed, affecting the pronunciation of the vowel sounds in other syllables of the word. Chapter 1 has covered how to analyze graphemes and syllable junctures to decode words. These skills aid readers in properly pronouncing words during oral reading. One must additionally learn where emphasis should be placed during pronunciation. This emphasis is called stress, and it is present in all multisyllabic words. It is an important feature of English orthography, as words must be properly pronounced to be spelled and read correctly. In linguistics, stress is the degree of force with which a syllable, word or phrase is uttered. Stress can be classified as prosodic (emphasis placed on a particular word or phrase) or lexical (emphasis placed on a particular syllable). We will focus on lexical stress.

In two-syllable words, only one syllable is stressed, but in words with three or more syllables, syllables have varying degrees of stress. Take a name, for example, and break it into its respective syllables. Where should the speaker place emphasis? Brittany (part of my first name) is technically a three-syllable name (brit-tan-y) although most people pronounce it in two syllables (brit-ney). The emphasis is placed on the first syllable and, thus, reads "BRĬT-t:n-e." However, my good friend Rachelle has a two-syllable name (rachelle), and stress is placed on the second syllable (ra-SHĔLL). We also refer to the syllable of stress as the accented syllable and the one that does not receive emphasis as the unaccented syllable.

How does one determine which syllable receives emphasis? Look for the syllables that seem to "sound louder" than the others. Another way to find the stressed syllable is to hold a hand under the chin when saying a multisyllabic word to feel where the jaw drops most. Try both methods with the following words to identify the primary stress:

photograph (pho-to-graph)   *photography* (pho-tog-raph-y)   *photographic* (pho-to-graph-ic)

In the first word, the first syllable is stressed (**PHO**-to-graph).
In the second word, the second syllable is stressed (pho-**TOG**-raph-y).
In the third word, the third syllable is stressed (pho-to-**GRAPH**-ic).

Stress is critical not only for proper pronunciation but also to distinguish between certain *homographs*—words that are spelled alike but have different meanings and, in many cases, different origins. Homographs like *record* and *record*, *present* and *present*, *subject* and *subject,* etc. can elucidate the point further:

I plan to *record* a *record* with a famous hip-hop violinist.

What type of *present* should I *present* to the emperor?

The scientists *subject* their *subject*, a white rabbit, to gruesome experiments to test cosmetic products.

After analysis and review, a pattern should emerge: in pairs of homographs, the difference in stress indicates the meaning of the word. Analyze the dictionary entries below:

With the stress on the first syllable of record (rē **cord**'), the word is a verb defined as "the act of indicating or registering for the purpose of again, preservation" (American Heritage, 2016). Stress on the second syllable of record (**rĕc**'ord) is a noun referring to an item with temporary or permanent information or an item or something on which sounds are recorded, both to preserve and make it available for future reference.

The words *present* (prĕz'ĕnt) and *present* (prĕ zĕnt') show the same distinction—the former a noun (both a thing and a state or condition), the latter a verb (to show). Where does the stress fall for each word? The noun form of present holds the stress on the first syllable, while the verb form holds it on the second syllable.

What about subject and subject? Where is the stress on the noun form? Where is the stress on the verb form?

One should note that linguists often analyze the degrees of stress in a word with three or more syllables. They look for the most emphasized syllable (*primary* stress) and the second most emphasized syllable (*secondary* stress). Some even search for a *tertiary* or third *stress*. For example, in the word *psychology* (psy-CHOL-o-gy), the primary stress is on the second syllable, but the secondary stress is on first syllable and tertiary stress on the penultimate (next to last) syllable.

As well as pronunciation and vocabulary comprehension, stress is also critical to learn during spelling instruction. While vowel sounds in stressed syllables are clearly heard, they are indistinguishable in unstressed syllables. These syllables are *reduced*, meaning that any vowel graphemes in the syllable represent the schwa. Look at the word *captain* (CAP'tain). The stress is placed on the first syllable /căp/, and the unstressed final syllable *tain* is pronounced /t:n/. The full word pronounced /căp-t:n/, despite the spelling phonetically representing /cap-tān/ (long a final syllable). It is most often the final unaccented syllables that reduced similarly to a schwa.

Words like *dental*, *fertile* and *noble* have the same second syllable sound (/əl/) and are unaccented. Again, the final syllable's vowel sound is reduced to the schwa, so it is difficult to determine how to spell the unaccented syllable; it can be spelled as *–al*, *–ile* or *–le*. Study and analysis of root words and affixes becomes particularly necessary for one to recognize the connection between a word's origin, word meaning and spelling.

Rule 6 Practice 1 — Identify the stressed syllable in each of the words below, and indicate the vowel sound (long a, short e, etc.).

Ex. symbol - first syllable (SYM bol); /ĭ/ or short i

1) magic   _____   _____

2) mistake   _____   _____

3) prefix   _____   _____

4) lemon   _____   _____

5) pilot   _____   _____

6) polite   _____   _____

7) music   _____   _____

8) tunnel   _____   _____

9) avoid   _____   _____

10) vowel   _____   _____

11) pencil   _____   _____

12) legal   _____   _____

13) eagle   _____   _____

14) suspect   _____   _____

(verb: to doubt the truth of something; to have an idea without proof)

15) suspect   _____   _____

(noun: a person thought to be guilty of a crime or offense)

Rule 6 Practice 2 — Identify the primary stress of the words in the list below; write each word in its corresponding column. An example is provided:

Ex. re-FIN-ish

1) demanding   2)   vacation   3)   grandfather   4)   awareness

5) uniform   6)   invalid (adjective: not true; not to be recognized by law.)

7) invalid (noun: a person who is not able to move)   8)   inflated

9) inflexible   10)   definition

Extension: Underline the syllable with the secondary stress. Circle the reduced syllables. (Hint: look for syllables that contain the schwa sound.)

1st syllable	2nd syllable	3rd syllable
	re-FIN-ish	

Rule 6 Practice 3 — Homograph Activity — Read the sentences to determine if the bolded words are nouns or verbs. Write noun or verb in the space after each sentence and underline the stressed syllable. An example is provided.

Nouns	Verbs
a. PRES-ent	b. pre-SENT

Example
a: I gave a birthday **present** to my favorite teacher. *noun*
b: Ms. Merriweather will **present** a lecture to students schoolwide about international travel. *verb*

1) The comedian knew he went too far when the women took his joke as an **insult**.

_____

2) Rebecca and John often **insult** their friends when they ask them how much their

parents make each year. _____

3) I grow most of my **produce** at home but sometimes buy melons at the local farmers'

market. _____

4) I plan to put together a great team to **produce** my next record. _____

5) Jonathan, a rising freshman in high school, must get a work **permit** if he wants to get

a summer job. _____

6) My mom and dad did not **permit** me to go to the school dance since I skipped school

last week. _____

7) I am wearing a facemask because I do not want to **contract** any illnesses before my

first day at a new school. _____

8) Never sign a **contract** without reading it first. _____

9) The Jaguars' loss to the Ravens was their worst **upset** of the season. _____

10) I asked Marquis to be careful not to **upset** the baby as it took an hour for her to fall

asleep. _____

Rule 6 Practice 4 — Reduced/Schwa stress– Read each word and identify the syllable that contains the reduced stress. Then, place the word in one of the following categories: /- əl/ (*normal*), /ət/ (*target*), r-influenced (*better*) or /ən/ (*captain*). Write the word phonetically (see examples below). If the word does not contain a reduced stress syllable, do not place it in any category.

Example: rocket, rifle, cellar, lesson

NORM-əl	TAR-gət	BĔT-ter	CĂP-tən
RĪ-fəl	RŎK-ət	SĔL-ler	ĂP-tən

1)	maple	2)	exit	3)	knowledge	4)	honey
5)	cookie	6)	travel	7)	dollar	8)	human
9)	cherry	10)	basket	11)	person	12)	flower
13)	pirate	14)	vital	15)	dolphin		

Rule 7: <u>Analyzing letters, sounds and syllables can help one decode unknown words.</u>

Knowledge of the basic components of words aids in decoding. Readers use unknown phonemes (vowels and consonants), graphemes or letters, sound-symbol relationships of English, syllabification and stress to decode single and multisyllabic words.

To decode and pronounce words:
a. Syllabicate
b. Analyze and determine the vowel sound in each syllable (long, short, ambiguous, schwa)
c. Analyze and determine the consonant sounds (digraph or blend? hard or soft g? etc…)
d. Determine the primary and secondary stress by testing where emphasis should be placed (particularly given a word's context)
e. Determine which syllables are reduced (typically unstressed syllables are reduced)
f. Pronounce!
g. (Optional) Write the word with diacritical marks

Rule 7 Practice — Complete steps A–G (see above) to decode the words below; write the word with diacritical marks:

Example: disgrace: dĭs-GRĀS
          giant: Jī-ent

1) picture   2) radio   3) exclaim

4) polar   5) thistle   6) marvel

7) homeless   8) good   9) matter

10) sunset

Rule 8: <u>Watch out for homographs and homophones.</u>

Chapter 1 has explored the pitfalls of homographs, but what about homophones? Literally meaning 'same sound' (homo 'same' + phone 'sound'), these are words that are spelled differently but are pronounced the same. The most famous set of homophones gives some of the great troubles in grammar: their/there/they're. Distinguish between the different usages of the homophones.

_____ going to Six Flags tomorrow with all of _____ cousins, but the meteorologist says _____ will be rain in the morning.

Some other examples include
- be/bee - flour/flower - steel/steal - sole/soul - vein/vane/vain

Rule 8 Practice — Homophones Activity– Fill in the blanks in the sentences below using the correct homophone. See an example below:

Example: [flee/flea]

Quick! We must _____ the area where my dog Fido gained a lot of _____s and tics to prevent my other pets from getting attacked.

Quick! We must **flee** the area where my dog Fido gained a lot of **fleas** and ticks to prevent my other pets from getting attacked.

1)   [knew/new] I _____ that Jenise could dance, but I did not know how good she was until I saw her _____ routine at the showcase.

2)   [male/mail] I don't know who lost your letter, but the person who delivered the _____ was indeed a _____.

3)   [pole/poll] For sociology class, I took a _____ on which flag we should hang from the _____: the school flag or the senior class flag?

4)   [cellar/seller] The _____ of the house added a _____ in the basement, so the price increased substantially.

5)   [main/mane] Did you see a lion with a long _____ on the _____ road? I think it escaped the zoo!

6)   [fir/fur] The dog ran through the woods and his _____ got caught in the thicket of _____ trees.

7)   [side/sighed] We enjoyed a hearty laugh until our _____s hurt; then, we _____ in happiness, thinking of the memories with our favorite high school teacher.

8)   [steel/steal] The construction worker tried to _____ _____ from the worksite, but the foreman caught him before he left.

9)   [foul/fowl] You cannot call a _____ in the game just because a strange _____ ran across the soccer field!

10)   [mall/maul] I do not want to go to the _____ because I am afraid a crowd of people will _____ me.

Rule 9: <u>Words comprise free and bound morphemes, which readers use to understand a word's meaning.</u>

Morphology is a branch of grammar that studies the structure of words and the way that morphemes operate in a language.

A **morpheme** is the smallest unit of meaning in a language that cannot be divided. *Horse*, *talk* and *happy* are morphemes, as they convey meaning. Adding *-s* onto 'horse' creates a new form of the word horse: *horses*. *Horses* is made up of two morphemes: *horse*, which represents the animal, and *-s*, indicating 'more than one horse.' Similarly, adding the morpheme *-ed* to the morpheme 'talk' creates the word form talked. *Talked* is not a morpheme because it can be divided into two separate units of meaning: *talk* and *-ed*. Adding the morpheme *un-* to the morpheme 'happy' creates the word *unhappy*. Unhappy is not a morpheme because it contains two units of meaning: *un-*, meaning 'not,' and *happy*.

Horse (a four-legged mammal) + **-s** (indicates more than one) = **horse<u>s</u>**
Talk (the act of speaking) + **-ed** (indicates past tense) = **talk<u>ed</u>**
<u>Un</u> (indicates negation or opposition) + **happy** (pleasure or contentment) = **<u>un</u>happy**

Morphemes are classified as free or bound. A **free morpheme** is one that can be uttered on its own while a **bound morpheme** is a grammatical unit that never stands by itself. In the words *horses*, *talking* and *unhappy*, <u>horse</u>, <u>talk</u> and <u>happy</u> are free morphemes while *-s*, *-ing* and *un-* are bound morphemes.

Word	Bound Morpheme	Free Morpheme
horses	-s	horse
talk	-ing	talk
unhappy	un-	not

A free morpheme is also called a **base word** or a **root word** (see Rule 11 for an explanation of root words). It is also considered a simple lexeme. It can have many forms; for example, *talking*, *talks* and *talked* are all lexical forms of the lemma *talk*.

Rule 9 Practice 1 — In the following word list, circle the lexemes that are free morphemes. An example is provided below:

1. play   2. playful   3. stretch   4. internal   5. interesting

Rule 9 Practice 2 — Underline bound morphemes and circle the free morphemes in the words that follow. An example is provided below:

1. slowly   2. bookstore   3. rewind   4. interested   5. signature

Rule 9 Practice 3 — Identify the number of morphemes in each of the following words. If there are at least two morphemes, write them on the line provided. An example is provided below:

Lexeme	No. of Morphemes	Morphemes in the Lexeme
footnote	2	foot; note
door		
doors		
view		
review		
basket		
interruptions		
polyamorous		
psalm		
irresistibility		
another		

Rule 10: <u>There are two main types of morphemes: inflectional and derivational.</u>

An **inflectional morpheme** changes a word's grammatical form to express number (singular/plural), possession, comparison and tense. **Tense** is the time in which an action took place (present, past or future). Below are examples of inflectional morphemes.

- *-ing* (indicates a noun formed from a verb)
- *-ed* (expresses tense)
- *-s* or *-es* (expresses number, as in rugs or a noun-verb agreement, as in "He speaks")
- *-er* and *-est* (expresses comparison)

Derivational morphemes are word parts (affixes) that are joined or "fixed" to a word to create a new word; thus, the new word is a derivative of the original word. Adding affixes alters the meaning of a word and can also change the word's part of speech. Below are examples of derivational morphemes.

- *pre-* in <u>pre</u>view (*pre-* meaning "before")
- *bi-* in <u>bi</u>annual (*bi-* meaning "two")
- *-ful* in play<u>ful</u> (*-ful* meaning "full of")
- *-ation* in present<u>ation</u> (*-ation* meaning "the act of")

Rule 10 Practice 1 — Add an inflectional and a derivational morpheme to each of the words that follow. An example is provided below:

<u>Word</u>	<u>Inflected ending</u>	<u>Derivational ending</u>
run	running	runner; rerun
phone		
sun		
carry		
trust		
front		
tract		
insist		
organ		
calculate		
repay		

Rule 10 Practice 2 — Add to or change the ending morpheme of the words below to create a new word.

1. symbol<u>ize</u>:
2. hypnot<u>ize</u>:
3. veget<u>ation</u>:
4. terr<u>or</u>:
5. person<u>ality</u>:

Rule 11: <u>Words contain words parts.</u>

Morphemes are often taught to children as word parts, which are used to build words of Greek, Latin and Germanic origin. There are three types of word parts: *prefixes*, *root* or *base words* and *suffixes*. Prefixes and suffixes are **affixes**, bound morphemes that attach to a root or base word and alter its meaning.

Root words are morphemes that represent the basic part of the word's meaning. For example, the root word of *tractor* is *tract*, which means 'to pull, drag or draw.' A tractor is "a powerful motor vehicle with large rear wheels, used chiefly on farms for hauling (pulling) equipment and trailers" (American Heritage Dictionary, 2016). Note that pulling (haul) is present in the word's meaning, which correlates to its root word. By utilizing the knowledge of root word meanings, one is able to begin to deduce the meaning of a word. Root words are also called stems or bases, although many teachers make a distinction between root and base words. Root words are said to be a bound morpheme while base words stand freely.

<u>Root word</u>	<u>Base word</u>
The word "re**ject**ion," with the root word *ject*, meaning "to throw." *Ject* is a bound morpheme because it cannot stand on its own as a word.	The word "**jump**ing," with the base being *jump*. Jump is a free morpheme because it can stand on its own as a word.

A Note About Root Words*

As stated above, the usage of 'root words' differs if not being used for reading and language arts instruction. In linguistics, the term 'root word' refers to a word from which word parts derive. For example, the stem *tract* comes from the Latin word *tractare*, meaning "to pull or haul; also, handle, manage and treat." In an effort to stay consistent with current educational terminology in this initial workbook, ER will refer to Latin- and Greek-derived word parts as "root words."

Affixes can be added to the beginning or end of a base or word or root word part to modify its meaning. Subsequent chapters of this book will cover more about these affixes.

Summary

A **word** is the smallest element in language that completely conveys _____. Words are made up of sounds called _____, and these sounds are classified as either _____ (sounds made without obstruction from lips, teeth and throat) or _____ (sounds made from blockages of air traveling through the vocal cords). A **lexeme** is a _____ in the lexicon of a language. A lexeme, such as frame, can have several _____, such as *framed*, *frames* and *framing*.

Consonants are categorized as _____ (lips), _____ (teeth) or _____ (throat) based on the method of blockage that creates the sound. **Vowels** can be classified as either _____ or _____ based on the position of the mouth as the sound is uttered. A _____ is a written or drawn representation of the phoneme. In English, we use the alphabet, where letters or letter combinations represent a given sound. Words are also divided into _____, a part of a word that contains only one vowel sound. Words also comprise _____ known as **prefixes**, **roots** and **suffixes**. _____ each carry the most basic part of a word's meaning; some are _____ morphemes that stand on their own as words, while others are _____ morphemes that must combine with prefixes and suffixes to formulate words.

Review

A.   Defining Key Terms

Terms

Directions: Match the following key terms on the left to the definitions on the right.

Definitions

1. word
2. phoneme
3. grapheme
4. morpheme
5. syllable
6. vowel
7. consonant
8. labial
9. dental
10. guttural

a. a consonant sound made by blockage of air via the lips

b. the smallest unit of meaning in a word; it does not stand alone

c. the smallest unit of sound in a word

d. a sound that is created without obstruction of air traveling through the vocal chords

e. the smallest unit of language that conveys complete meaning and stands on its own

f. the smallest unit of a written representation of a sound in a word; a letter

g. a part of a word that contains only one vowel sound

h. a consonant sound made by blockage of air via the teeth

i. a sound that is created by blockage of air traveling through the vocal chords

j. a consonant sound made by blockage of air via the throat

B.   Count the Phonemes

Directions: Identify the number of phonemes in each of the words below. Write your answers in the space provided.

1. sacred   _____

2. trust   _____

3. break   _____

4. theme   _____

5. nation   _____

C.   Lexical Classifications

Directions: Identify the lemma and the lexical unit for each of the following words. Write your answers in the space provided.

Word	Lemma	Lexical units
1. impeaching	_____	_____
2. reacted	_____	_____
3. shape's	_____	_____
4. tallest	_____	_____
5. roasts	_____	_____

D.   Count the Graphemes

Directions: Identify the number of graphemes in each of the words below. Write your answers in the space provided.

1. sash   _____

2. it   _____

3. I   _____

4. everlasting   _____

5. rational   _____

E.   **Classify the Consonants (initial)**

Directions: Classify the beginning consonant sound of each word. Tell whether the consonant sound is

a) a *labial, guttural* or *dental*;
b) a *liquid, nasal, plosive* or *fricative* and
c) *vibrating* vs. *non-vibrating* (if applicable).

For example, the initial consonant sound in black is /b/, which is a labial, plosive, vibrating consonant.

1.   linguist   _____

2.   destiny   _____

3.   religious   _____

4.   plenary   _____

5.   maple   _____

F.   **Classify the Consonant (final)**

Directions: Classify the final consonant sound of each word. Tell whether the consonant sound is

a) a *labial, guttural, dental* or *labiodental*;
b) a *liquid, nasal, plosive* or *fricative* and
c) *vibrating* vs. *non-vibrating* (if applicable).

For example, the final consonant sound in plan is /n/, which is a dental, nasal consonant.

1.   static   _____

2.   reach   _____

3.   cliff   _____

4.   conductor   _____

5.   empath   _____

G.   **Consonant Clusters**

Directions: Identify the consonant digraph or blend and write it in the space provided.

Example: The word <u>spray</u> contains the consonant blend (B) spr.

1. plenary   _____   2.   hyperlink   _____

3. abashed   _____   4.   amuck   _____

5. strategic   _____

H.   **Vowel Type**

Directions: Identify the vowel type(s) in each word below. The vowels will be long (L), short (S), r-influenced (R), a diphthong (D), or a schwa (ə). Write both the vowel(s) or vowel pair and the vowel type in the space provided.

Example: The word sprain contains a diphthong; the vowel pair is ai (D).

1. flow   _____

2. stint   _____

3. stark   _____

4. flaunt   _____

5. ball   _____

6. refresh   _____ _____

7. bonus   _____ _____

8. carpet   _____ _____

9. whirlpool   _____ _____

10. circumference _____ _____ _____ _____

I.   **Syllabification**

Directions: Divide the following words into their proper syllables. Write each syllable and syllable type on the lines provided.

Example: The word magical contains three syllables: mag-ic-al.

	SE (silent e)
	O (open)
	C (closed)
	VT (vowel team)
	DT (diphthong)
	RI (r-influenced)
	C-le (consonant + le)
	Schwa (schwa)

1. tea   _____

2. baseball   _____

3. better   _____

4. bundle   _____

5. voucher   _____

6. reflection   _____

7. phoneme   _____

8. strident   _____

9. inflammatory   _____

10. champion   _____

J.   **Stress**

Directions: For numbers 1–5, identify the primary stressed syllable and its vowel sound. For numbers 6–10, identify the reduced vowel(s) in the unstressed syllable. For example, the primary stress in the word <u>happy</u> is the first syllable (HAP-py). In the word <u>final</u>, the last syllable contains a schwa and is unstressed (FI-nal).

Example   happy   <u>HAP; short a</u>   Ex. final <u>–al</u>

1. reflex   6.   middle
2. behind   7.   fable
3. conserve   8.   tinsel
4. conservative   9.   captain
5. complex   10.   interrogation

K.   Homographs and Homophones

Part 1 Directions: Complete the sentences below using the homographs. With each given pair, determine which word goes in which part of the sentence.

1) {sweet/suite} They blushed when they ladies entered their hotel _____s as flowers and _____s lay poetically across their beds.

2) {chord/cord} Right as the guitarist was about to strum the final _____ in the song, someone tripped on an electrical _____ and the speakers were disconnected.

3) {mane/main} To commence the town parade, Lightning, the horse with the long and luxurious _____, marched proudly down the _____ road.

4) {waist/waste} Purchasing this new belt was a _____ of money as it did not properly fit my _____.

5) {praise/prays} Mary wakes up every morning, goes to church and _____ with the sick and needy. Then, she leads a _____ and worship service, singing songs and reading verses from the Bible.

Part 2 Directions: Complete the sentences below using the homophones. With each given pair, determine which word goes in which part of the sentence. When appropriate, identify the syllable of stress for each word. (Example: The thief <u>pro-CEEDs</u> to open a bank account with the <u>PRO-ceeds</u> from last night's benefit dinner.)

1) {wind (noun)/wind (verb)} As I hear the _____ begin to blow a bit stronger, I decide it is time to _____ up the kite's string and go home.

2) {tear (noun)/tear (verb)} When little Jamie saw a small _____ in the bright blue corduroy, she begins to _____ up as she was afraid she would get in trouble for ruining her new pants.

3) {des'ert (noun)/de-sert' (verb)} It would be cruel and inhumane to _____ a person in the middle of the _____.

4) {pro'ject (noun)/pro-ject' (verb)} To encourage investors to fund your business _____, you should show them that you _____ slow but positive growth during the first year.

5) {con'verse (noun)/con-verse' (verb)} I choose not to _____ with my colleagues for fear that my thoughts are the _____ of their own.

L.   Morphemes

Directions: Determine whether the following morphemes are free or bound. Write a word containing each bound morpheme in the space provided.

Morpheme	Free or Bound	Newly Formed Word (Bound Only)
1. ify	_____	_____
2. fix	_____	_____
3. bio	_____	_____
4. verse	_____	_____
5. intro	_____	_____

All About Prefixes

"By knowing just <u>some</u> of these prefixes...you can figure out the meanings of thousands of words without looking them up in the dictionary. For instance, more than 10,000 words can begin with the prefix <u>non</u>. Another common prefix, <u>pseudo</u>, is used in more than 400 words. As you can see, by learning only a few word parts, you can add many new words to your vocabulary." — ESSENTIAL READING SKILLS, P.140

A **prefix** is placed at the beginning of a word.

Example: *prefix* and *intercept*

Pre is the prefix of the word *prefix*. Circle the prefix of the word **prefix**.

Inter is the prefix of the word *intercept*. Circle the prefix of the word **intercept**.

Below is a list of 12 common prefixes and their meanings

a	sub	un	anti	re	inter	ex	re	trans	ad	con	dis

Practice #1: Circle the prefix of each of the following words:

1. antifreeze	2. subway	3. untie	4. confront
5. review	6. transport	7. interact	8. forecast
9. apolitical	10. disclose	11. avert	12. foresight
13. interference	14. antibiotic	15. subordinate	16. concurrently
17. undeniable	18. translucent	19. distraction	20. regenerate

Prefixes help us find the meanings of words. For example, review, preview and interview all have the same root but different prefixes that influence their meanings.

- *Preview* means to look **before**, since *pre* means *before*.
- *Review* means to look **back** or look **again**, since *re* means *back* or *again*.
- *Interview* means to look **between**, since *inter* means *between*.

When a prefix is attached to a root, it does one of the following things:

a) Adds direction to a given base or root word

b) *Negates* a base or root word (adds *not* to the meaning)

c) Adds a *numerical* meaning to the root or base word

d) *Intensifies* a root or base word by adding "very" or "thoroughly" to the meaning

Thus, prefixes can be organized into the following four categories:

- Prepositions that show direction
- Negation
- Numbers
- Intensifiers

Prepositional and Directional Prefixes

Most prefixes in English words are directional. They indicate the way or direction that the root travels, be it a noun or a verb. Additionally, prepositional prefixes can indicate a direction figuratively; that is, prepositional prefixes indicate the mental level and position of the base or root word. For example, consider words with the prefix *re*, meaning 'back or again.' The root or basic meaning of the word *retract* is <u>tract</u>, meaning 'to draw or pull.' To *retract* literally means to 'draw or pull **back**,' as the prefix *re* means back. *Retractable* claws are claws that animals can "*pull **back*** inside of their paw until they are needed." The opposite of the prefix *re* is *pro*, meaning 'forward.' The word *protraction* refers to 'joints or muscles that are being pulled or drawn **forward**.' By changing the prefix of a word, one is able to determine the direction of the word's root.

Another example of a directional prefix is *super*, meaning 'above or beyond.' *Superman* is a *superhero*, who is said to have *supernatural* powers. Let's analyze each of these words. *Superman* is a man who has powers **beyond** those of a typical human being—in other words, a *superhuman*. All heroes have courage and strength, but *superheroes* have powers beyond just those qualities. Their strength is also *supernatural*, an adjective that refers to 'existences above or *beyond* those of the natural world.'

The opposite of *super* is *sub*, which means 'below or under.' Thus, a *subhuman* is '**below** the natural abilities and activities of a human,' and a *subordinate* is that which is '**below** what is ordinary or apart of a **lower** class or **lower** in rank.'

Other examples:

Import is to carry **in**, while *export* is to carry **out**.

Transport is to carry across, while *report* is to carry back.

Try to fill in these examples:

Supernatant refers to swimming _____ or on the _____ of water.

Subterranean refers to that which is _____ ground.

Implode is to collapse _____.

Extend is to stretch _____.

Transcend is to pass or climb _____ or above.

Reverse is to turn and go _____.

Many Latin-based prefixes (prefixes derived from Latin language) are directional. These prefixes originally stood alone as their own words, as in the following Latin phrases. The prepositions-turned-prefixes are in boldface:

in memoriam– **inside** the memory   e[1] pluribus unum– **out** of many, one

pro bono– **for** the public   **ad** hoc– **to** this

post scriptum– **after** what has been written   **de** jure– **from** the truth

Practice #2: In the spaces provided, list additional examples of words with each prefix.

Prefix	Meaning	Example	Example 2	Example 3
ad	to	addition		
con, com, col, cor	with, together	conduct		
de*	away, down, from, removal, reversal	deflect, detach, depart, defrost		
e, ex, ef	out	eject, exit, effective		
fore	before	forewarn		
in, im, il, ir	in, into, on	influx		
inter	between	interstate		
pre	before	pretest		
post	after	posttest		
re	back, again	review		
semi	half	semicircle		
sub, suc, sur, sud, sup, suf	below, under	subway		
super	above, over	superior		
trans	across, over	transaction		
un	not, opposite	unnatural		
under	below, under	understand		

[1] The prefix *e* is an assimilated version of the Latin prefix *ex*; both mean "out."

Practice #3: Fill in each blank with the meaning of the listed word's prefix to complete the meaning of the boldfaced words below:

1. **produce**: to lead or bring _____

2. **reduce**: to draw or lead _____; to make less in amount, degree, or size

3. **induce**: to draw or lead _____, particular to a plot, plan or group

4. **educe**: to lead or bring _____; to develop

5. **adduce**: to lead one _____ the truth via facts and examples

6. **reject**: to cast or throw _____

7. **interject**: to throw _____; interrupt

8. **project**: to throw _____

9. **inject**: to throw _____

10. **eject**: to throw _____ (physically)

Numerical Prefixes

Prefixes can also identify an amount or a number. For example, the prefix **bi** means two. The word *bicycle* refers to a vehicle composed of *two* wheels held in a frame, one behind the other. On the other hand, a *unicycle* is a cycle with one single wheel, because the prefix **uni** means one. The prefix *mono* also means "one." *Monogamy* is being married to _____ person, while *bigamy* is having _____ spouses. A *millimeter* is a meter divided into 1,000 equal parts, while a *centimeter* is a meter divided into 100 parts. The prefix *milli* means '_____' and the prefix *centi* means '_____.'

Practice #4: In the spaces provided, list additional examples of words with each prefix.

Prefix	Meaning	Example 1	Example 2
uni; mono	one	unicycle; monocle	
bi; di/du	two	bicycle; diverge; duet	
tri	three	tricycle	
quad, quart; tetra	four	quarter; quadrant; tetrad	
quint; pent(a)	five	quintuplets; pentagon	
hex(a)	six	hexagon	
sept; hepat(a)	seven	September	
octo, octa	eight	October	
nov(em), non; ennea	nine	November; ennead	
dec/deci	ten	December; decimal	
centi; hecto	hundred	centimeter	
milli; kilo	thousand	millimeter	
multi; poly	many	multigrain; polygon	
equi	equal	equidistant	
hemi, semi	half	hemisphere, semisweet	

Practice #5: Circle the prefix in each of the words below and give the meaning of each prefix. Use the dictionary to check the words you are forming. An example is provided below:

Ex: bicycle   <u>2</u>   wheels

1) tetrachord	_____	*strings/tones*	2)	century	_____	*years*
3) octahedron	_____	*faces*	4)	decibel*	_____	*units*
5) kilowatt*	_____	*units*	6)	hemicycle	_____	*wheels*
7) polygamy	_____	*spouses*	8)	hectoliter	_____	*deciliters*
9) unify	_____	*to make*	10)	novena prayers for	_____	*days*
11) semisweet	_____	*sweet*	12)	hexameter	_____	*meters*
13) biannual	_____	*a year*	14)	equilateral	_____	*sides*
15) pentatonic	_____	*tones*	16)	quintuplet	_____	*at birth*
17) quadrilateral	_____	*sides*	18)	monocle	_____	*lens*
19) tripod	_____	*-legged*	20)	millipede	_____	*legs*
21) multitude	_____	*people or things*				

22) Septuagint _____ *times* 10 = _____ *Greek translators of the Bible*

*hints

4) *bel* is a measurement of sound named after Alexander Graham Bell

5) *watt* is a measurement of the rate of energy conversion over time, named after James Watt

13) *biannual* differs from *biennial*, which occurs every _____ years

Practice #6: Use definitions to fill in the blank and complete each blank and complete the words. Use the dictionary if you need help. An example is provided below:

1) _____ gon: an eight-sided figure

2) _____ meter: 1,000 meters
used in the metric system instead of the mile

3) _____ tone: one consistent sound; to not change in tone or sound

4) _____ glot: speaking many languages
such as Chinese, French, Japanese, English, Amharic, Arabic, etc.

5) _____ media: many media sources
such as text, audio, images, animation and interactive content

6) _____ corn: a mythical animal that has one horn in the middle of its forehead

7) _____ el: a fight between two people

8) _____ sect: to cut into three pieces

9) _____ syllabic: a word with more than one syllable,
such as "responsible," "interdisciplinary," or "reanimation"

10) _____ nox: a day of the year when night and day hours are equal; takes place on

the first days of spring and autumn

11) _____ sphere: half a sphere; half of the Earth

12) _____ -colon: half of a colon (;)

13) _____ nomial: contains two terms or names,
such as (2x +5) or homo sapien

14) _____ rivium: in classical education, three subjects taught after the trivium

stage, literally meaning "where the three roads meet." Subjects studied

are arithmetic; geometry; astronomy and music (vium comes from via,

Latin for road)

15) _____ grammaton: the four Hebrew words transliterated as YHWH (Yahweh)

16) _____ alogy: a compound literary body of narratives made up of six works

Extension: Learn new words by creating them. Replace the prefixes of the words from the previous exercise. Define and use in a sentence or draw a picture. Use the dictionary to check to see if your created words exist already.

Reversal and Negation Prefixes

A prefix can express opposition as either a **reversal** or a **negation**, depending on its usage. Below is a list of the prefixes that signify opposition. Practice #7: Complete the chart with word examples for each prefix listed.

Prefix	Meaning	Example 1	Example 2
a	not, without	apathetic	
anti	opposed, against	antiwar	
contra, counter	against	counteract	
in, im, il, ir	not	immature	
dis	away, apart, from	disregard	
mis	error, badly, wrongly	misbehave	
non	not	nondairy	
un	not	unhappy	
pseudo*	fake	pseudoscience	

A **reversal prefix** is a morpheme that indicates the "reverse of the action of the base or root word." For example, to *untie* means 'to reverse the action of tying something so that the object is not tied.' The prefix *un-* is now acting as a reversal, indicating to do the opposite of tie.

A **negation prefix** indicates the 'opposite state of being or oppositional description' as compared to the root or base word. To say a table is *unstable* means it is 'the opposite of stable'—shaky, weak, wobbly, etc.

More Examples

The following example shows a prefix used as a reversal:
- Please ***disconnect*** the wires.

In this case, the wires were initially connected; the speaker is asking for the condition of the wires to be ***reversed*** (not connected).

The following example shows the same prefix used as a negation:
- The radio will not work because the wire is ***disconnected***.

The condition of the wire is that it's ***not*** connected.

Practice #7: Read the following sentences and determine whether the prefix in each underlined word is functioning as a reversal (R) or a negation (N). Write your answer in the space provided.

1) The young man never showed <u>disrespect</u> to his mother; he was always listened when she spoke to him. _____

2) Do not <u>disrespect</u> your teacher in class. _____

3) Your sneakers are <u>untied</u>. _____

4) <u>Untie</u> your sneakers before you take your shoes off. _____

5) My mother told me to <u>defrost</u> the window so that I could see. _____

6) The window is now completely <u>defrosted</u>. _____

7) The <u>inactive</u> teen was encouraged to take up dance or art. _____

8) <u>Deactivate</u> the alarm before it goes off. _____

9) Please make sure you provide a ramp and elevator access for our <u>disabled</u> students. _____

10) Please be sure to <u>disable</u> the alarm system before you leave this evening. _____

Practice #8: Based on the context of each sentence, complete the bolded word by adding the correct prefix from the list. An example is provided below.

a	contra	anti	dis	il	in	ir	non	mis	pseudo	un

Example: Since your entire group did not turn in their project, I will give you a(n) ____**complete** grade until it is finished. (incomplete)

1. The claim that Christopher Columbus "____**covered** the New World" is false; for it is a land that was never hidden and always known by explorers and travelers throughout the world.

2. Many politicians have been found guilty of ____**managing** finances after authorities found errors and inconsistencies in their accountants' records.

3. In the evening, the guards usually ____**bind** the arms and legs of the prisoners and let them walk about freely in the yard.

4. On the east coast of North America, we have been experiencing ____**typical** weather all year; it snowed in late March and was 80 degrees in December.

5. A chaplain or imam of a military order is considered a ____**combatant** enemy during wartime as they do not physically fight in the war.

6. A(n) ____**toxin** works against a poison in the body that is of a biological origin.

7. When those holding political office violate the Constitution, their power becomes ____**legitimate** as they have now broken the law and are to be removed from office immediately.

8. The Israeli-Palestinian conflict seems almost ____**resolvable** as it is currently at an impasse; both parties adamantly claim ownership of the land.

9. Mark Twain is the _____(o)**nym** of the author whose real name is Samuel Clemens.

10. The ____**position** to the universal principles of truth, freedom and justice are falsehood, bondage and inequity.

Intensifier Prefixes

A prefix may function as an intensifier, making the base or root word stronger.

Example: confirm, constitution, obtain

Word	Prefix	Suffix
confirm	con	firm
constitution	con	stitution - the condition of standing
obtain	ob	tain - to hold

This is often tricky to decipher as intensifying prefixes hold other meanings as well. For example, *reread* means to 'read again,' while **re**search means to 'look at or search at something thoroughly.' When the prefix is an intensifier, it can also mean 'thoroughly.'

Practice #9: Read the list of words below. Using an American Heritage Dictionary, look up the definition (entry-level) and etymology of each word [see bracket] to determine the words that have intensifier prefixes. Write the definition on the line to the right and circle the words with intensifiers. An example is provided.

Example:
exit: to move out
exhausted: to be *thoroughly* drained

reinstate: _____

resolute: _____

congress: _____

comfortable: _____

persuade: _____

periphery: _____

deject: _____

desolate: _____

Practice #10: First, identify the prefix in each word. Next, determine whether the prefix is acting as an intensifier (I) or a non-intensifier (NI). Lastly, fill in the blank for the sentences that follow using the words from the list.

*Hint: The definitions give clues as to how the prefix functions. Read each one carefully.

Word Bank:

I a.   **confirmation:** a thorough spoken account of an event or situation <u>con</u>_____
  b.   **replete:** having much or plenty of something _____
  c.   **reactionary:** to act or do something in response or against a former act _____
  d.   **commentary:** the condition of making something firm or strong _____
  e.   **convocation:** the act of calling together _____
  f.   **exclude:** the act of closing or shutting out _____
  g.   **elucidate:** to make clear or intelligible or shed light or explain _____
  h.   **persist:** to stay or stand firmly or continuously; prolonged existence _____
  i.   **perimeter:** the measurement around a polygon _____
  j.   **declare:** to make clear _____
  k.   **demolish:** to take away beauty _____

Example: After receiving <u>confirmation</u> (a) that I was awarded a grant to travel overseas, I booked a ticket to Morocco.

1. History is _____ with examples of colonialism, namely in the Americas, Africa and Asia.

2. A _____ politician quickly voted down any efforts to change from the status quo.

3. After the documentary, we stayed to hear the director's _____ on the research it took to make the film.

4. The _____ ceremony brings friends and families together to celebrate the graduates of the school's first linguistics program.

5. If an African-American citizen tried to vote in the 1950s, the workers would _____ him based on his race.

6. Please _____ the science behind the Egyptians' construction of pyramids during the middle dynastic period.

7. The carpenter measured the _____ of the table in order to determine how many chairs could fit around it.

8. The pain in my left arm will _____ until I start working out and resting in the evenings.

9. The beautiful old building was _____ed because the contractors wanted to clear away the relics of the past to bring vibrancy and life to the city.

10. DC, Maryland and Virginia _____ d a state of emergency due to flooding after a major earthquake.

There are four important rules for you to know about **PREFIXES**.

Rule 1: <u>A prefix can change the meaning of a word.</u>

Example: *construct, reconstruct, deconstruct*

		con	+	*struct* (means to build **together**)
De	+	*con*	+	*struct* (to build **down** or take **apart**)
Re	+	*con*	+	*struct* (to build together **again**)

Rule 1 Practice — Add prefixes to the following base words below to make words. Some prefixes will not fit. Use the dictionary to see if your newly formed word is a real word. An example is provided below.

Base Word	mis	dis	re	de
calculate	miscalculate	~~discalculate~~	recalculate	~~decalculate~~
member				
locate				
pose				
take				
appoint				

Base Word	sub	pro	in	ex,e
tract				
stitute				
ject				
vert				
spect				

Rule 2: <u>A word can have more than one prefix.</u>

Example: ***Disconnect***

con	+	*nect*		*dis*	+	*con*	+	*nect*
(prefix)		(root)		(prefix)		(prefix)		(root)

Rule 2 Practice 1 — In the space provided, write the two prefixes in each of the words below. Give the meaning of the first prefix. *Note: One word has three prefixes; identify all three.

1) reintroduce   _____

2) discombobulate   _____

3) inaccessible   _____

4) decompose   _____

5) misinform   _____

6) deconstruct   _____

7) misrepresent   _____

8) irrelevant   _____

9) insurrection   _____

10) disregard   _____

Rule 2 Practice 2 — Complete each word below by adding the correct prefix within the space provided based on the definition that follows each word. Then highlight the other prefix and write its meaning in the space provided. An example is provided below:

Hint*: Use the following prefixes to complete the words below.

con   com   de   dis   ex   in   mis   re

_____describable: not able to completely write down or explain; not able to describe
<u>in</u>describable   **de**: completely; down
The word is "indescribable." The key word in the definition is "not." The second prefix means "down."

1. _____engage: to not engage; _____

2. _____instate: to bring back to the original state; _____

3. _____understand: to understand incorrectly; _____

4. _____compatible: not harmonious with another person; _____

5. _____conception: before a pregnancy; _____

6. _____efficient: not efficient; not able to be worked out; _____

7. in_____finite: lacking complete boundaries; that which does not

   come to an end; _____

8. re_____vene: to come together again; _____

9. mis_____municate: not able to exchange ideas with another

   person; _____

10. in_____plicable: not able to fully lay out an idea; _____

When a word has two prefixes, one is usually either negative (negation or reversal) or signifies repetition.

Remember the word *inaccessible* from our previous example?

It has two prefixes:

in	+	*ac*	+	*cess*	+	*ible*
(prefix)		(prefix)		(move)		(capable of)

The initial prefix in the word *inaccessible* signifies negation or the opposite of the word *accessible*. Thus, *inaccessible* means '**not** accessible' or '**not** capable of moving toward or approaching something.'

Another example: *reconvene*

re	+	*con*	+	*vene*
(again)		(with)		(come)

Thus, the initial prefix in the word *reconvene* signifies repetition as it means to '**come together again**.'

Rule 2 Practice 3 — Using the dictionary, write the meaning of each of the words below and highlight the meaning of the prefix(es). There are two examples below.

Inaccessible: <u>**not** accessible</u>   Reconvene: <u>to **come** together **again**</u>

1) nonconformist*   _____

2) irresponsible   _____

3) indistinguishable _____

4) reinstate _____

5) imperfect _____

6) decompose _____

7) reconfigure _____

8) misinform _____

9) disinvite _____

10) represent _____

*-*ist* is a suffix meaning one who (referring to a person)

Rule 3: <u>A prefix can change the part of speech of a word.</u>
— What are the eight parts of speech and their functions?

Part of Speech	Function	Example	Answers The Question
noun			who, what, where
pronoun			who, what, where
adjective			what type, kind, shape, color, etc., how much? whose?
verb			what did he/she/it do? what is his state of being?
adverb			how did he/she/it do something?
preposition			where, when, how, why
conjunction			
interjection			

These are examples of prefixes that change the part of speech of a word. They are generally of Germanic origin (versus Latin or Greek, which this book addresses in Chapter 5):

Word without Prefix	Word with Prefix
witch (noun)	bewitch (verb)
friend (noun)	befriend (verb)
throne (noun)	dethrone (verb)

Rule 3 Practice 1 — Read the sentences below and select the word in the parentheses that best completes each sentence.

1) I am determined to _____ my new neighbor's daughter because we are the same age. (**friend, befriend**)

2) Charlotte of Mecklenburg-Strelitz sat on the _____ as the Queen of Great Britain and Ireland; eventually, she became the queen of the United Kingdom. (**throne, dethrone**)

3) My grandfather tells anecdotes and stories to _____ our lives with tales of prosperity and happiness. (**rich, enrich**)

4) I'll be sure to set my alarm to _____ me up in the morning since I stayed _____ all night playing video games. (**wake, awake**)

5) I was taken _____ when the manager gave me _____ my wallet without any identification. (**back, aback**)

Rule 4: <u>A prefix can have many forms.</u>

Consider the prefixes *ad, con, dis, ex, in, ob, syn* and *sub*. When combined with base or root words, they create new words. For example:

ad + *junct* = <u>ad</u>junct	*con* + *tain* = <u>con</u>tain	*dis* + *rupt* = <u>dis</u>rupt
ex + *act* = <u>ex</u>act	*in* + *action* = <u>in</u>action	*ob* + *struct* = <u>ob</u>struct

However, sometimes a prefix's form must change before it attaches to a root. For example, the words *attain*, *assign* and *account* all have the same prefix: *ad-*. The prefix ad- changes its form by changing the final consonant *d* to *t*, *s* or *c* to match the base word that it follows, giving us *at-*, *as-* and *ac-*. Each of these prefixes is a variant of *ad-*.

The following chart shows how to use each variant and provides a word example. The final column offers a space to provide additional examples.

con (with; together)	co	vowels, h, w	coworker	
	col	l	collection	
	com	m, b and p	common, combine, companion	
	cor	r	correct	
in (opposite; not, inside)	i	gn	ignoble	
	il	l	illegal	
	im	m, b and p	immature, imbalanced, impossible	
	ir	r	irresponsible	
ad (to)	ac	c	access, acquiesce	
	af	f	affluent	
	ag	g	aggression	
	al	l	alleviate	
	an	n	annoy	
	ap	p	appear	
	ar	r	arrive	
	as	s and c	asset, ascertain	
	at	t	attack	
sub	suc	c	succeed	
	sud	d*	suddenly	
	suf	f	suffer	
	sug	g	suggest	
	sum	m	summary	
	sup	p	suppose	
	sus	c, p and t	susceptible, suspend, sustain	
	subter		subterfuge	
ob (away)	o	m	omit	
	of	c	offensive	
	oc	f	occur	
	op	p	opportunity	

syn (similar)	sym	m, b or p	symbol	
	syl	l	syllabus	
	sy	s and z	system	
ex (out)	e	on occasion*	erase	
	ec	c*	eccentric	
	ef	f	efficient	

The variant forms of a prefix are a result of assimilation. The verb assimilate means to become similar to something else. Assimilated prefixes become similar to their base/root word by changing the final consonant to match or blend well with the first letter of the base. Thus, ad becomes at when attached to tain, creating the word attain; ad becomes as when attached to sign, producing the word assign.

ad → at + tain = __at__tain   ad → as + sign = __as__sign
ad → ac + count = __ac__count   ad → ac + cent = __ac__cent

Prefixes assimilate to their base word to ease pronunciation and create euphony in language. Euphony is the quality of being pleasing to the ear (eu: pleasing + phony: sound). For example, attaching ad to tain creates adtain, an awkward word that is difficult to say. Below are examples of words with prefixes that were not assimilated. Read the words aloud and think about how they sound and how it feels to say them.

__ad__sign   __ad__count   __ad__cent

The variant forms of prefixes help a word's phonemes glide together, alleviating the strange sound and pronunciation from using the original prefix. These strange pronunciations existed in Latin over 2,000 years ago before, but over time prefixes absorbed a base word's initial consonant sound. Assimilated prefixes is one of many examples of phonetic change, a common feature of many languages.

Rule 4 Practice 1 — Identify the prefix of each word in the first column; next, give three words with a similar prefix (but in a different form). An example is provided:

Word	prefix	example 1	example 2	example 3
collateral	col; with	conducive	communal	coeducation
synonym				
eject				
invite				
obtain				
except				

illegitimate				
suffice				
sympathy				
oppose				
accept				

Rule 4 Practice 2 — Attach the correct form of the prefix to the root or base word to spell the intended word correctly. An example is below:

For example: in + possible: impossible
1. sub + plant: _____
2. con + passion: _____
3. ad + custom: _____
4. ad + tempt: _____
5. ad + certain: _____

Rule 4 Practice 3 — Select the correct form of the prefix to complete the words below. Next, fill in the blanks with the meaning of each word.

im + possible: impossible; meaning not possible
1. in + measurable: _____, meaning "_____ able to be measured"
2. ad + locate: _____, meaning "to place _____; to set aside for a special purpose"
3. in + plausible: _____, meaning "_____ plausible or possible"
4. ex + centric: _____, meaning "_____ of the center or norm"
5. syn + metalism: _____, putting "two or more metals _____ "
6. in + responsible: _____, meaning "_____ responsible"
7. in + describable: _____, meaning "_____ able to describe"
8. sub + press: _____, meaning "to press down or _____ "
9. in + logical: _____, meaning "_____ logical"
10. in + mobile: _____, meaning "_____ mobile or able to be moved"

Summary

A *prefix* is a word part attached before the root of a word that changes the meaning of a word. A prefix can indicate a _____ (such as *binomial, monologue*) or act as a _____ (such as *prepare, transact, interact,* etc...), a _____ (as in *indirect, illegal, unlawful*) or an _____ (as in *confirm, replete, obtain*). A word can have as many as _____ prefixes. Prefixes can have many variant forms, and the spelling of a prefix changes based on the _____ letter of the root or base word. The variant prefix forms are said to be _____ prefixes, as they absorb the initial consonant of its base word to maintain euphony.

All About Prefixes Review

Prefix Rules: Multiple Choice and True/False

1.   A prefix is placed at the _____ of a root.

   a.   beginning
   b.   middle
   c.   end
   d.   none of the above

2.   A prefix acts as which of the following (select all that apply)?

   a.   number
   b.   preposition
   c.   negation
   d.   none of the above

3.   T or F: All words have prefixes.

4.   T or F: A word can have two prefixes.

5.   A(n) _____ is a prefix that strengthens the meaning of the root in the word's definition.

Identifying, Classifying and Defining Prefix(es) in a Word

Directions: Identify the prefix(es) in the words in column 1 and write them in column 2. In column 3, classify the prefix(es) as either a preposition (p), a number (#), a negation (-) or an intensifier (i). Lastly, in column 4, give the meaning of the prefix(es). An example is provided below.

Column 1	Column 2	Column 3	Column 4
delete	de	P	away
trigonometry			
antidote			
biceps			
deplete			
preponderance			
quadrant			
innovation			
misinterpret			
convert			
polyglot			
subconscious			
reexamine			
transliterate			
disavow			
unilateral			
centennial			
duodecimal			
intermediary			
pentameter			
septennial			

Words in Context: Fill in the Blank

Complete each sentence by filling in the blank. Use the meaning of the prefix of the boldfaced word to assist you.

*Hint: Underline the prefix first, then determine the prefix meaning to fill in the blank. Use the dictionary to help you as well.

Example: To **delete** a word is to take it ___away___.

1. The word **quintessence** refers to the _____ highest element (after earth, water, air and fire) which makes up the heavens; the pure essence of something.

2. An **apathetic** individual is _____ feeling or indifferent.

3. It is easy to speak _____ an **affable** person.

4. A **multilateral** agreement is one participated in by _____ parties.

5. A **monarch** is the _____ and supreme ruler of a nation.

6. **Postnatal** care is given shortly _____ the birth of a child.

7. To **superimpose** is to lay one thing _____ another.

8. Authors of novels sometimes use **foreshadowing** to give hints about an event _____ it actually happens.

9. Someone who is **nonchalant** is very relaxed and appears _____ to be worried about anything.

10. An **equilateral** triangle is a triangle in which all the sides are of _____ length.

11. To be **semiconscious** is to be _____-conscious or partially aware.

12. A **tetrapod** has _____ feet, legs or leg-like appendages.

13. The star of David is an example of a **hexagram**, as it is a(n) _____-sided figure.

14. A **nonagon** is a(n) _____-sided figure.

15. An **octachord** is a(n) _____-stringed musical instrument or a series of _____ notes played in succession.

16. **Unleavened** bread is made without yeast so that it will _____ rise.

17. A person participating in a **decathlon** would complete _____ track and field events.

18. **International** affairs are conducted _____ nations.

19. To **transgress** is to go _____ a limit, law or commandment.

20. To **undersign** is to sign one's name at the _____ of a document.

Prefix Derivations

Directions: Based on the definitions that follow, select the correct prefix to complete each partial word.   Next, complete the sentences with words from each section.

Example   <u>dis</u>tract: to divert; to draw attention away

tract: to draw

_____tract: to draw together through written or verbal agreement

_____tract: to pull or draw back; to withdraw

_____tract: to draw or take away a desirable part; diminish

_____tract: to be drawn toward; to draw a thing or person toward you

_____tract: to draw or take out

1.   Maria's hideous attitude _____tracts from her natural beauty.
2.   Scientists are able to _____tract the most potent elements from plants to concoct oils and tinctures to make medicine.
3.   After the man cursed his sister, he wished he could _____tract his words; but it was too late as she had run to tell their mom of his blunder.

flect, flex: to bend or turn

_____flect: to bend or cast back; to turn back on one's thoughts

_____flect: to turn aside; to cause to deviate

_____flect: to bend in; to change, alter or influence

_____flexible: not able to bend

_____flex: bent in two directions or bends two ways

1.   The campaign manager tried to _____flect attention away from him when people realized money was missing from the account, but all eyes were on him.
2.   Word _____flections are most evident when making a noun plural. We typically add –s or –es and sometimes must drop ending vowels, replacing them when necessary.
3.   The gymnast's elbows are _____flex, which helps her hold difficult postures that require her joints to bend in two directions.

vert: to turn

_____vert: to turn inside out

_____vert: to turn from below; overthrow; destroy

_____vert: to turn aside; to prevent

_____vert: to turn toward

_____vert: to turn back; turn away

1. Please don't let Matthew_____vert your attention to the board where I am writing the notes you will need to study for tomorrow's quiz.

2. Although she refrained from meat for three days, she _____verted back to eating chicken after she went to a dinner for her high school reunion.

3. Those enslaved in South Carolina made a plan to _____vert their masters and obtain freedom for themselves.

sect: to cut
_____sect: to cut into three
_____sect: to cut into two
_____sect: to cut between
_____sect: to cut apart for investigation
_____sect: to cut across or divide by cutting

1. My favorite hiking trail _____sects a valley filled with lavender and blue-wild indigo.

2. I _____sected the pie so that my mother, father and uncle each received a portion.

3. The bus stops on Kennedy Street where it _____sects Georgia Avenue.

gress: to move, to step
_____gress: body of attendants; people coming together; meeting
_____gress: to step across, to step over
_____gress: to move forward
_____gress: to move back; return to a former state
_____gress: to go or move out; place of exit

1. The new building was beautiful but not functional; there were not enough ways to _____gress in case of a fire or emergency.

2. Representatives of the American and British governments _____gress to devise a treaty that will allow both parties to rule jointly over the land.

3. Although the medication will make her feel better temporarily, her illness will _____gress until she receives a more natural and holistic treatment.

Spelling Practice

Directions: Correct the spelling of each word below by indicating the proper prefix form.

Example: *subfocate*→*suffocate*

1. subpend: _____

2. subport: _____

3. conlusion: _____

4. conroaborate: _____

5. inlicit: _____

6. ingnore: _____

7. adlusion: _____

8. adgrandize: _____

9. exvoke: _____

10. exfulgent: _____

Intensifiers

Directions: Circle the word with the intensifier in each pair. Use the dictionary to assist you.

1. refine	recipient	6. perplex	perpetual
2. composure	committee	7. elicit	espouse
3. conversation	conscript	8. obverse	obtain
4. devalue	definite	9. occasion	occupation
5. correct	corrugate	10. conclude	consideration

All About Roots

"A single Latin or Greek root...can be found in and aid in the understanding (as well as decoding and encoding) of 20 or more English words." — Tim Rasinski

There are three important rules for you to know about roots:

Rule 1: A root carries the most fundamental meaning of a word.

The word *fundamental* carries a similar meaning as foundation. A foundation is "that which founds or is at the bottom of an object or concept." The foundation of a thing is generally understood to be firm and sturdy, providing a base upon which something can be built. Picture the foundation of a house. A strong foundation ensures that a house is sturdy and sound enough for safe dwelling. Without it, all other parts of the house are subject to fall apart. The foundation is critical for stability; it is the basis of the house's existence.

Now think about a plant and its roots. The roots are the foundation of the plant. Without them, the plant will not be securely embedded in the ground and will not vegetate. The seed is the source of the plant, sprouting roots from which the plant can grow. The foundation is the security of the house, and the roots are the power behind the plant's growth.

Thus, the root of anything is fundamental; it must be firmly understood because it holds the basic meaning of the word. It is akin to the root of a plant; though the plant's flowers, stems and leaves may be used for a variety of purposes, those parts are related through the root. The root is the mother of a plant and, subsequently, it is the mother of words as well.

This chapter addresses the most common roots or base words found in English words. These root words can derive from Germanic, Latin or Greek words (although words in the English lexicon come from a variety of sources). And the Germanic, Latin, and Greek words can be traced back to an even earlier source. The true root of a word traces back to the mother tongue of its lingual family. English is a part of the Indo-European family of languages, and its mother root is the Proto-Indo-European (PIE) root. This chapter introduces root or base words of Latin and Greek origin, which comprise 90% of the English language.

The next book of this series, "Getting to the Root of the Root," will trace these languages back to the Indo-European root and address their various cognates.

For now, let's explore the primary Latin and Greek roots.

Example: Report

Re is the prefix of the word **report**. Circle the prefix of the word **report**.

Port is the root of the word *report*. Underline or highlight the prefix of the word **report**. Port derives from the Latin word *portare* meaning "to carry."

The following chart contains a list of common roots and their meaning. Also listed are examples of words with each root. Using words from the list that follows the chart, write additional examples of words using the roots in the box below. *Hint: circle the prefixes in each word to identify the root.

Root	Meaning	Example 1	Example 2	Example 3
act, ag, igu	drive, go, move	action, agitate, ambiguous		
anim	breathe; mind	animation		
anthrop(o)	human	anthropology		
aqu, aqua	water	aquatic		
astro/aster	star	astronomy, asterisk		
audi	hear	auditory		
bio	life	biology		
cap, capt, cept	take, seize, get	capture, intercept		
chron(o)	time	chronology		
clude, clus	shut, close	exclusive		
corp	body	corporation		
cred	trust, believe	incredible		
dict	to speak or say	dictionary		

duc, duce, duct	draw	reduce		
fac(t), fec(t)	to make, to do	factory, affect		
flect, flex	to bend	reflect, flexible		
gen, gener	kind, type, or produce (birth)	genealogy, generation		
geo, gee	earth	geography		
graph	write	autograph		
ject	to throw	rejection		
leg, lex	law, to bind	legal		
log, logy, logue	word, study, science	logic, psychology, monologue		
meter, metri	measure	centimeter		
miss, mit	to send	mission		
path	to feel, to suffer, have a disease	sympathy		
port	to carry	transport		
scribe, script	to write	transcribe		
sens, sent	to feel	sensation		
spec	to see	spectacle		
ten, tend, tens, tent	stretch	tender, tension, tentacle		
the, theo	deity/"God"	theology		
therm	heat	thermal		
vis	to see	visible		

metric	captivate	agenda
pathetic	transact	animosity
interject	audit	introduce
examine	gene	lexicon
chronicle	thermometer*	aquamarine
spectator	thermostat	empathy
corpse	credit	dictate
prospective	tense	polytheistic
abduct	defect	aquarium
scripture	geology*	prescribe
credulous	recluse	attention
sentimental	submit	biopsy
thermos	unanimous	deflect
contradiction	astrology**	prologue
paragraph	caption	seclude
gender	etymology*	incorporate
biography	audience	legislature
inflection	synchronize	geometry*
manufacture	astronaut	anthropopithecus
monotheistic	missile	export
sensitive	misanthrope	portable
projectile	indicate	subaqueous
antibiotic	facile	supervision visual

*These words have two root words, but one functions as a root word.

Rule 1 Practice 1 — Circle the root of each of the following words.

1. benediction
2. agitator
3. privilege
4. important
5. inducement
6. permission
7. dissent
8. pathology*
9. contender
10. circumscribe
11. magnanimous
12. anachronistic
13. theocracy*
14. sentient
15. division
16. apogee
17. actuary
18. progeny
19. eulogy
20. disaster

Rule 1 Practice 2 — Match the words on the left to the roots on the right.

Words	Roots
transmission	gen
inclusive	fect
indictment	audi
indigenous	chron
antibiotics	clus
affectionate	miss
audition	cred
synchronize	anim
credential	**dict**
animosity	**bio**

Rule 2: <u>**A word can only have one root.**</u>

Example: Disconnect

con   +   *nect*
(prefix)   (root)

dis   +   *con*   +   *nect*
(prefix)   (prefix)   (root)

nect comes from the Latin word nectere meaning "to bind or tie." Thus, disconnect means

"to _____."

Example: contradict

Prefix				Suffix		
3P	2P	1P	0	1S	2S	3S
		contra	*dict*			

dict is a root meaning "to _____." Thus, contradict means "to

_____."

Sometimes, a word can have two parts that are common root words. However, only one of the roots functions as either a prefix or suffix.

Example:
<u>thermometer</u>
Thermo is a common root, meaning "heat."
Meter is a common root, meaning "measure."

Here, *thermo* is used as a prefix. It determines what is being measured (in this case, heat is being measured). A word can have up to three prefixes, although it typically has one or two. Also, a word can have up to three suffixes.

Rule 2 Practice 1 — Draw a line through the prefix(es) and suffix(es) or word endings. Then, in the space provided, write each word's root and its meaning.

*Hint: Use the list of roots on the previous pages to identify the root of each word.

Example: por~~table~~   port; to carry

1. anthropomorphic   _____

2. suspect   _____

3. aqueous   _____

4. adjective   _____

5. habeas corpus   _____

6. flexor   _____

7. capsule   _____

8. invisible   _____

9. graphology   _____

10. monotheistic   _____

Rule 2 Practice 2 — Complete each sentence by filling in the blank with the missing root (see options in parentheses at the end of each sentence).

Example: I try my best not to <u>contradict</u> (dict, ception) my mother's warnings to not multitask and pay attention while driving, but I often do find myself talking on the phone while driving.

1. Which type of science class would you prefer to take next semester? _____ology (bio, anthrop), the study of living organisms, or _____ology (bio, anthrop), which is the study of the development of humans.

2. In the Shakespeare play *Othello*, Othello the Moor gives a mono_____(logue, gram) professing his love for Desdemona to the Duke of Venice.

3. Jonathan wants to get involved in the pro_____tion (ject, duc) of films that teach youth about African cultural traditions.

4. The woman did not want to talk about the money she stole, so she de_____ed (flect, scrib) by talking about her promotion at work instead.

5. I have much sym_____y (metr, path) for families who are suffering from poverty and hunger. It hurts me to see them in such pain.

6. In 2013, I started a major educational _____ation (gener, corpor) with a body of experienced teachers.

7. The student's re_____ion (miss, tent) is based on the fact that he did not pass any of his final exams; he will have to go to summer school if he wants to go on to the next grade level.

8. The re_____ive (act, clus) old man had not left his house in over five years.

9. As I sat and watched the witnesses give their testimony, I began to _____ate (dicta, specul) about whether or not they were telling the truth.

10. Before one makes a lawful claim of right or address the lawfulness of an act or practice, one must ensure that he and all parties involved are of the same juris_____ion (dict, lex).

Rule 3: <u>A root can have many forms.</u>

Just like prefixes and suffixes, a root can have more than one form. A morpheme's form refers to the structure and letters that comprise that word part; in other words, roots can have multiple spellings. For example, in the "All About Prefixes" chapter, we learned that *sub* can also be written as *sug*, *suf* and *suc*. These prefixes all carry the same meaning, which is "beneath, below or after." Roots act in the same way.

<u>For example:</u>
Fac, *fact*, *fect*, *fic*, *fict* and *fy* are roots that bear the same meaning, which is "to do" or "to make." Some examples are below. Use your dictionary or an online source to add four more examples:

fac(t)	fec(t)	fic(t)	fy
factory	infected	efficient	verify
manufacture	defective	fiction	clarify

Each of the words above can be defined without a dictionary by using word parts.

In *factory*, the suffix *-ory* comes from the Latin suffix -orium meaning "place or room." Thus, a factory is a _____ where things are _____.

In *manufacture*: The prefix _____ means "by hand." The suffix -ure is Latin, indicating action. Thus, manufacture is

_____ .

Infect means to "put" or "do" within; once you _____ one substance or object into another substance or object, it spoils or stains the original thing. Think about arthritis or bronchitis; both are infections that develop from mucus placing itself in the joints and bronchial tubes, respectively.[1]

Efficient carries the adjectival suffix *-ent* and the prefix *ef*, which is a derivative of _____, meaning _____. Here, ef is an intensifying prefix. Thus, efficient means that which is _____ ; productive.

---

[1] The suffix *-itis* refers to inflammation; the arthr of arthritis comes from the Greek *arthron* meaning "a joint," while *bronchial* comes from the Greek *bronkhos* meaning "windpipe or throat."

Verify carries the verbal suffix *–fy* (but is derived from the root word fac(t)). Combined with the root *veri*, meaning 'true', *verify* means to _____

_____ .

Answers: A *factory* is a place where things are made; *manufacture* means to make something by hand; *efficient* means that which is thoroughly made or done. *Infect* means to put something into someone or something. Lastly, to *verify* means to make sure something is true.

It is failry easy to see how the root words *fac*, *fic*, *fec* and *–fy* are connected. However, some root words are more obviously connected than others. For example, gen and nat are root words that carry the same meaning, referring to "that which is produced or born." This is because both of these roots share a common Indo-European mother root. This makes gen and nat linguistic cousins. Linguistic cousins are also called cognates. Cognates will be addressed in future books in this series. Complete the chart below by providing word examples with the various roots and their cognates.

Root	Additional Roots	Words	Word Example
sta, stat (with; together)	sti, sist, syst	institute, insist, system	
gen (opposite; not)	kin, nat, nasc	kindred, nation, nascent	
fac, fact (inside)	fect, fict, fy*	affect, fiction, satisfy	
spec (to)	spic, spis, scop	suspicious, despise, microscope	
vis (to see)	vid, wit, wis, id	video, witness, wise, idea	
cap (to take)	cept, ceive	except, receive	
werg (work)	erg, urg, org, wr	energy, urgent, organ, wright	
port (carry, bear)	phor, pher, fer	metaphor, infer	

Rule 3 Practice 1 — First, identify the root of each word listed in the first column. Second, choose two words with a similar root from the list below and write them under Example 1 and Example 2. Lastly, think of an additional word with the same root word and record it under Example 3. It must be a word that contains a different cognate of the root. See the example below.

Word	Root	Example 1	Example 2	Example 3
defective	fect	*fiction*	*faction*	*artificial*
station				
reporter				
urgent				
specify				
generation				
provide				
captor				

fiction, faction	portfolio	inception
nativity	euphoria	microscopic
resist	evidence	advisor
deceive	emergency	kindergarten
disorganized	Constitution	inconspicuous

Rule 3 Practice 2 — Pick the right cognate or form to complete each missing word in the sentences below.

1)   The company promised to pr_____ [vise, vide] me with housing accommodations for at least six months.

2)   I received a C on my final paper because I did not go back and re_____ [vise, vide] or edit my work.

3)   Marcus has an interest in his family _____alogy [gene, nat] and learning about his lineage and heritage so that he may better understand himself.

4)   Moroccans and British officials met together to form an inter_____tional [gene, nat] treaty to ensure peaceful relations between the two countries.

5)   Although the grand opening was well-executed, I thought the new business would not be successful, since it was in an incon_____uous [spic, spec] location.

6)   Even though the investor liked my proposal, he was circum_____t [scop, spec] about investing so much money in the start-up.

7)   Use a helio_____e [scop, spic] to view the sun without straining and causing injury to the eyes.

8)   Without a firm foundation in petrology, you may be vulnerable to purchasing _____titious [fac, fic] gemstones and semi-precious jewels.

9)   My sister is ef___icient [fy, fic]; she planned our last family vacation all by herself and even booked travel and lodging accommodations for all our aunts and uncles.

10)   The scientist used microscopes to magni___ [fy, fac] the bacteria from hair samples to determine the root of the patient's ringworm.

Rule 3 Practice 3 — Complete the chart below by identifying the root, the root's meaning and the definition of each word below. Use the definitions below the chart to complete the last column. An example is included.

Word	Root	Root Meaning	Definition
nativity	nat	birth	*
concept			
unstable			
introspection			
liquefaction			
miscegenation			
capstan			
prefecture			
stethoscope			
desist			
renascence			

*   the occasion of a person's birth

a.   an instrument that "sees" within the chest to examine the heart and lungs

b.   office, authority or territory of an administration official; to "make before" in rank

c.   a device used to hold and wind rope, especially on ships

d.   to cease, stop; to abstain or stand down

e.   to be born again; revival

f.   not standing fixed; fluctuating

g.   an idea, thought; "taken together"

h.   the act of causing a solid or gas to become a liquid

i.   marriage between members of different ethnicities; to be born of mixed heritage

j.   having a tendency to look into one's own mind

Summary

The root of a word carries the most _____ meaning of the word. A word can only have _____ root word(s), and root words can appear in many _____, such as *tent*, *tend*, *tens* and *tain*, all meaning _____.

All About Roots Review Exercises

Identify the Root

Identify the root and its meaning in each of the words below.

Example: interactive   act: to move or go

- animadvert   _____

- conscription   _____

- lexicographer   _____

- tenacious   _____

- provisional   _____

Fill-in-the-blank activity 1

Fill in each blank with the literal meaning of the root of the italicized word in each sentence.

Example: to react is to "__go__ back" at someone or behave in a particular way in response to something.

- *Geology* is the study of _____.

- A *biopsy* is a microscopic examination of _____ tissue in a human body.

- *To genuflect* is to _____ the knees.

- A *portly* man would _____ a lot of weight around his stomach.

- An *insensate* patient would completely lack physical _____.

Match the Definition

Complete the chart below by

a) Identifying the root and its meaning of each word

b) Matching each word with its definition from the list below

Word	Root	Definition
counteract	act; move or go	*
equanimity		
relegate		
anthropomorphic		
disport		
retention		
inflection		
envisage		
sentient		
biotic		
circumscribe		

*   to move in opposition; to neutralize

a.   evenness of mind; calm temper

b.   to draw a line around; to encircle; to limit

c.   a change in pitch or tone of voice; a bend or curve

d.   relating to life; of living things

e.   relating to or characterized as having human characteristics, particularly objects, animals and deities

f.   to assign to an inferior position; to exile or banish under law

g.   to amuse, make merry; to "carry away" from work; also as a noun (amusement)

h.   the act of holding back; the continued keeping or possession of something; the fact of keeping something in one's memory

i.   of, having or capable of feeling or perception; conscious

j.   to confront; to view with the mind's eye

Complete the Sentence

Complete each sentence with the correct words from the previous exercise.

<u>Example</u>: In order to <u>counteract</u> police brutality, we must study law, history and politics to better understand our status in our own nation and recognize that without a nationality we have no standing in law.

1) One quality a great leader must develop is _____, which will allow him or her to deal with conflict with clear and balanced thinking.

2) After a long week, Ashley likes to go to karaoke for solace and _____.

3) Do not _____ children's creativity; give them time to freely explore their natural talents and interests and cultivate their curiosity.

4) As he read to the kindergarteners, Samuel's voice lacked _____, making his storytelling a bore to watch.

5) A _____ factor of any organism is the sun as a fuel source as it is necessary to live.

6) Final exams are used to measure a student's _____ of information taught throughout the year as they must remember and build upon it the following year.

7) The White Rabbit in Lewis Carroll's *Alice in Wonderland* is a(n) _____ Rabbit; as he wears clothing and speaks just like we humans do.

8) After the lead actors had been repeatedly late for rehearsal, the director decided to _____ them to the chorus and replace them with their understudies.

9) The blanket's touch seemed so like a human caress, I really thought it was a _____ being, capable of loving and having sympathy for me.

10) I _____ a school that teaches the truth about history, politics and culture and not watered-down curricula.

All About Suffixes

"...teaching ELLS the role of suffixes within words assists their reading fluency as well as their language development." — ANTONACO, O'CALLAGHAN AND BERKOWITZ, 2014

Rule 1: <u>Suffixes can be found at the end of a word.</u>

<u>Examples</u>: *hopeful*; *hopeless*; *magnetize*; *magnetic*

- *ful* is the suffix of the word **hopeful**. Circle the suffix of the word **hopeful**.

- *less* is the suffix of the word **hopeless**. Circle the suffix of the word **hopeless**.

- *ize* is the suffix of the word **magnetize**. Circle the suffix of the word **magnetize**.

- *ic* is the suffix of the word **magnetic**. Circle the suffix of the word **magnetic**.

Rule 1 Practice: Identify the suffixes of the following words:

Word	Suffix	Example
goodness		
lovable		
hopeful		
hopeless		
selfish		
selfless		
friendly		
friendship		
childish		
childhood		
instruction		
instructor		
empathetic		
empathize		

Extension: Think of another word with the same suffix as each of the words above and write a sentence using each word.

Rule 2: <u>Suffixes can change the part of speech of a word.</u>

By adding or removing suffixes from a word, it can change that word's part of speech. See the base word nation below:

Nation is a noun; adding the suffix -al produces the word national, which is an adjective. It describes a person, place or thing. National is "that which relates to or is a characteristic of a nation." See the sentence below for an example of the word used in context.

> **Although there are many languages spoken in Zambia, English is their official *national* language**

Adding -ly onto national creates the adverb nationally. It describes how an action takes place.

> **When running for president, you must campaign locally and *nationally* to educate constituents of your stance on key issues.**

Adding -ize to national produces the verb nationalize. It means "to make something distinctly national"; to give national character. It also refers to "a national body taking ownership of an industry."

> **In 1967, Tanzanian President Julius Nyerere *nationalized* the banks and other large industries. This means President Nyerere made it so that banks were owned by the nation as opposed to private citizens.**

Exercise: Fill in the middle column of the chart with words that contain the suffixes in the first column.

Suffix	Example	Part of Speech
able		adjective
age		noun
al		adjective
ate		verb
fy		verb
hood		adjective
ic		adjective
ish		adjective
ise/ize		verb
ity		noun
ly		adverb
ness		noun
ship		noun
ward		adverb
where		adverb

Rule 2 Practice — Identify the correct suffix usage by circling the best-fitting word in the sentences below. At the end of the sentence, indicate the part of speech of the word you chose. See the example below. Use the hints in italics to assist you with each sentence.

<u>Example</u>: Mark and his brother Michael (*quickly*, **quickness**) ran down the street to catch up with their friends on their way to school. *How did Mark and Michael run?* quickly, adverb

1. The professor asked the class a (**rhetorically, rhetorical**) question, but I felt inclined to respond. *What kind of question did the professor ask?*
    _____

2. The British, Spaniards and Portuguese (**unlawfully, unlawful**) denied people the right to life, liberty and property. *How did Europeans deny the people their rights?*
    _____

3. Dennis acted with (**kindly, kindness**) by sending Diana flowers and fine wine for her birthday. *What did Dennis act with?* _____

4. Please (**magnify, magnetically**) the picture to a larger font so that I can see it. *What are you being asked to do?* _____

5. Many people feel that animals are as equally (**lovable, lovingly**) as humans and should be treated with equal care. *How are the animals described?*
    _____

6. Although Ruth (**empathetic, empathizes**) with the protesters, she has decided to use the power of the pen and start a letter writing campaign. *What does Ruth do?*
    _____

7. The (**quality, qualify**) of your homework foreshadows whether or not you will pass this course. *What is this sentence mainly about?*
    _____

8. The woman's (**childish, childlike**) and playful attitude makes the other employee's feel at ease. Her co-worker, on the other hand, is (**childish, childlike**); she will not share her materials and only thinks about herself.
    _____

9. A person's (**nationality, nationalism**) is determined by their birth place and ancestry. If you are devoted to your nation, you are displaying attributes of
    _____ (**nationality; nationalism**).

10. One will never develop at least one meaningful (**friendship, friendliness**) in their life if they do not also develop an attitude of gratitude and (**friendship, friendliness**).
    _____

Rule 2 Practice Extension Activity — Make a list of the uncircled words from the previous exercise. Identify each word's part of speech and write a sentence with each word.

Rule 3: <u>A word can have as many as three suffixes. The word's part of speech is based upon the final suffix.</u>

Prefix			Suffix			
3P	2P	1P	0	1S	2S	3S
		con	sti(tu)	tion		
		con	sti(tu)	tion	al	
		con	sti(tu)	tion	al	ity

A word's part of speech is based on its final suffix.

Constitution is a noun (*ion*)

Constitutional is an adjective (*al*)

Constitutionality is a noun (*ity*)

Rule 3 Practice — Identify the suffixes of the following words and give each word's part of speech. Use the dictionary to assist you. The first one is done for you:

Word	Suffix(es)	Part of Speech
internationally	ion, al, ly	adverb
responsibility		
nationalism		
friendliness		
respectfully		
creativity		
truthfulness		
peacefully		
victoriously		
instantaneously		
regulatory		

Rule 4: <u>Adding suffixes sometimes changes the spelling of a word.</u>

A.   <u>When the root of a word ends in *y*, drop the *y*, replace it with an *i*, and add the suffix.</u>
<u>For example:</u>

-      happy :: happily

       happ<u>y</u> + -*ly* = happ<u>i</u> + -*ly* = *happ<u>i</u>ly*

-      fury :: furious

       fur<u>y</u> + -*ous* = fur<u>i</u> + -*ous* = *fur<u>i</u>ous*

-      friendly :: friendliness

       friendl<u>y</u> + -*ness* = friendl<u>i</u> + -*ness* = *friendl<u>i</u>ness*

Prefix			**Suffix**			
3P	**2P**	**1P**	**0**	**1S**	**2S**	**3S**
			hap	py		
			hap	p(i)	ly	
			friend	ly		
			friend	l(i)	ness	

B.   <u>When the root of a word or suffix ends in *e*, drop the *e* and add the suffix. For</u>
<u>example:</u>

-      instigate :: instigator
       investigat<u>e</u> + -*or* = investigat + -*or* = investigator
-      move :: movable
       move + -*ing* = mov + -*ing* = *mov<u>ing</u>*
-      conceive :: conceivable
       conceive + -*able* = conceiv + -*able* = *conceiv<u>able</u>*

Prefix			**Suffix**			
3P	**2P**	**1P**	**0**	**1S**	**2S**	**3S**
		in	sti	gate		
		in	st	at(e)	or	
			move			
			mov(e)	able		

C.   When the final consonant of a monosyllabic word follows a single vowel, the final consonant is doubled before adding the suffix. For example:

-    bag :: baggage
     b<u>ag</u> + -*ed* = bagg + -*ed* = *bagged*
-    cab :: cabbage
     c<u>ab</u> + -*age* = cab<u>b</u> + -*age* = *cabbage*
-    bed :: bedding
     b<u>ed</u> + -*ing* = bed<u>d</u> + -*ing* = *bedding*

Prefix			**Suffix**			
3P	**2P**	**1P**	**0**	**1S**	**2S**	**3S**
			bag	(g)age		
			cab	(b)age		
			bed	(d)ing		

D.   <u>If a multisyllabic word has one short vowel, one final consonant, and the final syllable</u> <u>is stressed, the final consonant is doubled before adding the suffix.</u> For example:

-    occur :: occurrence
     oc<u>cur</u> + -*ence* = occur<u>r</u> + -*ence* = *occu<u>rrence</u>*
-    transmit :: transmitted
     trans<u>mit</u> + -*ed* = transmit<u>t</u> + -*ed* = *trans<u>mitted</u>*

Prefix			**Suffix**			
3P	**2P**	**1P**	**0**	**1S**	**2S**	**3S**
			oc	cur	(r)ence	
			com	mit	ee	

As always, there are exceptions to this rule:

- Double the final consonant of multisyllabic words of Anglo-Saxon origin ending in -fit, regardless of the stress (see misfit and outfit → misfitted; outfitted)

- Double the final consonant of multisyllabic words that end in -fer unless there is a double f in the middle of the word (see refer → referred, but offer → offered)

Rule 4 Practice 1 — Add suffixes to the following roots or words below. Write the new word in the space provided. Follow the spelling rules outlined above to assist you and indicate which rule you used (A, B, C or D). An example is provided.

A: y changes to i | B: drop the e | C: double final consonant (single syllable) | D: double final consonant (multisyllabic)

Word	Suffix	New Word	Rule
Run	-er	Runner	C
Beg	-ar		
Cat	-y		
Execute	-ive		
Preside	-ent		
Pole	-ar		
Muse	-ic		
Pure	-ify		
Hope	-ing		
Office	-er		
Hop	-ing		
Rectify	-able		
Lug	-age		
Convene	-tion		
Likely	-hood		
Glory	-ous		
Busy	-est		
Commit	-ee		
Delegate	-ation		
Fancy	-ly		
Note	-ify		
Rate	-fy		
Artifice	-ial		
Simply	-city		
Lyre	-ist		
Seize	-ure		
Multiple	-y + cation		
Haste	-y + ly		
Wit	-y + ly		

Rule 4 Practice 2 — Add or remove suffixes to/from the following words in parentheses so that the overall sentence will make sense. An example is provided below. Use the hints in italics to assist you with each sentence.

Example: If you speak Spanish (fluency), you can travel to Honduras with the health and wellness team next year. *How must you speak Spanish to travel to Honduras?* <u>fluently</u>

1)   In technology class, we learned that robots and androids are forms of (artificially) intelligence programmed to operate like human beings. *What forms of intelligence are robots and androids?* _____

2)   I do not eat food products that are (artifice) made. *How are the food products made?*
_____

3)   Samaa's speech (inspiration) me to go out and start my own health and wellness business. *What did the speech do?* _____

4)   Marquis was writing a new song, but he could not think of any good lyrics, so he talked to his dad for some (inspire). *What did Marquis want from his father?*
_____

5)   When the wind stopped, all the (motion) crops stood in the field. *Describe the crops in the field.* _____

6)   The pageant winner's hideous attitude detracted from her physical (beautifulness).

7)   My doctor suggested meditation to help me feel less (restlessness).

8)   After exiting the plane, I immediately walked to (bag) claims to find my suitcase.

9)   Maryam and her sister sit (patient) and watch their mother make falafels tabbouleh salad for this summer's New Year's festival.

10)   To (atonement) for their wrongdoings, the people of the Effutu tribe hold a festival similar to Yom Kippur in Judaism.

Rule 5: <u>Suffixes have meanings.</u>

The following chart contains the meanings of commonly used suffixes, their part of speech, and a word example containing the suffix. Complete the chart by adding a second example in the last column.

Nouns (Person, Place, Thing, or Idea)

Suffix	Meaning	Example 1	Example 2
ary/ery/ory	place; thing	**jewelry** (a precious ornament with jewels) **cemetery** (graveyard; from Greek *koimeterion*, a sleeping place)	
arium	place	**planetarium** (a place to view planets and stars)	
oid	like, resembling, in the form of	**asteroid** (a star-shaped object; like a star)	
cle	small thing, like	**muscle** (from the Latin *musculus*, "little mouse"; like a mouse, as the shape/movement of some muscles resembles a mouse) **particle** (a small or minute portion of matter, from Latin *particula*, meaning "little part" or a small segment of something)	

ette	small thing	**cigarette** (a small cigar)	
let	small thing	**bracelet** (a little thing for the brachium, Greek for arm)	
ling	small thing	**seedling** (young plant from a seed)	
cy	quality, condition (idea)	**papacy** (condition of the Pope)	
age	belonging to, related to	**cabbage** (from Latin *caput*, meaning head of a vegetable or related to a head, as it has a similar shape)	
ence/ance	quality of being (idea)	**dominance** (having the quality of ruling and controlling, being lord and master over, as *dominus*=master of a home)	

ency/ancy	quality of being (idea)	**consistency** (quality of being consistent, meaning the quality of standing firm, con=intensifier + sist=standing)	
ety/ity/ty	quality or state of being	**poverty** (state of being impoverished or poor)	
dom	quality of being (idea)	**wisdom** (quality of being wise, meaning the ability to judge right from wrong; from the Indo-European root *weid* meaning "to see")	
hood	body of persons of a particular character or class (idea)	**neighborhood** (body of neighbors)	
cion, sion, tion	act of, state of, result of (idea)	**precision** (state of being precise; from the Latin *praecidere*, from *prae-* before and *cadere-* cut; the act of mentally cutting off or shortening)	

ic	dealing with, pertaining to, in the nature of	**magic** (from Latin *magus*, meaning power; dealing with a specific kind of special power or ability) **music** (pertaining to the art of the Muses, one of the nine deities of the arts) **classic** (from Latin *classicus*, "the highest rank"; a work in the nature of a perfect or early example of a particular style)	
ism	state or condition of; principles or doctrine of (idea); belief in; action, result of an action; conduct characteristic	**empiricism** (from the Greek *empeirkikos*, meaning "experience"; the belief that knowledge is derived from experience) **melanism** (the condition of having an increased amount of melanin; from the Greek *melas* or "dark")	
ment	act of, state of, quality of (idea)	**management** (act of managing or handling, from the Latin *manus*, meaning hand)	
mony	quality of or state of (idea)	**matrimony** (state of being and obtaining rights as a mother via marriage, see Latin *mater*, meaning mother)	

ness	state, quality or condition of (idea)	**restlessness** (the state of not being able to rest)	
sis, sus	state, quality or condition of (idea)	**basis** (the state of being the base or foundation)	
ship	state, quality or condition of (idea)	**relationship** (the state or quality of relating between two people, things or ideas)	
ure	state, act of, process and rank (idea)	**literature** (literary production or work, from Latin *literature*, meaning "writing formed with letters")	
ician	one who does, one skilled in (person)	**musician** (one who is skilled in music)	
or, er, ar	one who does (person)	**actor** (one who acts)	

ist, yst	one who professes or advocates a doctrine; one who makes a practice of or is skilled in a department of knowledge (person)	**etymologist** (one who is skilled in the area etymology) **atheist** (one who professes the doctrine of atheism, a belief that there is no God or supreme deity) **socialist** (one who advocates socialism)	
ee	one who does or is	**payee** (a person to whom money is to be paid)	

These suffixes are descriptive:

Suffix	Meaning		
al, ical, eal	pertaining to, like, belonging to, having the character of	**national** (of or belonging to a nation; having the characteristic of a whole nation) **musical** (of or relating to music)	
ar/ular	pertaining to, like belonging to, having the character of	**particular** (literally, "like a particle," having the character of a specific part of a whole)	

ic/tic	pertaining to, of the nature of, in the manner of, connected with or dealing with	**metric** (pertaining to measurement; of or relating to meter, from the Greek *metron*, meaning measure) **apostolic** (of or pertaining to the Apostles[1] or one who leads/advocates a new course; from the Greek *apostellein* "to send forth," and *apostolos*, "messenger") **quixotic** (in the manner of Don Quixote[2]; noble and chivalrous without practicality)	
ish	somewhat, somewhat prone to, or somewhat like; from the country of or belonging to the culture of	**Moorish** (belonging to the Moors) **bluish** (somewhat blue)	
ory	expressing, serving to, characterized by	**statutory** (serving as a statute, or standing in law)	
ive	having a tendency	**reclusive** (having the tendency of a recluse or one who shuts themselves out)	
escent	becoming, beginning, having	**iridescent** (becoming like an *iris*, Latin for rainbow)	

[1] An Apostle was one of the 12 chief disciples of Jesus Christ

[2] A character from the Spanish novel Don Quixote, characterized for his chivalrous deeds, setting out to undo wrongs and bring justice to the world

esque (style)	in the manner of, like or having the quality of; style	**arabesque** (in the manner or style of an Arab)	
able	capable of being, having qualities of	**relatable** (able to relate or have a connection)	
ible	capable of, tending to, inclined to	**audible** (capable of hearing)	
ile	able to, capable of, like, relating to	**facile** (capable of doing something quickly and easily)	
ful	full of	**grateful** (full of gratitude, grace or thanks)	
less	lacking; unable to	**restless** (unable to rest)	
ious, acious, eous	tending to, having, full of	**sagacious** (full of *sagus*, Latin for "wisdom")	
		righteous (tending to do that which is morally right or acceptable)	

Identify the suffix and provide the meaning of each of the words below.

astral	stellar	aqueous	graphic	mechanical	squeamish
compensatory	perceptive	crescent	Junoesque	reducible	ductile	gregarious

The following suffixes are used to turn words into verbs (verbification):

ate: to make something have a particular quality

dominate: to rule over, having the quality of a *dominus* or master

legislate: to make laws, from the Latin word *legis latio*, meaning "bearing or proposing of a law"

marinate: to pickle in sea brine, from the Latin word *marinus*, meaning "sea"

fy: to make or cause; to become; from the Latin word *facere*, meaning "to make or do." This suffix is mainly seen with noun bases.

rectify: to set right or literally "make straight or right," from the Latin *rectus*, meaning right; see Indo Europea root *reg*, meaning "straight"

calcify: to make stony and hard from calcium salts; to become inflexible and unchanging

indemnify: compensate for damage, loss or injury suffered; from the Latin *indemnis*, meaning uninjured (*in*=not, *dammum*=harm)

ise/ize: from the Greek *–izein*, which created *–izo* and *–izare*. This suffix carries the following meaning:

1) to subject to

baptize: to subject to dipping/sinking into water as a ritual washing, commonly practiced by various Christian sects; from Greek *baptein*, meaning to "dip or sink"

cauterize: to subject to burning via a branding iron from the Greek *kauterion*, a branding iron; from *kaiein*, to "burn; to render or make into"

sterilize: to make sterile or unfruitful; from the Latin *sterilis*, meaning "unfruitful"

tranquilize: to make tranquil or quiet or calm from the Latin *tranquilis*, meaning "quiet, calm still"; see *trans*, "over" + *quies*, rest

apologize: to render an apology; from the Greek *apologia*, "a speech in defense"; see *apo*, defense/against + *logia*, "speech"

oxidize: to combine with oxygen; also applies to intransitive verbs (verbs that do not take on a direct object, such as *laugh, flow, run, sneeze,* etc.)

   2) meaning to practice or carry on

     temporize: to carry on in speech or action in order to gain time or avoid an argument (from the Latin *temporizare, tempus, tempor,* meaning "time")

     botanize: to practice botany, the study of plants (from the Latin botanē, "plant")

Give two examples of a word that uses each verb suffix in the spaces provided below.

Suffix	Example 1	Example 2
-ate		
- ify/fy		
- ize/ise		

To make most adjectives into an adverb, simply add the suffix –ly

- quick→quick<u>ly</u>
- hope→hopeful<u>ly</u>
- late→late<u>ly</u>
- real→real<u>ly</u>

For words with more than one syllable ending in –y, replace the –y with i and add –ly

- angr<u>y</u>→angri<u>ly</u>
- eas<u>y</u>→easi<u>ly</u>
- voluntar<u>y</u>→voluntari<u>ly</u>

For words with more than one syllable ending in -le, drop the -le and add -ly

- nob<u>le</u>→nob<u>ly</u>
- id<u>le</u>→id<u>ly</u>
- capab<u>le</u>→capab<u>ly</u>

Rule 5 Practice 1 — Building Words: Read the instructions below to change the part of speech of each word. *Hint: may have to remove a letter or suffix first

A.   Turn the following words into nouns (things) by adding one of the following suffixes: *oid, let, ling, ette, cule/cle/ule*

   grumble _____   tablet _____   spring _____

   cubic _____   rose _____

B.   Turn the following words into nouns (ideas) by adding one of the following suffixes: *ment, cion/sion/tion, ancy/ency/cy, ness, ism*

   gentle _____   altruist _____   agent _____

   convene _____   move _____

C.   Turn the following words into nouns (people) by adding one of the following suffixes: *ar/er/or, ician, ist, ee*

   metaphysics _____   conduct _____   botany _____

   induct _____   aesthetics _____

D.   Turn the following words into adjectives by adding one of the following suffixes: *ic/itic, ive, ful, less, ar/ular* (use each suffix once)

   hope _____   spectacle _____   conduct _____

   spine _____   harmony _____

E.   Turn the following words into adjectives by adding one of the following suffixes: *escent, esque, able/ible, ory, al/ical/eal*

   predict _____   fluoride _____   picture _____

   mandate _____   magic _____

F.   Turn the following words into verbs by adding one of the following suffixes: *ate, fy/ify, ize/ise*

   real _____   quality _____   valid _____

   equal _____   liquid _____

Various suffixes can be attached to these bases.

<u>Extension</u>: Pick ten words from the lists above and use each one in a sentence, then use their derivatives in a sentence (that is, the newly formed words).

Rule 5 Practice 2 — Complete the sentences below with the correct version of the bolded word. An example is provided below.

<u>Example</u> - *explore*: exploratory, exploration, explorer, exploring, explore

    a.   Rachelle and I can often be found <u>exploring</u> the city for new places to hear good hip-hop and R&B music.

    b.   Many West African <u>explorers</u> traveled to America before Christopher Columbus searching for gold and other precious resources.

    c.   Marty took several classes on space <u>exploration</u>, learning about Katherine Johnson's monumental work with NASA during the Space Race of the 1960s.

    d.   During an <u>exploratory</u> phase of her life, Ariel left his job to travel throughout South America to learn more about his family's roots.

    e.   Imani and I often <u>explore</u> gardens in the spring, searching for a good place to sit and write short stories.

1.   *percept*: *perceptual, perceive, perceptible, perception, perceptive*

    a.   A person with _____ problems may have difficulty judging how far away something is.

    b.   Our _____ of the world is shaped by how we are raised and the ideas we are exposed to early in life.

    c.   To be confident, you must _____ yourself as capable and intelligent.

    d.   Although her mother tried to hide it, Deonna was able to provide a _____ account of her mother's financial struggles.

    e.   Since July 2015, there has been a _____ decline in unemployment as more and more people are finding work.

2.   *vivid*: *vivacious, vivacity, vividly, vivaciousness, vivaciously*

    a.   The singer won the talent show because her _____ set her apart from her competitors.

    b.   Ms. Gabriel is a _____ and exciting teacher, as she is always spirited and full of life.

    c.   Eager to relay the day's events, Maya _____ recounted how she scored the winning goal for her school's soccer team.

    d.   Once Marquis met Aisha, he was struck by her _____, humor, intellect and charm.

    e.   After his noon nap, the boy _____ awakes and sits up in bed, eager to go outside and play.

3. *prescript*: *prescribe, prescriptive, prescription, prescriptible, prescriptibility*

    a. If a statute or code is aligned to common law, then it has _____, as it represents a right that has existed for time immemorial.

    b. Doctors often _____ medicine that suppresses symptoms rather than cures diseases and illnesses.

    c. Freedom of speech is a constitutionally _____ right that can be limited in cases where speech is threatening or inflammatory.

    d. Naturopaths provide herbal _____s to help people naturally heal from their physical and mental ailments.

    e. Schools _____ ly punishes students without taking into account their individual circumstances and motivations.

4. *tension*: *tentative, tenacious, tenable, tenant, tenacity*

    a. To win the debate, you must have _____ arguments or else the opposing team will easily rebut your claims.

    b. I recently found a new _____ to rent my apartment.

    c. I am looking for a business partner with great fortitude and _____ as both are sustaining qualities necessary to start a business.

    d. She is a _____ worker, holding strong even when the going gets tough.

    e. Our _____ travel plan is to leave next week, barring any major storms that could detour our plans.

5. *substance*: *substantive, substandard, substantial, substantiate, substantially*

    a. I have a _____ amount of reading to do, so please do not disturb me.

    b. Giving little effort to studying and learning will surely give you a _____ knowledge base from which you can draw in general conversation.

    c. There are artifacts that can_____ the claim that Africans traveled to America prior to the trans-Atlantic slave trade.

    d. Almost all of the author's _____ works (poetry and prose) show that he has a true command and mastery of language, as he is skilled at selecting words that aptly convey his ideas.

    e. Studying etymology can _____ help students increase their vocabulary and reading comprehension with just a few weeks of study.

Rule 6: <u>When suffixes are added to some base words, the stress and pronunciation of various syllables can change.</u>

Remember, multisyllabic words contain primary and secondary stresses. Stress is the emphasis placed on syllables in a word. Sometimes, adding a suffix to a multisyllabic word changes the stress of the word; other times it does not. Overall, it depends on the suffix being added.

Suffixes can be divided into two classes: suffixes that cause the stress to be on the syllable before the suffix and suffixes that take on the stress.

	Suffixes that move stress onto the syllable before the suffix	Suffixes that take on the stress in a word
Syllable	(t)ion/(s)ion/(c)ion, eous/(i)ous, ic(al), ity	ee, er, eer, ese
Example	**Vacate** + (t)ion = vacation **legal** + ity = legality **Harmony** + ous = harmonious **Parasite** + ical = parasitical	

A final note on stress: Dropping the *e* automatically changes the syllable pronunciation because e, as the silent vowel marker, has been removed. Typically, the long vowel sound in the base word will change to a schwa or a short vowel sound.

Com<u>pe</u>te- com<u>pe</u>titive (long e to short e)
Man<u>date</u>- man<u>da</u>tory (long a to schwa)
Pre<u>side</u>- pre<u>si</u>dent (long i to schwa)

Rule 6 Practice 1 — Add a suffix to the base words below and circle the stress of the base word and the word derivative. Lastly, determine if the stress remained the same or changed. If the stress did not change, write NC. If the stress changed, determine if the suffix itself absorbed the stress (SS) or if the stress is on the syllable prior to the suffix (BS).

gui**tar** + ist= gui**tar**ist (NC)

1. similar + ity =
2. refer + ee =
3. general + ize =
4. astronomy + ical =
5. fulfill + ment =

Rule 6 Practice 2 — Sort the following words into three categories:
revelation, indication, Chinese, national, beautiful and *racketeer*

- Words with suffixes that changed stress (1)
- Words with suffixes that move stress onto the syllable before the suffix (2)
- Words with suffixes that take the stress onto themselves (3)

1: No Change	2: Move Stress- Before Suffix	3: Move Stress- Onto Suffix

Summary

A suffix comes at the _____ of a word. It helps define a word by telling its

_____; for example, the word **vindicate** is a(n) _____, while

vindication is a _____. A word can have as many as _____ suffixes, as in the

word **intentionality**. The suffix changes the meaning of a word; for example, **actor** means

"_____ acts or moves," while **action** means "_____ of acting

or moving."

All About Suffixes Review

Suffix Rules: Multiple Choice and True/False

1.   A suffix is placed at the _____ of a root.
    a.   beginning
    b.   middle
    c.   end
    d.   none of the above

2.   A suffix indicates the _____ of a word.
    a.   basic meaning
    b.   part of speech
    c.   origin
    d.   none of the above

3.   T or F: All words have suffixes.

4.   T or F: A word can have two suffixes.

5.   A(n) suffix can change the _____ in a word such as *interview* and
    interviewee.

Identifying, Classifying and Defining Suffix(es) in a Word

Directions:
Column 1: Underline the suffix(es) in the word.
Column 2: Write the suffix(es).
Column 3: Classify the final suffix: give its part of speech using one of the following symbols:
noun (n), verb (v), adjective (adj), or adverb (adv). Column 4, Give the meaning of the
suffix(es). One example is done for you.

Identifying, Classifying and Defining Suffix(es) in a Word

Directions:

Column 1: Underline the suffix(es) in the word.

Column 2: Write the suffix(es).

Column 3: Classify the final suffix: give its part of speech using one of the following symbols: noun (n), verb (v), adjective (adj), or adverb (adv). Column 4, Give the meaning of the suffix(es). One example is done for you.

Word(1)	Suffix(es) (2)	Type of Suffix/Part of Speech (3)	Suffix Meaning (4)
anim<u>ate</u>	ate	V	to make
belligerency			
conversationalist			
anthropomorphize			
religiously			
strategic			
grotesque			
solarium			
diversify			
accommodate			
ineluctable			
native			
miraculously			
nationalize			
boorish			
knowledgeably			
suffragette			
respectfully			
inculpate			
nationally			
cubicle			

Words in Context: Fill in the Blank

Complete each sentence by filling in the blank, using the suffix of the boldfaced word to assist you. Hint: Circle the suffix so that it stands out for you.

<u>Example</u>: An aud<u>ible</u> sound is one _____ <u>capable of</u> being heard.

1. Greek mythology and the Haitian Vodun are two examples of **polytheism**, _____ in many gods.

2. To **solidify** a plan would be to _____ it solid or firm.

3. To **mesmerize** is _____ one hold their attention or _____ a person transfixed upon people, places, things or ideas.

4. An **endless** supply would be one _____ an end or limit.

5. A **precarious** situation would be one _____ hazards or dangers.

6. One who **speculates** _____ a theory without firm evidence to promote their ideas or thoughts.

7. To **amplify** would be _____ louder in sound or _____ a thing or idea more intense.

8. A **refugee** is _____ takes refuge or seeks to take shelter.

9. **Sensitivity** is _____ of being sensitive.

10. A **pubescent** teen is one who is _____ a mature adult.

11. One who is a **tactile** learner must be _____ of touching educational materials to truly learn content and skills.

12. Mental **reflection** is _____ bending or turning back upon one's thoughts.

13. A **semantician** is _____ in the meaning and significance of words.

14. A **bountiful** harvest is one that is _____ goodness or abundant.

15. To **rectify** is _____ right, correct and straight; to amend.

Spelling Practice

Turn the following words into nouns by adding one of the following suffixes: *ment, mony, ness, ship, ure* (you may have to remove a letter or suffix first)

- govern _____
- scholar _____
- holy _____
- acrid _____
- cult _____

Turn the following words into adjectives by adding one of the following suffixes: *al, esque, ic, ish, ory* (you may have to remove a letter or suffix first)

- majesty _____
- digit _____
- sense _____
- statue _____
- knave _____

Change the words below into verbs by adding one of the following suffixes: *ate, fy/ify, ize/ise* (you may have to remove a letter or suffix first)

- code _____
- fabric _____
- digit _____
- vivid _____
- invalid _____

Turn the following words into adverbs by adding *ly* or *ically*

- mature _____
- probable _____
- politic _____
- whole _____
- civil _____

Suffix Derivations

1. **empath**: *empathetic, empathize, empathetically, empathy, empathizer*
    a. Black Americans should _____ with others oppressed by colonial powers due to their shared struggle to exercise the right to live freely and practice cultural rituals and norms without molestation.
    b. When making her decision, the judge _____ considered the defendant's rough upbringing. She decided to give him probation with mandatory counseling and a mentor and entered him in a vocational program instead of jail.
    c. Although I am _____ to your difficulties, they are still no excuse for you to treat others with contempt and malice.
    d. When students fail tests due to lack of understanding, we should demonstrate _____ and support them.
    e. An _____ would feel the pain of another person and take the time to understand them.

2. **hydra**: *hydrant, hydrate, hydrated, hydration, hydrator*
    a. After a long hike, Maria _____s with alkaline water soaked in rosemary and cucumbers.
    b. Since staying _____ is vital to our existence, the government must address the lack of clean drinking water in poor communities.
    c. Our _____ is vital to our existence and, thus, we must look at the poor drinking water in many urban centers throughout the land.
    d. The fire department hooked their hoses up to the _____ in front of my house to put out the fire in my neighborhood.
    e. Put your vegetables in the _____ in the refrigerator, as it will keep them fresh and prevent moisture loss.

3. **litigate**: *litigation, litigator, litigable, litigant, litigating*
    a. The _____s in this case chose to represent themselves but were not prepared or well-studied on matters of the law.
    b. Tony will be _____ his first criminal case this afternoon.
    c. After years as a public defender, Alicia became a _____, representing immigrants in danger of being deported.

    d.   Selma had a _____ case, but she could not afford a lawyer so she studied and presented her own defense.

    e.   Instead of settling out of court, the two parties decided to proceed with _____.

4.   **respond**: *responsible, responsibility, responsive, responder, respondent*

    a.   Each neighborhood should have their own program where they train people to be first _____s who will provide medical aid in the event of a natural disaster.

    b.   In law, the term _____ is synonymous with defendant, as it is one who answers the claim of a plaintiff

    c.   The United Nations appears to be _____ to the claims filed by indigenous people of North America as they have issued declarations to end colonialism and the mistreatment of the aboriginal worldwide.

    d.   The fraternity organized a group of _____ young men to start a food co-op in food deserts throughout their city.

    e.   Each morning, we each have one _____ to carry out to ensure the success of our school garden, and we do the work because our lunch depends on it.

Putting It All Together: Practice with Affixes and Roots

"Awareness of morphology has been shown to be a strong indicator of and positive influence upon reading comprehension." — SOIFER, 2005

Analyzing morphological[1] components of a word is critical to deepening vocabulary skills. To do this, the reader should identify prefixes, roots and suffixes to determine the meaning of a word.

Rule 1: Identify a word's prefixes, roots and suffixes to determine the meaning of words without using a dictionary.

Prefix				Suffix		
3P	2P	1P	0	1S	2S	3S
			sta	(t)ion		
			sta	ble		
	re	con	sti	(t)ute		
		in	act	ive		
		re	ceiv(e)	able		
	in	con	ceiv	able		
			nat	ion	al	
		de	nat	ion	al	ize

---

[1] *morph*: shape or form + *logical*: pertaining to the study of = pertaining to the shape or form of a word, particularly roots and affixes

How to Put Prefix, Roots and Suffixes Together to Find the Meaning of a Word

1) Determine the root. Place the root at **0**.

2) Identify the prefix(es). Place the first prefix on **1P**. Then place the second prefix on **2P**. Place the 3rd prefix on **3P**. If there are no prefixes, move on to step **3**.

3) Identify the suffix(es). Place the first suffix on **1S**. Place the second suffix on **2S**. Place the 3rd suffix on **3S**. If there are no suffixes, move on to step **4**.

4) Identify the meaning of each word part. Combine the meanings of the word parts to determine the meaning of the word.

Example 1

	1P	0	1S
Station:		sta	(t)ion

1) *Sta*: to stand.
   a. to be or remain in a generally upright position, supported on the feet or foot;
   b. to take, maintain or be in a position, attitude or course;
   c. to remain unchanged, intact, effective or valid;
   d. to be placed;
   e. be situated;
   f. to remain where situated, built, etc.;
   g. to be of a rank, degree or the like.

2) *tion*: the condition of, quality of

   Sta + *tion* = station: the condition or quality of standing (whether it be on foot, in a position, in a place, or in a situation in which one is situated; also the condition of holding a rank or degree; the condition of being unchanged or effected).

Example 2

	1P	0	1S
Inactive:	in	act	ive

1) *in*: not (negation)

2) *act*: to do; to set in motion; to drive, draw out or forth, move

3) *ive*: having a tendency to, having the quality of, characterized as

In + *act* + *ive* = *inactive*: having a tendency to not do anything; having the quality of not being set in motion; characterized as not moving.

Analyzing a word's morphemes to determine its meaning is called morphemic analysis. Combined with context, readers can learn the basic meaning of a word without a dictionary.

Define the rest of the words below using the prefix-root-suffix line, the rules and the definitions of each prefix, root and suffix. Check your answers in the American Heritage Dictionary.

1. stable	2. supervise	3. postscript
4. receivable	5. reconstitute	6. inconceivable
7. aqueduct	8. reanimate	9. envision
10. benediction		

Rule 1 Practice 1 — Use morphemic analysis to define the following words. Match the words on the left to the meaning on the right. *Hint: the meaning of the morphemes are bolded in each definition.

_____ 1. deportment
_____ 2. subject
_____ 3. symbiosis
_____ 4. apathy
_____ 5. disjection
_____ 6. delegate
_____ 7. deportee
_____ 8. portage
_____ 9. legality
_____ 10. exopathic
_____ 11. legalize
_____ 12. autobiographer*
_____ 13. abject
_____ 14. antibiotic
_____ 15. psychopathic

a. the **act of throwing** apart or asunder; scattering
b. **pertaining** to a **disease** having its cause or source **outside** the body
c. to be "**cast off**" into extreme lowness of station
d. **one** who **writes** a memoir of their **own life**
e. **characterized** by serious personality defects; having a "**diseased**" **mind**
f. **harmful** to **life**; destroying the growth of bacteria
g. to **throw** someone **below** or **under** someone's control; to subjugate
h. **the act of** organisms **living** as one or **together**; or mutually living off each other
i. **quality, condition or state** of being **lawful**
j. cost of **carrying**, carrying of boats over and between navigable waters
k. to **make lawful**
l. **the manner or quality** of how one "**carries**" themselves; behavior
m. **one who** is dispelled or **carried away** from a country
n. **lack of** interest or **feeling**; indifference
o. to entrust the authority to make or execute the **law**; to entrust a role or task to a person

Rule 1 Practice 2 — Use the words above to complete the sentences below.

1.   Education does not just help students develop academic skills but also improve their
        _____; in school, they learn to carry themselves with dignity and respect.

2.   During the 1500s, Spain and Portugal stole land from and _____
        American indigenous people to forced labor.

3.   After hearing about two animal attacks in less than a month, Monica began to have
        more _____ toward PETA's cause as she felt compelled to help children over
        animals.

4.   The city created a plan for the _____ of groups of protesters, as they were
        fearful that crowds would turn to looting, destruction of property and violence.

5.   It is important for the leader to _____ roles and responsibilities to the
        members of the group.

6.   The _____ that comes from China via ship must be counted to ensure that
        proper tariffs are charged.

7.   Marcus Garvey was an American freedom fighter who became a _____ as he
        was unjustly forced back to his homeland of Jamaica.

8.   The United States Supreme Court hears cases that challenge the _____
        of federal circuit court rulings, leading to the establishment of new case law.

9.   _____ factors that cause disease include improper diet, poor water and air
        quality, stress and lack of exercise.

10.   Child psychologists often look at _____ behavior as precursors to murder
        and other heinous crimes.

11.   Although some states have recently _____d marijuana, the Food and Drug
        Administration (FDA) still raids medical marijuana facilities.

12.   Assata Shakur is one of my favorite _____s, as reading her memoir further
        solidified what I knew about injustice at the hands of the United States.

13.   Colonialization has placed many nations in _____ poverty despite the abundant natural resources available throughout the land.

14.   A doctor suggested that I get _____ medication to kill infections I might get overseas.

15.   A natural _____ exists between consumers and producers as they both rely on each other for their livelihood and their needs to be met.

Rule 2: <u>Every word has only one root word.</u>

Sometimes a root can act as a prefix, as in the words *geometric,*[2] *graphology,*[3] and *aqueduct,*[4] where *geo*, *graph* and *aque(a)* act as prefixes. However, the main meaning of the word is found in the single root, while the root-influenced prefix further adds distinguishing features to the term. *Geometric* does not just pertain to measurement; it's the measurement of the **earth**. *Graphology* is not just any study; it's the study of **handwriting**. It also refers to the **written** and printed symbols in a **writing** system. An *aqueduct* is a channel that <u>leads</u> **water**, which differs from a *caliduct*, which is a pipe <u>leading</u> **heat** to warm up a space via a furnace for the whole house. These examples are important to understand so that we can properly identify the word parts, their meaning and their function in a word.

Rule 2 Practice — Identify and define the prefix(es) and root in each of the words below; record responses in the second and third columns of the chart. Read the definitions on the next page in the space provided; match the provided definitions to the words and record your responses in the final column. An example is provided.

Word	Prefix(es)	ROOT (JUST ONE!)	Meaning (see below)
genealogy	gene- birth/kind/origin	log- word, study, science	
thermometer			
tensiometer			
vociferous			
hydroscope			
thermostat			
theopathy			
philologist			
pathology			
liquefaction			
animadvert			

[2] (geo/metr/ic)
[3] (graph/log/y)
[4] (aque/duct)

a.   the study of family lineages or the birth and family origin

b.   the act of making a solid or gas into liquid

c.   an instrument used for measuring the tightness or tension of a wire

d.   great feeling or zeal from religion; excitement of a mystical source

e.   one who is fond of literature and/or linguistics; a lover of words

f.   to turn critically "to the mind"; to take notice; to censure

g.   an instrument used to look underwater

h.   an instrument used to measure temperature, particularly heat

i.   the study of diseases

j.   an apparatus that keeps an instrument stable or regulated, particularly a heating unit

k.   tending to carry a loud voice or outcry

Rule 3: There are 11 different prefix/root/suffix combinations that are found throughout the English language.

Remember, each word has only one root, but it can have up to three prefixes and three suffixes.

Combination 1: Root + Suffix
Examples: Fixture, Station, Question, Current

2P	1P	0	1S	2S	3S
		Fix	ture		
		Sta	tion		
		Quest	ion		
		Cur	rent		

Combination 2: Root + Suffix + Suffix
Examples: Stationary, Flexibility

2P	1P	0	1S	2S	3S
		Sta	tion	ary	
		Flex	ibil	ity	

Combination 3: Root + Suffix + Suffix + Suffix
Examples: Nationalization, Vertically, Standardization

2P	1P	0	1S	2S	3S
		Natio(n)	al	iz(e)	ation
		Vert	ic	al	ly
		Stand	ard	iz(e)	ation

Combination 4: Prefix + Root
Examples: Construct, Invent, Endure, Enterprise

2P	1P	0	1S	2S	3S
	Con	struct			
	In	vent			
	En	dure			
	Enter	prise			

Combination 5: Prefix + Prefix + Root
Examples: Reconstruct, Discontinue

2P	1P	0	1S	2S	3S
Re	con	struct			
Dis	con	tin(ue)			

Combination 6: Prefix + Root + Suffix
Examples: Construction, Tradition, Application

2P	1P	0	1S	2S	3S
	Con	struct	tion		
	Tra	di	tion		
	Ap	pli(c)	ation		

Combination 7: Prefix + Root + Suffix + Suffix
Examples: Conditional

1P	0	1S	2S
Con	di	tion	al

Combination 8: Prefix + Root + Suffix + Suffix + Suffix
Examples: Denationalize, Jurisprudence, Instrumentalism

1P	0	1S	2S	3S
De	nat	ion	al	ize
Juris	prud	ent	ial	ly
In	stru	ment	al	ism

Combination 9: Prefix + Prefix + Root + Suffix
Example: Unacceptable, Unremarkable

2P	1P	0	1S
Un	ac	cept	able
Un	re	mark	able

Combination 10: Prefix + Prefix + Root + Suffix + Suffix
Examples: Unconstitutional

2P	1P	0	1S	2S	3S
Un	con	sti(tu)	tion	al	

Combination 11: Prefix + Prefix + Root + Suffix + Suffix + Suffix
Examples: Disproportionableness

2P	1P	0	1S	2S	3S
Dis	pro	por(t)	ion	able	ness

Rule 3 Practice — Identify the type of combination (1–11) present in each word below and write it in the space provided.

1. native ____
2. postnatal ____
3. inadmissible ____
4. supervise ____
5. interventionist ____
6. nativity ____
7. rationalize ____
8. imperfect ____
9. denationalize ____
10. inconsistently ____
11. illegalization ____

Rule 4: <u>Morphemic analysis helps readers learn the denotation or literal meaning of words; this sometimes differs from the connotation or modern-day, implied meaning.</u>

Identifying and defining some words by their word parts do not provide a clear definition. This is because the meaning of the word's morphemes may not always match the dictionary definition or the everyday meaning of that word.

For example, the word *disaster* etymologically breaks down to mean "a bad star." However, the definition, according to the Oxford Concise English Dictionary, is "a sudden accident or a natural catastrophe that causes great damage or loss of life; an event or fact leading to ruin or failure."

Using word parts to find its meaning produces the word's denotative or literal meaning. The word *denotation* refers to a symbol, sign or indication used to derive meaning. When denoting a word's meaning, the word parts or morphemes are symbols of meanings, explicitly representing persons, places, things, ideas, directions, grammatical usage, etc. The root of denotative, *nota*, means "mark," referring to the symbol (a graphic marking.) A denotative meaning is based explicitly on the meanings of the word's morphemes that are then combined to indicate the word's overall meaning. Denotations are also referred to as the literal meaning. (Literal derives from the Latin *litera, literalis*, morphing to the Middle English *literal*, means "pertaining to the letter.") Thus, a reader must analyze a word's morphemes to identify its literal meaning. Analyzing a word's meaning for its word parts is **parsing** the word. Parsing a word reveals denotations and gives insight into its modern-day meaning.

Meanings of yesteryear may seem unnecessary; however, knowing denotative word meanings provides insight into the thoughts and perspectives of past societies as ideas and, thus, words that represent those ideas are constantly evolving.

In contrast to the denotation, the **connotative** meaning of a word refers to its modern-day usage; connotations are implied meanings that differ from the original meaning. The literal meaning of *connotative* is "added mark." What is added is another way to use the word. The connotative meaning is an additional or shaded meaning, as the prefix con meaning "with" (added, together) and the root word nota indicate. The connotation is a secondary meaning *in addition* to the denotative meaning. It is not based on the original meaning of the word but on a meaning that people have attached to the word over time. Thus, the connotation of *disaster* is "a sudden accident or a natural catastrophe that causes great damage or loss of life; an event or fact leading to ruin or failure"; this meaning is secondary to the denotative (bad star). The dictionaries tend to use connotative meanings as definitions of words as they represent modern-day usages. However, some dictionaries do make note of denotative meanings in what are known as etymological brackets []; these are found below a word's connotations or the entry-level meanings. The next chapter addresses this in greater detail. For now, use word parts to analyze the morphemes and learn a word's denotation. Use the prefix/root/suffix line to parse words and a dictionary to find denotative and connotative word meanings; an example is provided below.

<u>**Example 1**</u> *prescribe*
Denotation: to "write before"

Prefix				Suffix		
3P	2P	1P	0	1S	2S	3S
		pre	scribe			
		before	write			

Connotation:
- to advise and authorize the use of medicine or treatment
- to recommend as something beneficial
- to state as a rule that an action or procedure should be carried out (rules prescribing proper grammar and word usage)

Sometimes, the denotation is similar or relates to the connotation in some way to help you recall the meanings of words.

<u>**Example 2**</u> *generous*
Denotation: of a high or noble birth

Prefix				Suffix		
3P	2P	1P	0	1S	2S	3S
		gener	ous			
		(noble) birth	having the quality of			

Connotation:
- liberal; showing a readiness to give more of something than is strictly necessary
- showing kindness toward others
- exhibiting qualities regarded as belonging to high birth

In the previous example, one can see how the original meaning pertains to the present day. The root gen refers to "birth," often the birth of one with a high status in society. People of high birth were expected to be kind and willing to give time and money to others, as noblemen had the resources to do so. While all noblemen did not act in this manner, the expectation was for them to be chivalrous and to act with dignity and manners. The word *gentleman* follows a similar path. Connotatively, a gentleman is "a man who treats other people in a proper or polite way." Denotatively, it refers to "a man characterized as being of noble birth." Again, nobles are characterized as proper and polite, thus elucidating the connection between the denotation and connotation of the word gentleman.

Rule 4 Practice 1 — Complete the chart below by a) identifying and defining the word parts; b) determining the denotation based on the meanings of those parts; and c) determining the connotative meaning based on prior knowledge. An example is provided below.

Roots to Note
foli: leaf (foliage)　　　　*habeus*: you shall have　　　　*manu*: hand

Word	Denotation	Connotation
generous		
speculate		
spectacular		
special		
habeus corpus		
portfolio		
animosity		
manumission		
emotion		
provisional		
nationality		

Denotations
a. pertaining to a (noble) birth
b. that which carries leaves (original source of paper)
c. the act of sending to another hand
d. better than ordinary, thus easily seen; pertaining to an appearance or sight (that stands out because it is particular)
e. to look or see (from a vantage point, like a watchtower)
f. pertaining to something prepared or arranged to be seen or displayed

g. (words of writ stating) "you shall have the body"
h. quality of a spirited (or bold) mind
i. the state that pertains to conditions of birth
j. characterized as the act of seeing forward
k. to move out or stir up

Connotations

l. tending to be kind and liberal in giving time or money
m. intense bitterness of mind
n. a case for carrying loose papers, list of stocks, bonds
o. different from what is normal or usual; especially important or loved
p. temporary; viewed as suitable but subject to change
q. to meditate or reflect on a subject (hence observe the subject closely); to make a risky trade; a venture or gamble
r. the state of being a member of a group of people that share common history, traditions and language; living in a particular country
s. causing wonder and admiration; very impressive
t. liberation from slavery
u. a strong feeling
v. a writ obtaining release of a person from unlawful restraint

Rule 4 Practice 2 — Use the words above to complete the sentences below.

1) The _____ benefactor donated $5,000 to the school so that each student could have their own copy of the class novel.

2) Jack believed Harry stole $500 from him and watched him with distrust and _____.

3) Mustafa has held his Egyptian _____ while living in the United States of America over the past 15 years.

4) Frederick Douglass fought for the _____ of all those forced into servitude, as he believed the institution of slavery to be unjust and immoral.

5) When her mom asked about her brother Nykolas, Alexis could only _____ about his whereabouts since she wasn't sure where he had gone.

6) Before her interview for art school, Shayla prepared a _____ of her work, including the sketches she had done for an art competition in middle school.

7) Since it was her anniversary, Sophia prepared a _____ dinner for her husband to show her appreciation of their love.

8) While she was still in graduate school, Reka obtained a _____ teaching license until she finished her teacher licensure program.

9) Eamon's lawyer demanded that he be released _____ since the police illegally searched his home and arrested him.

10) Iniejah made a _____ run at the football game, scoring the game-winning touchdown after a 45-yard drive down the field.

11) While she appreciated the range of human _____s that she experienced, Delilah felt uncomfortable with the feelings of guilt and shame.

Summary

All words are made up of word parts or _____, _____, and _____. By combining the meaning of each of the word parts, you can _____ a word without a dictionary. When defining words, be sure to distinguish between the _____ or literal meaning (based on the word parts' meanings) or the _____ meaning (the meaning that words have acquired over time).

In lieu of a review section, a set of morphemic analysis activities follows. These skill-and-drill activities aid in mastery of a) parsing, b) defining words without a dictionary, and c) using newly learned words in context.

Name: _____ Date: _____

Root Focus: <u>act/ag, anim, anthro, aqua</u>   Root Meaning: _____

Prefixes		Roots		Suffixes	
mag	non	phil	-ology*	-ate	-eous
_____	_____	<u>love</u>	_____	_____	_____
pro	re			-ic	-ile
_____	_____			_____	_____
sub				-ity	-ive
_____		*Root is log; y is the suffix		_____	_____

Directions: In column A, identify the elements in each word by circling roots and underlining prefixes and suffixes. Then match each word with its correct meaning from column B.

COLUMN A | COLUMN B

1. activate — a. having the quality of acting or moving beforehand

2. agile — b. having the quality of being underwater

3. aquastat — c. very small living creature, especially one microscopic size

4. animalcule — d. having a great and noble mind

5. anthropoid — e. not pertaining to, living in, or needing water

6. magnanimous — f. to bring back to life

7. misanthrope — g. to make or cause a thing to be alive

8. nonaquatic — h. an apparatus for regulating or keeping the temperature of water stable

9. philanthropic — i. able to move with ease

10. proactive — j. human-like; in the form of or resembling a human

11. reanimate — k. the quality of having love for humans; charitable

12. subaqueous — l. a person who dislikes humankind and avoids society

Directions: Choose the best word from column A for each sentence. Use each word only once.

1) A(n) _____ volcano is a volcano built beneath freshwater that never builds above lake level.

2) With regard to matters of law, it is best to be _____ , not reactive; for example, you should place your national status on public record to protect yourself.

3) LeBron James is a(n) _____ basketball player, moving with ease and firmness across the court.

4) The old woman was indeed a(n) _____; she does not speak to her neighbors and shuns the children who try to help her walk across the street.

5) Rachelle donates 10 percent of her finances to a(n) _____ organization that provides free education to girls around the world.

6) Many local fish stores inadvertently sell _____ plants as aquarium decoration because they are not plant specialists who can easily identify aquatics.

7) George Washington regarded Muhammed Ibn Abdullah, Emperor of Morocco, as a(n) _____ ruler, as he was gracious enough to recognize the United States of America as a nation independent of Great Britain.

8) Bacteria are examples of _____s, as they are microscopic and cannot be seen by the human eye.

9) When the _____ broke, the water boiler overheated, despite the fact that the thermostat indicated the water was already hot enough.

10) You must eat the proper foods and drink plenty of water to _____ your glandular system for optimal brain performance.

11) Though deflated from their loss, the team became _____d when they received word that they were still in the playoffs.

12) The troglodyte niger is a(n) _____ with limbs and organs similar to those of humans.

Name: _____   Date: _____

Root Focus: <u>bio, aster/astr, aud, cap(t)/cept</u>   Root Meaning: _____

Prefixes		Roots		Suffixes	
anti	in	soci(o)	-ology*	-al	-cle
_____	_____	<u>people</u>	*the study of*	_____	_____
inter				-ence	-ible
_____				_____	_____
				-ic	-ion
		Root is log; y is the suffix		_____	_____
				-isk	-ive
				a thing	_____
				-y	
				_____	

Directions: In column A, identify the elements in each word by circling roots and underlining prefixes and suffixes. Then match each word with its correct meaning from column B.

<u>COLUMN A</u>   <u>COLUMN B</u>

1. amphibious   a. one who seizes by force or stratagem

2. antibiotic   b. pertaining to stars

3. asterisk   c. microscopic examination of living tissue, especially for medical diagnosis

4. astral   d. the study of or a branch of science concerned with the sense of hearing

5. astrology   e. anything used to hold or receive something

6. audience   f. a star-shaped symbol used in print as an annotation or to stand for omitted

       text

7. audiology   g. a thing or person described as unable to be heard

8. biopsy   h. the act of taking something from between two people or things

9. captor   i. literally "having a double life"; being able to live on land and in water (as a

       frog); joint land and sea military operation

10. inaudible   j. harmful to life; destroying the growth of bacteria

11. interception   k. a formal hearing; a group of people assembled to

hear and watch a lecture or performance

12. receptacle   l. the study of the stars and their influence on human

behavior and society

Directions: Choose the best word from column A for each sentence. Use each word only once.

1) When slaves were caught trying to escape, their _____s would return
them and receive a reward from their owners.

2) Writers often use a(n) _____ when providing a footnote to define a word
or provide background information in a literary work.

3) In Octavia Butler's *Parable of the Sower*, heroine Lauren Olamina introduces a religion
titled Earthseed that aims to create a(n) _____ society on other planets and
amongst the stars.

4) Moringa is a natural, herbal _____ that kills harmful bacteria that cause
diseases such as malaria, pneumonia, and tuberculosis.

5) Regina attempted to pass a note to tell me about the surprise party, but the teacher's
_____ of her note gave everything away.

6) Markel decided to study _____ and research methods of restoring one's
hearing.

7) To study _____ is to learn how particles from the sun, moon, and stars
interact to manifest human beings as well as energies that result in physical
phenomena on earth.

8) A best practice when giving a speech is to write and deliver your speech based on the
needs and interests of your _____. This will help you hold their attention
and ensure they hear your message.

9) While in Jamaica, I rode a(n) _____ motorcycle throughout the city and
on the water, where it converted into a jet-ski.

10) It is common practice for doctors to order a(n) _____ to examine tissue cells when they suspect a patient may have inflammatory conditions.

11) Zambia is a country with very few _____s to hold trash and rubbish, so most of the garbage is strewn throughout the streets.

12) I was extremely excited to hear Kojo Nmamdi's radio show, but static made the segment _____.

Name: _____   Date: _____

Root Focus: <u>cred, chron, clud/clus, corp</u>   Root Meaning: _____

Prefixes		Roots	Suffixes	
ana	dis	meter	-ate	-eal
backward	_____	_____	_____	_____
ex	in		-iblility	-it
_____	_____		_____	_____
se			-ive	-ulous
_____			<u>a noun</u>	_____

Directions: In column A, identify the elements in each word by circling roots and underlining prefixes and suffixes. Then match each word with its correct meaning from column B.

COLUMN A   COLUMN B

1. anachronism   a. literally, "to shut in or to enclose"; to bring a person into an activity or bring parts into a whole

2. chronology   b. literally, "the quality of shutting a thing or person out of a group"

3. chronometer   c. the act of placing something in the wrong time period

4. credibility   d. a body of people authorized to act as a single entity in trade and politics

5. credulous   e. the state of being closed away from society

6. corporation   f. an instrument used to measure time

7. corporeal   g. pertaining to the body

8. discredit   h. to make a body of people into a single legal entity.

9. exclusive   i. the study of historical records to establish dates in the past; the arrangement of events in order of the time they took place

10. include   j. the state or condition of being trustworthy or believable

11. incorporate   k. having or showing the quality of believing too easily; gullible

12. seclusion   l. to cause a person or thing to be unbelievable; to make invalid.

1) Metaphysicians believe that we are all spiritual beings first and have incarnated in flesh so that we may be challenged in our _____ existence.

2) I plan to take a trip to the Ozark Mountains by myself for a week so that I can meditate in _____ and remove myself from all the distractions of city life.

3) As the CEO of an educational _____, I am honored to unite with a body of educators working to establish etymology as the basis of all learning.

4) Many credit card companies take advantage of young, _____ college students who don't often read the fine print on the applications by giving rewards and gifts just for signing up.

5) I plan to _____ yoga and boxing in my daily workout regimen.

6) In historical sketches, avoid _____s; for example, George Washington Carver should not be shown using a computer to compile research data about the peanut.

7) In debate, one can easily attack evidence if the _____ of the source is in question, for it will be difficult to confirm whether or not the information is true.

8) Doctors are often quick to attempt to _____ naturopaths and herbalists, despite overwhelming evidence that herbs and healthy living alone can both prevent and cure most diseases. (discredit)

9) While fraternal organizations are designed to be _____, temples, mosques, and churches are supposed to _____ all members of a community that seek to learn and develop their moral character and strength.

10) _____s were first developed for marine navigation, as they were designed to keep accurate time in spite of motion or variations in temperature, humidity, and air pressure.

11) When one studies the _____ of the Spanish Inquisition, it is interesting to note that Columbus "discovered" America in the same year that the last Moors were expelled from Spain.

Name: _____   Date: _____

Root Focus: <u>dic(t), duc(t), fac/fic/fec, flec(t)</u>   Root Meaning: _____

Prefixes		Roots	Suffixes	
ab-	aqu-*		-ment	-ious
_____	_____		_____	_____
bene-	bi-			
_____	_____			
contra-	ver-			
_____	_true_			
*Root is acting as a prefix				

Directions: In column A, identify the elements in each word by circling roots and underlining prefixes and suffixes. Then match each word with its correct meaning from column B.

<u>COLUMN A</u>   <u>COLUMN B</u>

1. abduction   a. literally, to "turn away"; to cause to deviate

2. aqueduct   b. something that is made up

3. benediction   c. literally, a "true saying," particularly in law and justice; a decision or

     judgment

4. benefactor   d. the act of saying something in opposition to another statement

5. biflex   e. a person who does good things for another; a patron or a person who funds a

     project, organization, research, etc.

6. contradiction   f. literally, a "good saying"; words or the rite of a solemn blessing

7. deflect   g. that which leads one into an action or to do something, often fraudulently

8. fictitious   h. the quality of bending back; turn back and ponder one's thoughts

9. inducement   i. a pipe or channel that leads water from a distant source

10. infectious   j. the state of leading someone away by force; kidnapping

11. reflective   k. literally pertaining to "making in"; likely to cause contamination

12. verdict   l. bent in two directions; having two bends

1) I invested in a quality pair of sunglasses to _____ the sun as I travel through Mexico this summer.

2) When the _____ canal of a sheep is infected, it is unable to bend its joints and, thus, can only walk on its knees.

3) After listening to both arguments, the jury assessed the facts and unanimously gave a guilty _____, as it was truly evident that the public servants violated their oath.

4) Be cautious when traveling through Paris; news media reports several _____s of healthy men and women for the selling of their vital organs on the black market.

5) An effective teacher is not only a great planner and presenter, but also is _____, thinking about how to improve their instructional methods to yield better results. (reflective)

6) The young mayor illegally promised the labor union leader a significant _____ in return for encouraging the union to vote him into office again.

7) George Orwell's *1984* is a(n) _____ novel, but many of the book's events and concepts can be observed in real life. (fictitious)

8) To start our school, we will need to receive donations and investments from local _____s that believe in our mission and want to help the community.

9) Phrases such as "liquid ice," "independent colony", and "dark light" are examples of _____s in terms, as the combined words are in conflict with one another.

10) The Union Arch Bridge contains a(n) _____ that carries the public water supply to DC and parts of the surrounding neighborhoods. (aqueduct)

11) A person with a positive attitude and a smile is just as _____ as a person with a bad cold, and can spread joy to all those whom that they touch.

12) There is great power behind making a(n) _____ before traveling, as it can bring protection from angels and other divine energies.

Name: _____ Date: _____

Root Focus: <u>graph, gee/geo, gen, ject</u> Root Meaning: _____

Prefixes		Roots	Suffixes
apo-	choreo-	cide	-ous
<u>away</u>	<u>dance</u>	_____	_____
hetero-			
<u>different</u>			

Directions: In column A, identify the elements in each word by circling roots and underlining prefixes and suffixes. Then match each word with its correct meaning from column B.

<u>COLUMN A</u>   <u>COLUMN B</u>

1. apogee   a. the study of the history and structure of the solid earth, including its rocks and changes over time

2. choreography   b. literally "one writing"; something written about one particular subject

3. geocentric   c. relating to or measured from the earth's center, or representing the earth as the center

4. geology   d. to throw between; in grammar, an exclamation thrown into a sentence

5. genocide   e. the highest point in the development; movement or orbit of something

6. graphology   f. the killing of a race or group of people born within the same bloodline

7. heterogeneous g. pertaining to a thing produced by light; an image easily captured by camera

8. interject   h. written representation of various dance movement; the art of dancing

9. monograph   i. to throw back or discard; to refuse to acknowledge

10. photogenic   j. to throw below; to force someone to act on the commandment of a person; a person that is forced to do the will of another

11. reject   k. the study of handwriting

12. subject   l. different or opposite in parts and quality

Directions: Choose the best word from column A for each sentence. Use each word only once.

1) Aristotle and Ptolemy taught we lived in a(n) _____ universe, but Copernicus believed that the sun was the center and all the planets rotated around it.

2) The moon's orbit is an eclipse that places its _____ at 251,968 miles away from the Earth.

3) Katherine Dunham, Josephine Baker, and Alvin Ailey are famous _____ers who composed dances throughout the 20th century.

4) "And," "but" and "or" are _____s that are used to connect two or more subjects in a sentence.

5) Some experts in _____ , like Antonio Snider-Pellegrini, believe that America and Africa once fit together as Pangea before being separated.

6) The beach scene is very _____, particularly with the sun glistening off the clear blue water; I would love to take our engagement pictures with this as the backdrop.

7) Doctors were confused as to why the patient's body _____ the antidote, and had to find an alternative method of curing him.

8) Stanley Poole's *Moors in Spain* is a classic _____ illustrating a golden age in Spanish history in which the Moors brought technological and political advancements to the country.

9) New York City has a(n) _____ that comprises people of a variety of nationalities, languages, and overall cultural preferences.

10) The British often used physical force, intimidation, misinformation and coercion to _____ indigenous people to their European customs, policies and overall culture.

11) The Portuguese, British, and Spaniards were responsible for the colonization and _____ of indigenous peoples of North America, and thousands were killed.

12) The forensic psychologist hired a(n) _____ expert to determine whether the signature was real or fake.

Name: _____   Date: _____

Root Focus: <u>lex/leg/log, meter, miss/mit, opt</u>   Root Meaning: _____

Prefixes		Roots
e- eu- _____ _good_ neo- peri- _new_ _____		-optos* -thermos* _eye_ _heat_ -privus* _private; individual_ *a root used as a prefix

Directions: In column A, identify the elements in each word by circling roots and underlining prefixes and suffixes. Then match each word with its correct meaning from column B.

<u>COLUMN A</u>   <u>COLUMN B</u>

1. emit   a. an instrument for measuring and indicating temperature

2. eulogy   b. law in favor of any individual; favor granted to a person or group of people

3. legislation   c. a new word or new meaning for an established word

4. lexical   d. words at the beginning of a play or poem, as an intro; a forward

5. neologism   e. the act of lawmaking

6. optometry   f. to send out

7. perimeter   g. the measurement around a shape/geometric figure

8. privilege   h. that which pertains to words or law

9. prologue   i. words of high praise, especially for those that have passed away

10. promissory   j. the science of measuring and testing one's vision

11. remission   k. literally, "the act of sending back"; to restore, pardon, or forgive

12. thermometer   l. conveying or implying a declaration that one will do a particular thing or

that a particular thing will happen

Directions: Choose the best word from column A for each sentence. Use each word only once.

1) On February 27, 1965, the actor and singer Ossie Davis gave a beautiful _____ at the funeral for Malcom X.

2) Paulo Coelho's *The Alchemist* begins with a(n) _____ that features the alchemist himself reading a variation the Greek myth "Narcissus."

3) Bi-metallic stem _____s are often used to measure the temperature of steamed liquids, particularly when cooking.

4) A doctor of _____ must measure the space between the pupils of your eyes to ensure your eyes match up with the optical center of your lenses.

5) In the 16th and 17th centuries, the Catholic Church encouraged confessions and paying penance for the _____ of sinful activity.

6) The empress gave each soldier a(n) _____ note, indicating that they would receive $5,000 after completing their military services in defense of the empire.

7) A dictionary provides _____ definitions, which often differ from the etymological meaning of a word.

8) The word *google*, a(n) _____ of the 21st century, means "to use an online search engine" to look up information on the internet.

9) While American nationals have the right to obtain property to build a place for domicile, the governor is given special _____ to live in a specified residency during their term in office.

10) Cars _____ harmful gases that affect the environment and contaminate our air. (emit)

11) While the president enforces and executes law, Congress is responsible for creating _____ in accordance with the Constitution of the United States of America.

12) Circumference, a measure of the linear distance around the outside of a circular object, is one example of _____.

Name: _____   Date: _____

Root Focus: <u>sta(t)/stas/stain, spec(t), ten(d), therm</u>   Root Meaning: _____

Prefixes		Roots	Suffixes	
ab-	mono-		-ism	-ive
_____	_____		_____	_____
pan-	retro-		-ion	-ious
_____	_____		_____	_____

Directions: In column A, identify the elements in each word by circling roots and underlining prefixes and suffixes. Then match each word with its correct meaning from column B.

<u>COLUMN A</u>   <u>COLUMN B</u>

1. abstain   a. a belief in one God and one God only

2. monotheism   b. literally "to hold away"; to withhold oneself from participation; to refrain

3. pantheon   c. a bottle, flask, or jug for maintaining liquids at an original temperature

                       particularly warm drinks and soups

4. retrospective   d. the act of stretching something tightly; nervous strain

5. specimen   e. literally, "looking back" being concerned about the past

6. spectator   f. an instrument for measuring temperatures

7. tenacious   g. a person that studies religion and deities

8. theologian   h. a temple for all deities or gods; all the deities of a people or religion

                       collectively; a group of exalted figures

9. tension   i. an apparatus for regulating temperature, especially of a heating unit

10. thermos   j. a part intended to show the quality of the whole; a sample

11. thermostat   k. inclined to hold fast; adhesive or cohesive

12. thermometer   l. a person who watches or views, as in an event or activity (as opposed to one

                       who participates) that a particular thing will happen

Directions: Choose the best word from column A to complete each sentence. Use each word only once.

1) Bailee _____ly fought through rejection and disappointment before being invited to show her art at a prestigious art gallery.

2) Saron _____s from eating meat, dairy, or eggs for 40 days before Ethiopian Christmas on January 7th.

3) A guest _____ delivered a sermon at First Baptist Church in an effort to promote interfaith worship and community connections.

4) Although his forehead felt quite warm, the _____ indicated his temperature was 98.6 degrees.

5) Toni Morrison is one of the most prolific writers in the _____ of great American authors.

6) Writing a memoir is a _____ process that not only entertains and informs the reader but can be a source of healing for the author.

7) In the winter, I usually set my _____ no higher than 68 degrees.

8) In the early 2000s, scientists studied a _____ found by Michael Farmer in Erfoud, Morocco to determine whether it indeed came from Mars.

9) I felt a great deal of _____ between Mark and Maya after their argument about sharing household responsibilities.

10) Many folk religions around the world are not adherents of _____ as they worship several different deities.

11) A _____ is the perfect winter gift to keep soup and tea warm throughout the workday.

12) They would have preferred to participate, but since they lost the semi-finals, D'Andre and Jackson were _____s of the final round at the policy debate Tournament of Champions.

Name: _____   Date: _____

Root Focus: <u>path, port, scrib/scrip(t), sens</u>   Root Meaning: _____

Prefixes	Roots	Suffixes	
sym <u>together</u>	*folio* <u>leaf. including papyrus or paper</u> *psycho* <u>mind</u>	-ee _____ -y _____	-orium _____

Directions: In column A, identify the elements in each word by circling roots and underlining prefixes and suffixes. Then match each word with its correct meaning from column B.

<u>COLUMN A</u>   <u>COLUMN B</u>

1. apathy

a. a room for writing, particular in a monastery

2. circumscribe

b. able to perceive; marked by having or showing sound judgment

3. consensus

c. literally, "pain suffering of the mind"; a mental disorder or illness (or a person suffering from one)

4. deportee

d. literally "written after"; an afterthought added to a completed letter

5. portfolio

e. the condition of having no feelings

6. postscript

f. the act of carrying across from one place to another; the means by which people or goods are carried to another place

7. psychopathy

g. to draw a line around; to encircle; to limit or restrict

8. scriptorium

h. literally "the condition of feeling the same as another"; feelings of pity or sorrow for someone else's misfortune

9. sensible

i. literally, to "perceive together"; general opinion

10. sensitive

j. one who is "carried away" from a nation to their homeland

11. sympathy

k. to perceive or be affected by slight changes, signals, or influences, including sights, sounds, smells, tastes, touches, or emotions

12. transportation

l. literally, a case for "carrying loose papers," often pieces of creative work to display one's skills; a range of investments held by a person or an organization

Directions: Choose the best word from column A to complete each sentence. Use each word only once.

1) My dream home would include a library and a _____ for reading and writing, respectively.

2) Despite her drunken state, Samantha was _____ enough to take a Lyft and not drive home.

3) Ngozi was born in Nigeria and raised in America; however, she was added to the list of _____s because her family never applied for permanent residency.

4) After deliberating for two days, the jury determined they could not come to a _____ as to whether the defendant was guilty or innocent.

5) Without a car, Selah had to rely on public _____ to get around the city.

6) Greg's _____ at his workplace impacted his work performance, as he was utterly uninterested in his job.

7) Prior to the 1920s, the United States government unjustly _____d women's right to vote.

8) Nyko's _____ contained paintings, photography, and mixed media art pieces; he plans to showcase his work to a panel of artists next week.

9) Since we recently lost my grandmother, my neighbor offered their _____ and brought cooked meals to our home.

10) Catfish are said to be one of the most finely tuned creatures on earth; they have tiny hairs that are very _____ to earthquake vibrations.

11) Dr. Smalls studied _____ in college because he wanted to provide free treatment for those with mental health struggles in low-income communities.

12) In a letter to her cousin, Ginger added a _____ saying that she will visit soon.

All About Word Origins

"Language is like a flowing stream sweeping onward with few discernible breaks in the flow" (The Miracle of Language).

When we are able to speak a language without breaks and with great confidence and ease, we say we are "fluent," with the root flu meaning "to flow." When we study word origins, we ask for derivatives, literally pertaining to where words are picked up "from the river" of said flowing language.

derivative= de (from) + riv (from Latin rivo, meaning river) + (a)tive (adj)

Rule 1: <u>To study word history is to study world history.</u>

Learning word origins provides a glimpse into a former world, and original meanings reveal perspectives of their time. Words represent thoughts and their meanings shift to reflect the births of new ideas and the deaths of antiquated ones. As the lexicographer Sol Steinmetz (2008) notes, "objects, institutions, ideas and scientific concepts change over the course of time, but the words remain—only their meanings change" (p. xi) Sometimes the changes are so drastic that a word's morphemes give no indication of its sense. For example, consider, meaning "to think or ponder about something," comes from the Latin *considerare*. Its morphemes *con*, meaning "with," and *sider*, meaning "star," reflect *consider's* original meaning "to observe with the stars." The denotation of consider shows readers a glimpse of the ancient Roman world, where astrological divination was a common practice. In this sense, words are linguistic artifacts that etymologists unearth and reconstruct to better understand history.

Word histories also show the cultural origin of concepts prevalent in the English-speaking world. Cartoons are Italian creations, *lemons* are Persian and *kindergarten* is a German design where teachers cultivate learning in a "garden" (*garten*) of "children" (*kinder*). English then becomes the infectious carrier of culture, albeit through cooperation and conquest. Trade, global conflict and colonization introduced new labels for new ideas and English speakers eagerly welcome linguistic innovation. Etymology and historical linguistics also highlight the politics of language. While English speakers typically embrace new words, they may also reject them as a political statement. During World War I, the United States and Great Britain suffered from a crushing case of "Germanphobia,"* where *hamburgers* became "Salisbury burgers" and dachshunds "liberty puppies."

In 2003, former Representative Bob Ney renamed French fries "freedom fries" in response to France's opposition to an Iraqi invasion post-9/11. Freedom fries fell out of use as national support for the Iraq War waned. Despite their brief existence, these patriotic cognomen further support the idea that language represents culture and political sentiments.

Rule 1 Practice — Place the following events in chronological order in the boxes below, with the earliest event in the leftmost box and the most recent event in the rightmost box.

A-   The Normans invade England, bringing with them Norman French.
B-   English experiences the first usages of words such as *hashtag* and *internet.*
C-   The Industrial Revolution brings the development of new technological terms.
D-   British colonization brings new words to the English tongue.
E-   Germanic tribes invade the British Isles, giving England its name.

Rule 2: <u>Most prefixes, roots and suffixes in the English language are of Latin, Greek or Germanic origin.</u>[1]

English began on the isles of Britannia; today, it is the most widely spoken language on the planet with over one billion speakers. How is it that a language born from a remote civilization becomes the lingua franca of the twentieth and twenty-first centuries? And how do languages throughout the world influence English?

English is a Germanic Language

Languages throughout the world are divided into families. Linguists systematically compare languages to find correspondences between them. If languages hold phonetic, syntactical and semantic similarities, they are assumed to be related. This is evident amongst Spanish, French, Italian and Catalan-Romance languages that derive from Latin. Language families are said to span vast regions, such as Eurasia, the Ural Mountains, North America, southern and eastern areas of India and northern Pakistan and the southern part of Africa. Historical relationships between languages are represented as a tree, akin to a family tree; hence, corresponding languages are said to be family.

---

[1] Germanic, Italic and Hellenic are sub-families of the Indo-European languages. Sub-families indicate that languages within it follow similar spelling and grammatical rules. English, Dutch and Yiddish are all similar because they are Germanic languages, while French, Latin and Spanish are common languages under the "Italic" category.

Languages within a family can all be traced back to a constructed mother tongue known as the proto-language of the family. For example, languages spoken in the Horn of Africa, North Africa, the Sahel and much of the Middle East are part of the Afroasiatic family of languages and derive from Proto-Afroasiatic. Linguistic commonalities between East Asian, Southeast Asian and South Asian languages are from Proto-Sino-Tibetan. English and other languages spoken in Europe and on the Indian subcontinent are Indo-European and derive from Proto-Indo-European.

Families are divided into subfamilies or stocks, which are further broken down into subdivisions or linguistic branches. For example, linguists trace Spanish and French to the Latin branch, which is under the Italic stock. The Italic stock is apart of the Indo-European family. Italic is the subfamily, and Latin is the branch. English is of the Germanic stock and can be traced through the West Germanic branch, again under the Indo-European family.

English is a Germanic language, born in Celtic land

The Celts were the original inhabitants of modern-day England, and they spoke Insular Celtic, an Indo-European stock language that branched into modern-day Gaelic and Welsh. This differs from Continental Celtic, a proto-language spoken throughout most of Europe and Asia Minor. The term Celtic refers to an ancient people who emerged in south-central Europe around the 5th century B.C.E. These were the first Indo-Europeans to spread across Europe; their culture is known as La Tene, named after the Swiss archeologist who discovered a site with Celtic artifacts. The Celts who spread to present-day France, northern Italy and northern Europe were known as the Gauls. Those who immigrated to the Balkans and Asia Minor were the Galatians, while the Celts who moved into Spain were the Celtiberian (hence the term Iberian). Those who moved into the British Isles and northern France are Insular Celts and were divided into two groups: the Goeldic of ancient Ireland and the Brythonic of southern England, Wales and the northern-French province Brittany. Linguists speculate as to when the Celts first settled in the British Isles and from where they immigrated; however, it is commonly agreed that they were the first inhabitants of England. In 55 B.C., Roman troops invaded Britain, occupying it for 400 years. While the Romans left their cultural mark, Celtic[2] remained the dominant language of the region.

Germanic tribes began invading the British Isles in roughly 410 A.D. The Jutes, the Angles and the Saxons (source of the term "Anglo-Saxon") established bases in Great Britain, bringing their culture and their respective languages. All three Germanic tribes spoke distinct languages that derived from the West Germanic branch of the Indo-European language family.

---

[2] Words such as *glean, piece, flannel, clan, shamrock* and *clock* are Celtic in origin, while *neighbor, bequeath* and *cheap* are from Old English or Anglo-Saxon.

The common features of these three tongues made it easy for them to merge to create "Old English" with most features deriving from the dominating Angles and Saxon tribes.

Words of Anglo-Saxon or Germanic origin comprise 25 percent of Modern English (Cevasco, 1977, p.261). These are often practical words such as *sun (sunne)*, *water (wæter)*, *earth (eorthe)*, *drink (drinc)*, *sleep (slēp)* and grammatical words such as *the, she, have, of* and *you*.

Old English featured a grammatical form, spelling patterns and vocabulary that differed drastically from Celtic and the Germanic languages. Although modern-day English has retained many words of Celtic origin, most everyday English words are Germanic. Remnants of Celtic include English place-names *Avon* and *Thames* and words of little use, such as *glen (glenn)*, *bog (buggo-)* and *banshee (ben síde* meaning "woman of fairies").

Eventually, the Germanic tribes displaced the Celts, driving them north to Scotland, Wales and Ireland. Originally called Britannia, the land the Anglo-Saxons invaded and took on a new name: England named for the Angles, as England derives from the Old English *Engla-land*, or "land of the Angles."

(The Vikings contributed a great deal to English.)

In the late eighth century, the Vikings or Norsemen from Sweden, Norway and Denmark invaded England. The Vikings, who spoke Scandinavian languages, were known to be fierce competitors and eventually occupied Russia, Iceland, France, Greenland and North America. They wrestled the English for control of England for 200 years until King Alfred checked the Vikings raids and established Danelaw treaty. The treaty split England, giving the Danes control of the north and the English control in the south. English adopted many Scandanavian words, such as *get (geta)*, *hit (hitta)*, *scream (scræma)*, *law (lag)*, *egg (eggen)*, *dazzle (dasask* meaning "to become weary") and *freckle (freknōttr)* and Old Norse grammatical structure, seen in the pronouns *they*, *them* and *their*.

With mostly Greek and Latin vocabulary

Latin

English borrowed Latin-derived words during four periods in history, and English developed into two of its three historical forms: Middle English and Modern English. In the Early Middle Ages, Roman merchants and soldiers brought 200 Latin words to the lexicon; words such as *dish (disc)*, *wall (vallum)* and *pepper (piper)* remain in Modern English.

Since the use of Latin was limited to cities and the wealthy, Latin did not replace the Celtic language as a whole. Under attack from the Germanic tribes, the Romans left Britain in 436 A.D. Most of their language and culture left with them. Britons did not experience Latin influence again until St. Augustine and his missionaries ventured to the Anglo-Saxon kingdoms to convert the Germanic tribes to Christianity in 601 A.D. They brought Latin words that pertained to the church, such as *priest, vicar* and the word *church* itself, and even some domestic words such as *fork* (*furca*), *cook* (*coquus*) and *rose* (*rosa*). Romans also introduced a new grapheme system, replacing the Anglo-Saxon Runes with the Roman alphabet.

English experienced the largest influx of Latin-based words during the Middle Ages after the Norman invasion of England in 1066. The Normans were Germanic Vikings who settled in northern France 200 years prior and originally spoke Old Norse. Over time, they began to speak a rural version of French mixed with Old Norse, but by 1066 Norman French had lost most of its Germanic influence and, thus, was primarily a derivative of Latin.

Initially, Norman French (also called Anglo-Norman) was the language of nobility in England, and the peasantry continued to speak Old English. It would be 300 years after invasion before the Normans began to intermix with the English, producing Middle English. The Normans imparted more than 10,000 words to English, three-fourths of which are still in use (Bryson, p. 53, 2015). Norman French and Latin were the languages of the educated, high class and, thus, loaned English words related to nobility (*crown, duke, castle*), government (*city and parliament*), war and authority (*army, obedience, enemy*), law (*court, justice, sentence*), high living (*jewel, beauty, sauce*) and art (*literature, poet, color*). Latin continued to infiltrate the English lexicon during the English Renaissance of the 14th through 17th centuries. England, alongside most other European nations, placed a great emphasis on learning Latin and Greek and translating classical texts from these languages. This introduced new terms such as *fictitious, manuscript, comedy, gradual, specimen, skeleton, invention* and *orbit* to the lexicon. The addition of Latin words during the English Renaissance differed from previous instances of adoption as the additions were deliberate and not a result of a conquering or a "top-down" decree.

English experienced a surge in neologisms[3], or newly formed words, by way of the Industrial and Scientific Revolution in 1760. The Industrial Revolution was a time when scientific discoveries and technological innovations developed exponentially in both England and the United States. New forms of transportation developed, giving rise to the word train, which derives from the Latin verb tragīnāre, and the past participle tractus, meaning "to pull" (see root word tract). Scientists also coined new words based on discoveries that required new systems of measurement, like centigrade, the original term for Celsius.

[3] neologisms: *neo* is a Greek root acting as a prefix, denoting "new"; *log* is also a Greek root denoting "word"; and *ism* is a Greek suffix denoting "act of, belief in."

Centigrade is literally "_____ degrees" (hint: identify the numerical prefix to fill in the blank). These words differ from other Latin-based words, as they are not loanwords, but newly formed using both Latin and Greek morphemes. Other scientific and technological neologisms include bacteria, lens, caffeine, factory, vacuum and airplane.

Greek

Many English words also derive from Greek. There are three main methods by which Greek entered the language:

—Latin: many Latin roots, and words derive from Greek. For example, the Latin root *lexi* comes from the Greek word *lexis*, from *legein*, meaning "to say," producing the words *lexicon*, lexicographer and lexus. Other Greek roots that came through Latin include Latin *nomen* from the Greek *onym*, meaning "name" Latin *nauticus*, *navis* from the Greek *nautikos*, *naus* meaning "sailor"; physics from the Greek *physiko*, meaning "natural things"; iambic from the Greek *iambikos*, *iambus*, meaning "a verbal attack"; and *lithic*, from the Greek *lithikos* meaning "stone."

—Arabic: Islamic scholars once translated Greek writings on science and philosophy, adding their own research and understandings. Words such as *elixir, chemist* (from *al-chem ist*) and *alembic* are evidence of this.

— Coinages, particularly from the Industrial and Scientific Revolution. Greek loaned English words like telescope, where both *tele* and *scope* are Greek roots meaning "far" and "see," respectively). Other words include hydraulic, claustrophobia, chronometer, chromo some, biology and entomology. Most words of Greek origin entered English via this method.

Three charts on the following pages list common English morphemes of Greek or Latin origin.

...with global influences

Throughout the 18th, 19th and 20th centuries, trade and globalization, global conflict and cooperation, and imperialism and colonization facilitated the incorporation of foreign words into the English lexicon. These are called "borrowed words," and they are prevalent throughout the English language. "Tea," for example, is a word of Chinese origin: It came into the English language in the 16th or 17th century when the English took to the seas in search of land and resources to conquer. Tea was and is still a staple in Chinese culture but was unheard of to the English until they first reached China. Similarly, Spanish and Arabic share several words because the Moors brought Arabic into Al-Andalus (presently known as Spain) when they conquered it in 711 A.D. For example, the Spanish word for "orange" is naranja; it derives from the *naranj*, the Arabic word for "bitter orange." The Russian term *glasnost* is an international policy that derived from the fall of the Soviet Union; it refers to openness and government transparency (which was uncharacteristic of the Soviet Union at that time).

English words originate from languages all over the world, never rejecting a word based on creed or national origin (Lederer, 25). English continues to expand, and today, its speakers create new words and terms, such as *internet*, *hashtag* and *tweet*, three words that evidence the rise of technology in the 21st century.

Root	Origin	Latin or Greek Word	Word Meaning	Word Example
anim	Latin	anima	mind, soul life	animation
bio	Greek	bios	life	biome
terra	Latin	terra	land	territory
gee, geo	Greek	gaia, ge	earth	geothermal
spec, spect	Latin	specere, spectus	to see	inspect
scope	Greek	skopein	to see	telescope
son	Latin	sonus	sound	sonogram
phon	Greek	phone	sound, voice	telephone
aqu	Latin	aqua	water	aquatic
hydr, hydro	Greek	hydor	water	hydraulic

Prefix	Origin	Meaning	Word Example
pre-	Latin	before	prevail
fore-	Germanic	before	forego
bene-	Latin	good	benefit
eu-	Greek	good	euphoria
con-	Latin	with, together	connotation
syn-	Greek	with, together	synergy
multi-	Latin	many	multitude
poly-	Greek	many	polymorphic
super-, supr-	Latin	above	supreme
hyper-	Greek	above	hyperthermia
over-	Germanic	above	override
sub-	Latin	below	substitute
hypo-	Greek	below	hypothermia
under-	Germanic	below	underneath
be-	Germanic	intensifier	become

Suffix	Origin	Meaning	Word Example
-able, ible	Latin	capable of	responsible
-ation	Latin	state or condition of	reservation
-(a)gogue	Greek	leader, one who drives	demagogue
-gon	Greek	shape, form	polygon
-ful	Germanic	full of	colorful

Mathematical Prefixes: Which One Do I Use?

Determining whether to use a Latin or Greek form of a prefix can be confusing. The following are guidelines on how to use numerical prefixes:

A.	Typically, we use Latin and Greek prefixes with Latin and Greek roots, respectively. For example:

a. *Uni* and *mono* both mean "one." Universe and **mono**poly both have prefixes that mean one. However, the root of *universe* is *verse*, from the Latin verb *versus*, meaning "to turn." Thus, the universe refers to all the planets and star systems that turn or move in one direction. The *poly* root of *monopoly* comes from the Greek word *polein*, meaning "to sell." Thus, a monopoly refers to a market with one seller.

B.	We sometimes use Latin prefixes with Greek roots and Greek prefixes with Latin roots. This is particularly the case for words formed during the Scientific Revolution.

Number	Latin	Greek
1	uni	mono
2	duo/bi	duo/di
3	tri	tri
4	quad	tetra
5	quint	penta
6	sex	hex
7	sept	hept
8	oct	oct
9	non	ennea
10	dec	dec
20	vigint	icosa
30	trigint	triconta
40	quadragint	tetraconta
50	quinquagint	pentaconta
60	sexagint	hexaconta
70	Septuagint	heptaconta
80	octogint	octaconta
90	nonagint	enneaconta
100	cent	hect
1000	milli	kilo
many	poly	multi

Many of our words can be traced directly back to Old English and other older languages of the Germanic family, like Frankish Norse, Dutch, etc. Below are examples of words that have Germanic origins.

Word	Origin	Latin or Greek Word	Word Meaning
watch	Old English	*waeccan, wacchen*	to be awake
mingle	Old English	*mengan*	to mix
egg (verb)	Old Norse	*eggja*	to incite
anger	Old Norse	*angr*	sorrow, grief
blaze	Middle Dutch	*blasen*	to blow/swell up

A Note on Dictionary Usage, the Matrix of a word, and Etymological Brackets.

An important component of vocabulary study is dictionary usage. We mostly just look at the entry-level meanings, but a dictionary entry conveys a wealth of information. To truly understand a word, it is important to always look for its matrix. The matrix of a word refers to its mother tongue/origin. It will answer the following questions:

What is the word's function? (see part of speech)

From where did the word derive?

What is the original meaning and usage of the word?

What are the modern-day word usages?

You can find the answer to these questions using a dictionary with decent etymological references (American Heritage Dictionary works best for this example; also see Oxford English Dictionary and Eric Partridge's Origins). For now, we will use the American Heritage Dictionary (AHD) of Indo-European roots.

When looking up words in the dictionary:

First: Identify the word's proper pronunciation by using the decoding rules from Chapter 1 (looking at how the word is phonetically syllabicated and the diacritical marks used). For example, the word *synagogue* is phonetically spelled *sĭn-ə-gŏg'*. Notice that there is an accent over the last syllable, indicating that the first syllable receives the primary stress. The second syllable is reduced to the schwa, and the third syllable is a short o. Both the g's in the word are hard sounds. This spelling should give you enough clues as to how to pronounce the word.

Second: Identify the word's part of speech.

Third: Look for the [brackets] at the end of the entry-level meanings, where **you will see a) the word's morphemes, and b) the language of origin and the languages through which the word can be traced before reaching English**. Synagogue comes from [Middle English, from Old French *sinagoge*, from Late Latin *synagōga*, from Greek *sunagōgē*, assembly, synagogue from *sunagein*, to bring together: sun, syn + agein, to lead; see ag- in the Appendix of the Indo-European roots].

Fourth: Finally, read the entry-level definition of the word. It is best to start from the last entry and work your way up, as the definitions closest to the etymological meaning are at the bottom, buried beneath the connotative modern-day meanings.

Here is a visual example of a dictionary entry for the word *ventilate*:

ven·ti·late (věn´tl-āt´)
tr.v. -lat·ed, -lat·ing, -lates
  1. To admit fresh air into (a mine, for example) to replace stale or noxious air. 2. To circulate through and freshen: *A sea breeze ventilated the rooms.* 3. To provide with a vent, as for airing. 4. To expose (a substance) to the circulation of fresh air, as to retard spoilage. 5. To expose to public discussion or examination: *The students ventilated their grievances.* 6. To aerate or oxygenate (blood). [Middle English *ventilaten*, to blow away, from Latin *ventilāre*, *ventilāt-*, to fan, from ventulus, diminutive of ventus, wind. See we- in Appendix I.]

Some word entries do not list origins, generally because the word is a derivative of a word that already has its origin listed elsewhere. For example, the origin of the word *mismanage* might be found under *manage*, as the former is a derivative of the latter. If this is the case, simply look up *manage* or the cognate of the word in question.

You will need to use the etymological brackets to complete many of the exercises in this chapter.

Rule 3: Some English words were borrowed from languages other than Germanic tongues, Latin and Greek, due to colonization of lands and trade with cultures worldwide.

On the next page there are words with origins other than Germanic, Latin or Greek. These are often called **loan words** or **borrowed words** because they are directly taken from tongues outside of the Indo-European family of languages (as opposed to transliterated and developed over time).

Rule 3 Practice 1 — Answer the following comprehension questions about the ways in which Latin and Greek have influenced the English language.

1)   Latin first entered the English language by way of
    a.   when the English invaded Rome, which brought Latin back to the British Isle;
    b.   the Scientific Revolution, which ushered in words such as *telescope* and *psychology;*
    c.   the Roman invasion of Celtic lands; and
    d.   the Norman French invasion of Great Britain.

2)   Although English derives from the _____ branch of the Indo-European family of languages, the original inhabitants of England spoke a _____ language.
    a.   Germanic Italic
    b.   Germanic, Celtic
    c.   Italic, Celtic
    d.   Celtic, Hellenic

3)   Most Greek words came into the English language as
    a.   coinages, particularly from scientific and technological advancements and discoveries
    b.   direct loanwords of Modern Greek origin
    c.   Arabic translations of Greek writings
    d.   via Latin words of Greek origin

4)   Which of the following had the greatest influence on English vocabulary?
    a.   Proto-Germanic, the mother tongue of the Germanic language
    b.   Proto-Celtic, the mother tongue of the Celtic language
    c.   Latin
    d.   Greek

Rule 3 Practice 2 — Sort the following words based on their language of origin (Germanic, Latin or Greek). Write the word in the respective spaces below. The first three are done for you. Use the dictionary and etymological brackets to assist you.

1.	today	2.	subscribe	3.	antithesis	4.	king
5.	identical	6.	meal	7.	baptize	8.	pandemic
9.	malefactor	10.	tenacious	11.	hoof	12.	philanthropic

13. cosmogony   14. lady   15. conviction   16. contrary

17. podium

Germanic	Greek	Latin

Rule 4 — <u>Some English words were borrowed from languages other than Germanic tongues, Latin and Greek due to colonization of lands and trade with cultures world-wide.</u>

On the next page there are words with origins other than Germanic, Latin or Greek. These words typically enter the English language via invasions, conquest and colonization, trade or political allied relationships.

Look at the following table of words. Consider the words borrowed from Arabic, Hebrew, Asiatic languages (Mandarin, Japanese, etc.) or tongues of the aboriginal American (Algoquin, Choctaw, etc.). Compare the words below to words that are directly borrowed from Greek, Latin and the Romance languages or Germanic.

Word	Origin	Original Word	Original Word Meaning
decipher	Arabic	*sifr*	zero
admiral	Arabic	*amir*	head, commander
cherub	Hebrew	*kerubh*	one who blesses
amen	Hebrew; Kemetic	*amen*	Kemetic deity
chipmunk	Odawa (Algonquin)	*chitmunk, jidmoonh*	red (striped) squirrel
geisha	Japanese	*gei + sha*	person (sha) of the arts (gei)
ketchup	Chinese (Mandarin)	*kê-chiap*	pickled fish (kê) juice (chiap)
ballet	French	*(serge) de Nîme*	worsted fabric from (de) Nime
kindergarten	German	*Kinder + garten*	a garden of children
psychic	Greek	*psukhikós*	pertaining to the mind or soul
yoga	Sanskrit	*yogah*	binding; union or joining
bandana	Hindu	*bandhna*	a tie

Rule 4 Practice — Complete the chart below by identifying the language of origin and meaning of the words in the first column. Use the American Heritage Dictionary, particularly the information found at the end of each entry in the [etymological brackets] for assistance.

Word	Origin	Original Word	Word Meaning
consider	Latin	considerare	to address the stars, lit "with the stars"
sophisticated	Greek	sophistikos	of or pertaining to a wise man
teach			
almanac			
hallelujah			
monolith			
alkaline			
bagel			
moose			
expulsion			
quartz			
avocado			
nice			
plunder			
cider			
subterranean			
glitch			
hurricane			
sofa			

Words for additional practice

- microscope	- sequoia	- concurrent	- motivate	- cay
- prescription	- tapioca	- expire	- squash	- pecan
- piranha	- chemistry	- interject	- chronological	- alleviate
- cognition	- terrapin	- guacamole	- mutate	- lime
- sugar	- phonetics	- persimmon	- lemon	- cashew
- papaya	- bibliophile	- monsoon	- cyclone	- dynamite
- magnetic	- alpaca	- llama	- sequin	- progressive
- democrat	- politician	- science	- subsequent	- artichoke
- chocolate	- tomato	- potato	- skunk	- Judas
- cocaine	- residual	- savannah	- demographic	- conductor
- monotheistic	- iguana	- galilee	- syrup	- judicial
- podiatrist	- petunia	- babel	- bisector	- monogamy
- bayou	- algorithm	- cayenne	- photograph	- primordial
- cannibal	- admiral	- barbecue	- claustrophobia	- kosher
- bethesda	- lemon	- savannah		

Rule 5: Compound and Portmanteau words are created by putting two or more words together.

Compound Words

These words are created by combining two whole English words to form a new word. For example:

dog + house = doghouse   *star + fish* = starfish

Some of the meanings of basic compound words are obvious. A doghouse is a shelter or house specifically for pet dogs. A starfish is a fish that is shaped like a star.

The meanings of other basic compound words are not so obvious until it is deconstructed into the two original words. For example,

rain (wet, shower) + *bow* (bend) = **rainbow**, the result of light reflecting in water droplets after a rain shower (note: *flect*, the root of reflecting, means "to _____," which fits the definition of rainbow, as sunlight is bending in the raindrop).

break (spring out) + *fast* (firmly fixed against eating) = **breakfast**, literally the first meal eaten after not eating all night, facilitating one springing out of their fast.

Rule 5 Practice 1 — Break the following compound words down into two individual words. Use the space provided to show your answer.

Example: **matchbook** = *match* + *book*

1. keyboard   2.   firefly   3.   makeup   4.   notebook

5. daydream   6.   headline   7.   headfirst   8.   stomachache

9. viewpoint   10.   whirlwind

Rule 5 Practice 2 — Write the meaning of each of the following compound words in the space provided.

Example: redhead <u>a person with high levels of reddish pigmentation in his or her hair</u>

1. milestone _____
2. icebreaker _____
3. drawback _____
4. wallpaper _____
5. pigeonhole _____

Blended or Portmanteau Words

Portmanteau words blend two words, one of which is usually shortened, to form a new word. For example:

lion + *tiger* combine to form *liger*, dropping the *–on* ending of "lion" and the *ti-* beginning of "tiger."

smoke + *fog* combine to form *smog*, by dropping _____ in "smoke" and the _____ in "fog."

The train company *Amtrak* is derived from the words "America" and "track," dropping the *–erica* from America and *c* from track.

The term "portmanteau" derives from the French (*porte manteaux*) and originally referred to a suitcase that opened into two equal compartments. It carried (*port*) coats (*manteau*) and other articles of clothing on one side and smaller bags on the other. It was first used as a linguistic term by Lewis Carroll in the book "Through the Looking Glass" in 1871. The character Humpty Dumpty used the blended words *slithy* and *mimsy* in the poem "Jabberwock."

When Alice inquired to the meaning of *slithy*, Humpty answered: "You see, it's like a portmanteau—there are two meanings packed into one word." Carroll himself said he loved creating words because "he loved to scrunch two words into one as clothes are crammed into a port, or traveling bag" (Lerderer, 118).

Rule 5 Practice 3 — Combine each pair of words into a portmanteau word.

1.   breakfast + lunch = _____

2.   motor + hotel = _____

3.   spoon + fork = _____

4.   web + log = _____

5.   skirt + shorts = _____

6.   vital + mineral = _____

7.   emotion + icon = _____

8.   malicious + software = _____

9.   hazardous + material = _____

10.   Pocket + Monster (hint: a well-known anime show) = _____

Rule 5 Practice 4 — Determine the two words that have been combined to make the portmanteau words listed below. Write your responses in the spaces provided. An example is provided below.

1.   alphanumerics = alpha + numerics

2.   paratrooper = _____ + _____

3.   infomercial = _____ + _____

4.   multiplex = _____ + _____

5.   Eurasia = _____ + _____

6.   mathlete = _____ + _____

7.   sitcom = _____ + _____

8.   redox = _____ + _____

9.   Comcast = _____ + _____

10.   sheeple = _____ + _____

11.   telemarket = _____ + _____

Rule 5 Practice 5 — Sort the following words into the appropriate boxes. For the portmanteau words, write the two original words in parentheses in the appropriate box. The first two have been completed to provide examples.

1.   *backpack*

2.   *moped*

3.   bash

4.   football

5.   layman

6.   forklift

7.   podcast

8.   webinar

9.   sharecropper

10.   hindsight

11.   camcorder

12.   televangelist

Compound Words	**Portmanteau/Blended Words**
backpack	moped (motor + pedal)

Summary

Words in English have a variety of origins. English is a language that derives from the
_____ branch of the Indo-European family of languages. However, most
roots, prefixes, suffixes and words in general come from _____ and
_____, two European classical languages. Because of _____ and
_____, Modern English contains words from around the world. Some words in
English are the combination of two existing words, _____
_____ words are two whole words put together to create a new word (such as
handyman). _____ or _____ words are parts of two words
combined to create a new word (such as webinar).

Review

A.   Which is a Word?

Directions: Circle the word(s) in the list below.

1.   meter
2.   ex
3.   ball
4.   I
5.   b

B.   Germanic, Latin and Greek Sort

Directions: Sort the following words into the proper boxes based on their language of origin.
Remember: Old English words derive from Germanic stock.

1.   tomorrow   2.   biography   3.   myriad
4.   maternity   5.   mother   6.   law
7.   legal   8.   beef   9.   cow
10.   microcosm   11.   orthodox   12.   vitality

Germanic	Latin	Greek

C.   Word Origins

Directions: Complete the chart below by identifying the language of origin and meaning of the words in the first column. Use an etymological dictionary and the information found at the end of each entry meaning in {etymological brackets} to assist you.

Word	Origin
safari	
savanna	
pet	
jubilee	
ebony	
caucus	
cashier	
magazine	
tycoon	
guru	

D.   Building Compound Words

Directions: Using the list of single words below, create compound words and write them in the spaces provided. Each word can only be used once. One example is completed for you.

long   draw   *earth*   cross   time   board
walk   line   card   bridge house   *quake*

1.   earthquake
2.   _____
3.   _____
4.   _____
5.   _____
6.   _____

pass   key   spread   hill   bank
turn   port   snow   foot   bed

7.   _____   8.   _____
9.   _____   10.   _____
11.   _____

E.   Defining Compound Words

Directions: Define the following compound words and write your responses in the space provided.

1.   lifeguard

2.   pancake

3.   ballroom

4.   watermelon

5.   scapegoat

F.   Creating Portmanteau Words

Directions: Combine the word pairs below to create portmanteau words in the spaces provided. Use the hints in parentheses to assist you.

1.   international + network= _____ (global system of interconnected computer networks)

2.   velvet + crochet= _____ (a company responsible for making fastening products)

3.   cybernetic + organism= _____ (a person with robotic body parts)

4.   British + exit= _____ (Great Britain's 2016 exit from the European Union)

5.   Tanganyika + Zanzibar= _____ (a present-day African nation)

6.   botulinum + toxin= _____ (a drug used to treat certain muscular conditions and cosmetically remove wrinkles by temporarily paralyzing muscles)

7.   E. Gerry + salamander= _____ (to manipulate district boundaries to establish political advantage for a group or party)

8.   beat + beetles= _____ (software used to disrupt a computer)

9.   hazardous + material _____ (dangerous goods)

10.   ethyl + alcohol _____ (a psychoactive drug found in alcoholic beverages, causing intoxication)

11.   endogenous + morphine= _____ (released from the pituitary gland for euphoria and relief)

G.   Dividing Portmanteau Words

Directions: Divide the following blended words in the spaces provided.

1.   Jazzercise = _____ + _____

2.   urinalysis = _____ + _____

3.   workaholic = _____ + _____

4.   affluenza = _____ + _____

5.   docudrama = _____ + _____

6.   biopic = _____ + _____

7.   newscast = _____ + _____

8.   electrocute = _____ + _____

9.   blog (short for weblog) = _____ + _____

10.   Microsoft = _____ + _____

Post-Test

Directions: Select the best answer to the following questions about words and their basic components and structure.

1) What is a **phoneme**?
   a. an utterance of sound conveying complete meaning on its own
   b. the smallest unit of sound that does not convey meaning
   c. the smallest unit of written language
   d. the smallest unit of meaning in a word that cannot stand on its own

2) What is a **grapheme**?
   a. an utterance of sound conveying complete meaning on its own
   b. the smallest unit of sound that does not convey meaning
   c. the smallest unit of written language
   d. the smallest unit of meaning in a word that cannot stand on its own

3) What is a **morpheme**?
   a. an utterance of sound conveying complete meaning on its own
   b. the smallest unit of sound that does not convey meaning
   c. the smallest unit of written language
   d. the smallest unit of meaning in a word that cannot stand on its own

4) What is a **syllable**?
   a. unit of sound in a word that contains a vowel sound
   b. the smallest unit of sound that does not convey meaning
   c. a letter
   d. the smallest unit of meaning in a word that cannot stand on its own

5) What is a **word**?
   a. an utterance of sound conveying complete meaning on its own
   b. the smallest unit of sound that does not convey meaning
   c. the smallest unit of written language
   d. the smallest unit of meaning in a word that cannot stand on its own

6) Sort the following lexeme and lexical units into their respective groups; write the lexemes in the circles and the lexical units in the spaces below the circles.

sprinkle   accessorize   accessed   sprinkled   access

sprinkling   accessory   sprinkler   sprinkles   accessing

_____   _____

_____   _____

_____   _____

_____   _____

_____   _____

7) Circle the free morphemes and put a box around the bound morphemes.

ment   mint   tract   fract   cry   ly   fin

fine   trine   in

8) True or False: the word *transformation* has a derivational ending. _____

9) The English language contains vocabulary mostly of _____ origin.
   a. Latin
   b. Germanic
   c. Celtic
   d. Greek

10) How many *vowel sounds, consonant sounds, phonemes, graphemes, morphemes, and syllables* are in each of the listed words?

Word	Vowels	Consonants	Phonemes	Graphemes	Morphemes	Syllables
sleep						
shell						
mash						
test						
refraction						

11) What type of vowel sound is in the word *slip?*
a.   long
b.   short
c.   r-influenced
d.   diphthong

12) What type of vowel sound is in the word *file?*
a.   long
b.   short
c.   r-influenced
d.   diphthong

13) What type of consonant sound is in the word *tea?*
a.   labial
b.   dental
c.   guttural
d.   semi-vowel

14) What type of consonant sound is underlined in the word *sky?*
a.   labial
b.   dental
c.   guttural
d.   semi-vowel

15) List the **vibrating consonants** in each of these words:
a.   bin _____
b.   melt _____
c.   ring _____

16) List the **plosives consonants** in each of these words:
a.   jump _____
b.   thumb _____
c.   flee _____

17) What type of syllable is underlined in the following words?
a.   dip<u>per</u> _____
b.   <u>sni</u>per _____
c.   bub<u>ble</u>_____

18) What is the origin of each of the following words?
a.   testify
b.   umbrella
c.   admiral

19) Complete the prefix/root/suffix chart below. Be sure to give the meaning of the prefix and root, and the part of speech of the suffix.

Word	Prefix + meaning	Root + meaning	Suffix + POS
ingenious			
inclusion			
untenable			
important			
intercontinental			

For your convenience, I have included a collection of charts with reading and orthography information. These are reproducibles that are to be used for educational purposes.

Stages of Reading (Bear et al., 2016)

STAGES	READING	WRITING/WORD STUDY	SUGGESTIONS
Preemergent	Pretend reading; cannot segment speech stream; no phonemic awareness or COW-T; inconsistent alphabetic knowledge	Pretend writing; writing progresses from random scribbles to letter-like figures or letters (though they do not match these to sounds to attempt to spell words)	Develop oral language; develop phonological and phonemic awareness and COW-T; build letter identification and letter writing; build ability to identify the onset and rime of a word. Have students engage in dramatic play; engage in drawing, retelling, rereading, think and read alouds, and learning rhyme.
Beginning	Word-by-word reading; oral reading is choppy; readers progress from basic to firm COW-T; focus is on building phonemic awareness; readers attend to sounds in a word for decoding; readers build sight word knowledge	Word-by-word writing; writers spell using letter names and vowel sounds; writers are fully alphabetic and use sound-symbol relationships to spell words Spells words with short-vowel patterns; learning beginning and final consonants and consonant blends	Harvesting sight words; partner reading; repeated readings; echo readings; dictations; learning to preview and make predictions before reading text; answer plot repeated questions; engage in independent reading and writing; engage in partner reading and writing; sentence writing; word study focusing on short vowel patterns, digraphs, consonant blends and word families

Transitional	Consolidated alphabetic phase (where readers recognize patterns and chunks to analyze unfamiliar words); they read more words and have more sight word knowledge; they are phrasal, fluent readers and begin reading with expression and prosody; less word-by-word reading and more whisper or silent reading; students read independently and are taught with materials at their instructional reading level	Fluent writing; can spell more words automatically; greater speed and less conscious attention to spelling; better organization (can write multiple paragraphs); more time to concentrate on ideas Uses but confuses silent vowel markers and vowel patterns (ambiguous, long, and diphthong)	Vocabulary is key! The goal is to build *wordsmiths* or *word warriors* (readers and writers who are word conscious or curious about words) Students should read 20 minutes a night
Intermediate	Readers develop expanding interests; explore new topics and genres; sharpen use of strategies; develop background knowledge, strategies and vocabulary for content area reading; develop greater fluency due to attention to punctuation for phrasing; display expressive and prosodic reading	More confidence due to greater automaticity and fluency; more attentive to ideas; more prominent voice; writes for an audience; able to work on longer pieces over days and can revise and edit writing Unaccented final syllables; syllable juncture; affixes and spelling-for-meaning connections	Focus on building background knowledge by reading a variety of types of text; instructional focus should be on reading to learn (versus learning to read)
Advanced	Readers develop word knowledge through generative process or morphemic chunking; critical reading is a major area of focus; vocabulary increases through wide reading and study of specific content areas	Writers able to produce many forms and genres of writing for different functions and purposes; expanding vocabulary improves word choice; better able to revise work Learn morphemes and etymologies of words to increase vocabulary comprehension	Generative and word specific vocabulary instruction; engage in wide reading; explicitly taught how to learn vocabulary; provide readers with engaging text to increase their level of background knowledge; instructional focus should be on critical thinking and reading

Emergent/Pre-literate:
Pretend reading; pretend writing; developing concept of word in text (COW-T), begins to develop phonological and phonemic awareness; developing alphabetic knowledge

Beginner:
Learning and using letter-sound correspondences to and decode and spell words; read aloud; word-by-word, finger-point reading; decoding; word-by-word writing, letter-name spelling; writing moves from a few words to paragraph in length; rudimentary-firm COW-T and firm phonemic awareness

Transitional:
Growing sight word knowledge; approaching fluent and prosodic oral reading; increased phrasal fluency; emergence of silent reading (whisper reading); writing is approaching fluency, more organization in writing, can write several paragraphs

Intermediate:
High sight word knowledge; fully fluent and prosodic oral reader; engage in silent and independent reading using; wide reading of several genres; writing with more automaticity and speed; more concentration on ideas; more sophisticated writing and composition; more specific vocabulary

Advanced:
Greater word knowledge from generative process and morphemic chunking; engaged in critical reading of a variety of reading styles based on text type and purpose for reading; writing contains different forms and structures for different functions and genres; greater word choice and better revisions due to expanding vocabulary

Components of Language

Phonology: the study of the sounds that comprise lexemes of a language	**Graphology:** the study of a language's written system	**Syntax:** the study of how words and phrases of a particular language are arranged to create well-formed sentences	**Morphology:** the study of the shape or form of words in a language	**Semantics:** the study of the meaning of words

	Definition	Units	Number of units in "wishful"
phonology	the study of the principles that govern how sounds are organized in languages	phoneme: the smallest unit in sound in a word	/w/ /i/ /sh/ /f/ /u/ /l/ (6 phonemes)
graphology	the study of written and printed symbols and of writing systems	grapheme: a letter; the smallest written unit in a word	W-i-s-h-f-u-l (7 graphemes)
morphology	a branch of grammar that studies the structure of words and the way that morphemes operate in a language	morpheme: the smallest unit of meaning in a language that cannot be divided	wish-ful (two morphemes)

Types of Morphemes: Free and Bound

Free *a morpheme that can be uttered on its own*	**Bound** *a grammatical unit that never stands by itself*
play horse (n) talk	play<u>ing</u>, play<u>ed</u>, play<u>s</u>, play<u>ful</u>, play<u>fully</u> horse<u>s</u> talk<u>ing</u>, talk<u>ed</u>, talk<u>er</u>, talk<u>ative</u>

Types of Morphemes: Derivational and Inflectional

Eight Most Common Derivational Morphemes	Eight Inflectional Morphemes
Prefixes dis- (negation/reversal), im/in/il/ir- (negation/reversal), re- (again, back), un- (negation/reversal) *Suffixes* -ly (adverb and adjective)- like or having the characteristic of), -al (adjective- pertaining to), -able/ible (adjective- able to), -tion (abstract noun- quality or condition of)	-s (noun plural) -s (noun possessive) -s (verb present tense) -ed (verb past tense) -ing (verb present participle) -en (verb past participle) -er (adjective comparative) -est (adjective superlative)

Types of Vowel Sounds

Type of Vowel	Examples
short vowel	<u>a</u>pple <u>E</u>d the <u>e</u>lephant <u>i</u>tch <u>o</u>ctopus <u>u</u>mbrella
long	n<u>a</u>me bay weigh br<u>ai</u>d cl<u>ea</u>n tr<u>ee</u> f<u>igh</u>t k<u>i</u>te c<u>oa</u>t m<u>o</u>de c<u>u</u>te
r-influenced	c<u>ar</u> b<u>are</u> h<u>air</u> st<u>eer</u> cl<u>ear</u> t<u>ier</u> p<u>er</u> st<u>ir</u> f<u>ire</u> sh<u>or</u>t c<u>ore</u> r<u>oar</u> w<u>ar</u> f<u>ur</u> <u>ear</u>n w<u>or</u>d
diphthong	b<u>oy</u> andr<u>oid</u> c<u>ow</u> cl<u>ou</u>d
schwa	sep<u>a</u>rate en<u>e</u>my subst<u>i</u>tute compr<u>o</u>mise inst<u>i</u>gate

Types of Prefixes

Type of Prefix	Examples	
prepositional/ directional	<u>re</u>play <u>super</u>man <u>intro</u>vert	<u>pre</u>arrange <u>sub</u>way <u>ex</u>trovert
numerical	<u>uni</u>cycle <u>tri</u>angular <u>quin</u>tuplet	<u>bi</u>cycle <u>quad</u>rilateral <u>sex</u>tuplet
negation	<u>il</u>legal <u>un</u>tie <u>dis</u>abled	<u>ir</u>regular <u>anti</u>dote <u>mis</u>understand
intensifier	<u>be</u>wilder	<u>ex</u>uberant

Root Words (bound morphemes)

Latin Roots	Greek Roots	Anglo-Saxon Roots
aud: to hear (*audience*)	auto: self (*autonomous*)	bitan: bite (*bite, bait*)
ben: well (*benefit*)	bio: life (*biology*)	
gen: to create, to give birth (*generate, progeny*)	chrono: time (*chronology*)	earg: cowardly, disgusting, lifeless (*irk, irksome*)
	geo: earth (*geology*)	
jur/jus: law (*justify, jury*)	graph: write/draw (*graphic*)	
manu: hand (*manual*)	log: word/speech/science (*logic*)	cunnan: know (*cunning, keen*)
temp: time (*temporary*)	morph: shape/form (*morpheme*)	
terr: earth (*terrarium*)	lith: rock (*monolith*)	god: good (*goodwill, gospel*)
scrib: to write (*describe*)	poli: city (*politics*)	
vita: life (*vital*)	phon: sound (*telephone*)	laewede: lay, unlearned (*layman, laity*)

"Root Words" and its multiple forms	Examples
cap/cip/cept: take, hold	captive, capture; municipal, anticipate; accept, deception
fact/fic/fect: make, do	factor, factitious; benefice, efficient; infection, confectionary
mit/miss/mise: send, throw	remit, transmit; remission, missile; surmise, promise
reg/rect/rig/ress: rule, straight, arrange	regal, regimen; corrective, rectangle; incorrigible; address, redress
sta/stat/sist: stand	station, standard; status, statement; insistent, persist
spec/spect/spic: look, see, appear	speculate, species; introspective, perspective; suspicious, conspicuous
ten/tent/tin/tain: hold	tenure, untenable; detention, intent; abstinence, retinue; abstain, maintain
vid/vis: see	video, evident; visible, revision

Suffixes

Part of Speech	Suffixes	Word Examples
noun	-tion/sion, -ment, -ness, -ity, -or/er, -ist, -ance/ence, -ancy/ency	tradition, inclusiveness, specificity, actor, artist, relevance, complacency
adjective	-al, -ous, -ive, -ic/ical, -ful, -less, -able/ible, -ish, -esque, -y, -ent	traditional, judicious, inclusive, specific, artful, artless, Arabesque, hazy, relevant, complacent
verb	-ate, -ize/ise, -ify/fy, en	vacate, vitalize, specify, awaken
adverb	-ly, -where	specifically, vitally, hazily, everywhere, anywhere, somewhere

Subgroup	Languages
Albanian	Albanian (dialects: Gheg, Tosk, Arbëresh, Arvanitika)
Armenian	Armenian
Balto-Slavic	*Baltic*: Lithuanian and Latvian *Slavic*: Bulgarian, Russian, Polish, Czech, Slovak, Montenegrin, Macedonian, Bosnian, Croatian, Serbian, Slovenian, Ukrainian, Belarusian and Rusyn
Celtic	Welsh, Cornish, Scottish Gaelic, Irish Gaelic and Manx
Germanic	English, Frisian, German, Dutch, Danish, Swedish, Norwegian, Afrikaans, Yiddish, Low German, Icelandic, Faroese
Hellenic	Greek
Indo-Iranian	*Indo-Aryan*: Sanskrit, Hindustani, Punjabi, Bengali, Nepali, Romani, Sindhi, Kashmiri, Gujarati, Marathi, Konkani, Sylheti, Bhojpuri, Odia and Sairiki *Iranian*: Persian, Ossetian and Kurdish
Italic	*Latin and Romance languages*: Spanish, Portuguese, French, Italian, Catalan and Romanian
Language subgroups that are extinct	Anatolian and Tocharian

Bibliography

Baumann et al. (1998). Where are teachers' voices in the phonics/whole language debate? Results from a survey of U.S. elementary classroom teachers. *The Reading Teacher* 51(8): 636-50.

Bear, D. R., Invernizzi, M., Johnston, F. R., and Templeton, S. (2015). *Words their way: Word study for phonics, vocabulary, and spelling instruction*. Edinburgh Gate, Harlow, and Essex, England: Pearson Education Limited.

Beck, I., McKeown, M., and Kucan, L. (2002). *Bringing words to life*. New York, NY: The Guilford Press.

Bruner, Michael S. (1993). *Reduced Recidivism and Increased Employment Opportunity through Research-Based Reading Instruction*. Washington, DC: Department of Justice Office of Juvenile Justice and Delinquency Prevention.

Camera, Lauren. (2016, January 13). Achievement Gap Between White and Black Students Still Gaping. *US News and World Report*. Retrieved from www.usnews.com

Cooper, K., Furry, A., and Van Vleck, S. (2008). *What to Look For- Supervision of Vocabulary and Comprehension*. Nashville, Tennessee: Western Regional First Technical Assistance Center.

Drakeford, William (2002). The Impact of an Intensive Program to Increase Literacy of Youth Confined to Juvenile Corrections. *Journal of Corrective Education*. Retrieved from http://www.jstor.org/stable/41971101

Gould, S. J. (1996). *The mismeasure of man*. New York, NY.: Norton.

Gunning, T. G. (2013). *Creating literacy instruction for all students*. Boston, MA: Pearson.

Harris, T. L. & Hodges, R. E. (Eds.). (1995). *The literacy dictionary: The vocabulary of reading and writing*. Newark, DE: International Reading Association.

Hierbert, E. H., and Kamil, M. L. (2005). *Teaching and Learning Vocabulary: Bringing Research to Practice*. Mahwah, NJ: Lawrence Erlbaum Associates.

International Literacy Day 2016 (2016, June 9). Retrieved from http://uis.unesco.org/en/news/international-literacy-day-2016
Invernizzi, Marcia. (2017). Reading Foundations lecture.

Keene, E. K., & Zimmerman, S. (1997). *Mosaic of thought: Teaching comprehension in a reading workshop*. Portsmouth, NH: Heinemann.

Kidder, R. (1990, April). Should schools pay the price of prison? *Christian Science Monitor*. Retrieved from https://www.csmonitor.com/1990/0423/dkid23.html

Ladson-Billings, G. (1994). *The dreamkeepers*. San Francisco, CA: Jossey-Bass Publishing Co.

National Reading Panel (U.S.), & National Institute of Child Health and Human Development (U.S.). (2000). *Report of the National Reading Panel: Teaching children to read: an evidence-based assessment of the scientific research literature on reading and its implications for reading instruction: reports of the subgroups*. Washington, DC: National Institute of Child Health and Human Development, National Institutes of Health.

O'Cummings, M., Bardack, S., & Gonsoulin, S. (2010). *Issue Brief: The Importance of Literacy for Youth Involved in the Juvenile Justice System*. Washington, DC: National Evaluation and Technical Assistance Center for the Education of Children and Youth Who Are Neglected, Delinquent, or At Risk (NDTAC). Retrieved from http://www.neglected-delinquent.org/nd/docs/literacy_brief_20100120.pdf

OECD (2013). *OECD Skills Outlook 2013: First Results from the Survey of Adult Skills*. OECD Publishing. Retrieved from http://dx.doi.org/10.1787/9789264204256-en

Rasinski, Timothy. (2004). *Assessing Reading Fluency*. Honolulu, HI: Pacific Resources for Education and Learning.

Rasinski, Timothy. (2012). Why Reading Fluency Should be Hot. *The Reading Teacher* 65(8): 516-22.

Rasinki, Timothy. (2014). *Greek and Latin Roots: Keys to Building Vocabulary*. Huntington Beach, CA: Shell Education Publishing.

Strickland, D. 1994. Educating African American learners at risk: Finding a better way. *Language Arts* 71(5): 328–36.

The Impact of an Intensive Reading Program on Literacy Skills of Youth in Juvenile Corrections (2017). *In The National Center on Education, Disability and Juvenile Justice (EDJJ)*. Retrieved from http://www.edjj.org/litSkills.html

U.S. Department of Education, Institute of Education Sciences, National Center for Education Statistics, National Assessment of Educational Progress (NAEP). (2015). "NAEP — 2015 Mathematics & Reading Assessments." *NAEP 2009 High School Transcript Study: Gender, Grade Point Average*. Retrieved from www.nationsreportcard.gov/reading_math_2015/

Weaver, C. et al. (1996). *Creating Support for Effective Education*. Portsmouth, NH: Heinemann.

Weiser, Beverly. (2013). *Effective Vocabulary Instruction for Kindergarten to 12th Grade Students Experiencing Learning Disabilities*. Overland Park, KS: Council for Disabilities.

Glossary

Abjad: a writing system in which a grapheme represents a consonant only with no symbol for vowels, such as Arabic

Abugida: a writing system in which a grapheme represents a consonant and vowel, such as Ethiopian Ge'ez

Accuracy (reading): reading a text without errors

Active vocabulary: words that a person both understands and uses

Affix: a morpheme (prefix and suffix) that is placed before or after a root word to alter the root word's original meaning

Allophone: the multiple sounds a grapheme can represent depending on its position in a word

Alphabet: a writing system in which letters represent consonants and vowel sounds, and are combined and arranged to make words

Alphabetic code: the application of the letter-sound relationship

Alphabetic principle: the understanding that words comprise letters that represent sounds and that there are systematic and predictable relationships between letters and sounds

Alphabetics: the science dealing with the representation of the spoken sounds with letters; emphasis is placed on developing a child's alphabetics (phonemic awareness and phonics) when beginning to learn to read

Assimilated prefix: a prefix that changes its final letter according to the first letter of the base it is attached to (con changes to com when attached to mand, giving us command)

Automaticity: is the ability to read and decode words accurately and effortlessly or automatically

Basic Compound word: words are created by combining two whole English words to form a new word such as doghouse (dog and house) or starfish

Compound word: words created by putting two words together such as rainbow (rain and bow) and motel (motor and hotel)

Connotation: an additional meaning of a word that has derived from changes over time; it is a secondary meaning of a word that often reflects its present-day usage.

Consonant: a speech sound produced by providing stricture or obstructing the flow of air from the lungs; friction is created by restricting or blocking air from coming through the nose, lips, teeth, or throat

Consonant blends: two or more consonants in a word that make a distinct consonant sound, such as sl in sleep and scr in screech

Context clues: a strategy in which the reader closely studies the words in a sentence to determine the meaning of a particular word in a sentence

Concept of Word in Text (COW-T): the ability of a reader to match spoken words to written words while reading

Denotation: the literal and original meaning of a word, often conveyed via a word's morphemic composition

Dental: a consonant sound that is produced by obstruction or stricture to the air flow via the teeth

Derivational morpheme: word parts (affixes) that are joined (or "fixed") to a word to create a new word or a new form of a word and alter the meaning of a word

Digraph: two letters that represent one sound; examples include sh (like in shoe), ck (like in truck), or ai (like in braid)

Diphthong or ambiguous vowel: complex vowel sounds made by gliding from one vowel sound to another within the same syllable, as in joy, joust, and jaw; two vowel sounds that blend to make one vowel sound

Elaboration Strategies: comprehension strategies employed while reading to facilitate additional processing of text; includes making inferences, visualizing text, producing questions about text, and evaluating the author's message

Etymological bracket: brackets found in a dictionary at the end of a word's entry-level meanings that contain the word's morphemes and origin. For example, the etymological brackets for the word cordial would read as follows: [Middle English, of the heart, from Medieval Latin cordiālis, from Latin cor, cord-, heart; see kerd- in the Appendix of Indo-European roots.]

Etymology: the study of the origin of and change in the pronunciation, spelling, and meaning of words

Expressive language: a person communicates their wants and needs, using of words, sentences, gestures, and writing to convey meaning and messages

Fluency: the ability to read a text free from word identification problems that impede text comprehension in both silent and oral reading; includes accurate, smooth, and prosodic oral reading

Fricative: a consonant sound produced by forcing air through a narrow passage (partial obstruction) to create friction

Grammar: the rules about the way the sentences of a language are constructed and the function of each word in a sentence

Grapheme: the smallest unit in a writing system; a letter

Guttural: a consonant sound that is produced by obstruction or stricture to the air flow via the throat

Homograph: two words that have the same spelling but different pronunciations, meanings, and word origins

Homophone: two words that have the same pronunciation but different spellings, meanings, and word origins

Ideograph: a glyph or an image that represents an idea or concept, such as many Mesoamerican languages

Inflectional morpheme: a morpheme that changes the form of a word to express grammatical contrasts in sentences, such as singular/plural and present/past tense

Intensifier/intensifying prefix: a prefix that strengthens or intensifies the meaning of the root word; it often carries the meaning "very" or "thoroughly"

Intonation: changes in tone and pitch based on the meaning of the text

L-blends: a consonant blend found at the beginning of a word that ends with the letter l, such as bl, cl, sl, etc.

Labial: a consonant sound that is produced by obstruction or stricture to the air flow via the lips.

Labiodental: a consonant sound that is produced by obstruction or stricture to the air flow via the lips and teeth

Lax vowel: vowels articulated with shorter duration and a widened mouth, such as /ɪ/ (as in kit), /ʊ/ (as in foot), /ɛ/ (as in dress). Phoneticians refer to tense vowels as long vowels, which differs from reading teacher's definition of long vowels (see long vowel for the reading teacher's definition)

Lexical stress: emphasis placed on a particular syllable in a word

Liquid: a consonant sound produced by air flowing through a partial closure of the mouth; it similar to a vowel in that it takes little friction to produce the sound.

Logogram: a glyph or an image that represents an idea (by way of a word or morpheme), such as Chinese

Long vowel: (according to English orthography) a vowel that sounds like the name of the letter that represents it; for example, long a sounds like the name of the letter A, as in braid; long i sounds like the name of the letter I as in bright (see tense vowel for the phonetician's definition)

Metacognitive Strategies: comprehension strategies employed during and after reading to check one's comprehension; includes monitoring comprehension, reviewing and evaluating reading, and repairing and correcting comprehension difficulties

Morpheme: the smallest unit in language that represents meaning, such as both the word horse and the -s in horses

Morphemic analysis: the ability to identify word meanings based on affixes and roots, as well as word derivations

Morphology: a branch of grammar that studies the structure of words and the way that morphemes operate in a language

Multisyllabic: a word with two or more syllables

Nasal: a consonant sound that is produced by air flowing through the nose

Negation or negating prefix: a prefix that shows the negation or reversal of the root word's meaning (illogical meaning "not logical" or untie meaning "to loose or unfasten; cause something to not be tied")

Numerical prefix: a prefix that identifies an amount or a number with regard to the root word (as in biennial means "every two years" or triangle means "three angles")

Onset: the initial consonant sounds in a monosyllabic word (/p/ in pat, /k/ in cat, /ch/ in chat, etc.) in contrast to the rime

Organizational strategies: comprehension strategies employed during reading to organize information; includes identifying the main idea, distinguishing important details, sequencing and organizing details, and paraphrasing and summarizing text

Part of speech: eight classifications that words are divided into based on their meaning, form, and syntactic function; includes noun, verb, adjective, adverb, preposition, conjunction, and conjunction

Passive vocabulary: words that a person understands but does not actively use

Phoneme: a single sound found in a given language that does not convey complete meaning on its own

Phoneme blending: a strategy in developing phonemic awareness in which students listen to a sequence of sounds in a word and combine the sounds to form a word. Ex: A teacher asks students to blend the sounds /b/, /ā/, and /r/, and the students respond "bar."

Phoneme categorization: a strategy in developing phonemic awareness in which students recognize the word in a set of three or four that has the odd sound. Ex: A teacher asks students which word does not belong: pat, pot, or tack? Students respond tack because it does not begin with the /p/ sound.

Phoneme deletion: a strategy in developing phonemic awareness in which students recognize that removing a sound from a word creates a different word. Ex: A teacher asks students what is paint without the /t/. The students respond "pain."

Phoneme identification: a strategy in developing phonemic awareness in which students recognize the same sound in different words. Ex: A teacher asks students what sound is the same in tar, tab, and tap, and the students respond /t/.

Phoneme isolation: a strategy in developing phonemic awareness in which students identify specific phonemes in monosyllabic words (initial, medial, or final). Ex: A teacher asks students to isolate the initial sound in cat, and the students respond /k/.

Phoneme segmentation: an aspect of phonemic awareness in developing phonemic awareness in which students break a word into separate sounds and say each sound by tapping or counting them out. Ex: A teacher asks students to segment the sounds in black, and students respond saying /b/, /l/, /ā/, and /k/

Phonemic awareness: the ability to perceive and manipulate individual phonemes or sounds that make up a word

Phonics: a method of beginning reading instruction in which students learn the alphabetic code (the sound-symbol relationship between phonemes and letters) in order to decode words. See in contrast to whole language

Phonological awareness: ability to tend to and manipulate the sounds within words, including syllables, onset and rime, and phonemes

Plosive: a consonant sound produced by completely stopping or blocking air flow (complete obstruction)

Portmanteau word: blend of two words, one of which is usually shortened, to form a new word. For example liger is a blend of lion and tiger. Smog is a blend of smoke and fog.

Prefix: a morpheme (affix) that is placed before a root word to alter the root word's original meaning; for example, the prefix in the word interview is inter-, and the prefix in the word immature is im-.

Preparational Strategies: comprehension strategies employed before reading; includes previewing, activating background knowledge, making predictions, and setting the purpose for reading a text

Prepositional or directional prefix: a prefix that indicates the way, or direction, that the root travels both literally (rewind meaning 'to wind back') and figuratively (predict meaning 'to say before') In addition, prepositional prefixes can indicate a direction figuratively

Primary stress: the most emphasized syllable in a multisyllabic word

Prosodic stress: emphasis placed on a particular word or phrase when reading a passage

Prosody: to use pitch, stress, and timing to convey meaning when reading aloud; evidence that a beginning/transitional reader is making meaning of the text.

R-blends: a consonant blend that ends with the letter r, such as br, dr, tr, etc.

Reading rate: the speed at which one is able to read a text; the number of words one is able to read per minute

Receptive language: a person's ability to understand the gestures and words they see, read, and hear

Reduced vowel: a vowel in an unstressed syllable that is reduced to the schwa (/[g/) sound

Rime: the medial vowel and final consonant sound in a monosyllabic (-at in pat, cat, and chat) in contrast to the onset

Root: a morpheme in a word that carries the basic meaning; for example, the root of the word interview is view, and the root of the word running is run.

S-blends: a consonant blend that begins with the letter s, such as st, sl, sk, etc.

Schemata: units of organized knowledge about concepts (plural of schema)

Schema theory: the idea that readers rely on schemata to comprehend the text and use what they already know or background knowledge to make predictions, ask questions, and make inferences about the text

Schwa: a German sound that is not a long or short vowel, but rather, a mid-central vowel sound; often represented as /g/

Secondary stress: the second most emphasized syllable in a multisyllabic word

Semantics: the science of the meaning of words

Semi-vowel: consonant sounds that are akin to vowels in that there is little obstruction of air to produce the sound

Short vowel: (according to English orthography) a vowel that does not sound like the name of the vowel that represents it; for example, short a sounds like the vowel sound in bat; short i sounds like the vowel sound in bit (see lax vowel for the phonetician's definition)

Situational model: the theory of reading that views comprehension as a process of building mental models of the information, situations, and events depicted in the text

Stress or accent: the degree of force with which a syllable, word, or phrase is uttered

Suffix: a morpheme (affix) that is placed after a root word to alter its original meaning; for example, the suffix in the word running is -ing; concentrate is -ate

Syllabic: a system in which one letter represents an individual syllable, such as Cherokee

Syllabic analysis: the division of words into syllables for the purposes of word attack or word decoding

Syllabication: see syllabic analysis

Syllable: a unit of pronunciation having one vowel sound with or without surrounding consonants, forming the whole or part of a word

Syllable juncture: the places in which a multisyllabic word is divided

Syntax: the study of the arrangement of words and phrases to create well-formed sentences

Tense vowel: vowels articulated with greater duration and with greater narrowization of the mouth, such as /i[g/ (as in fleece), /u[g/ (as in goose), /[g[g/ (as in nurse); phoneticians refer to tense vowels as long vowels, which differ from reading teacher's definition of long vowels (see long vowel for the reading teacher's definition)

Tertiary stress: the third most emphasized syllable in a multisyllabic word

Textbase: a surface-leveled meaning of text conveyed by words and syntax

Text comprehension: making meaning of a text by actively engaging in making connections between the text and their own thinking

Tier 1 vocab: high-frequency words that often appear in oral language; they are most often learned by listening to and engaging in everyday speech; also known as 'basic, general vocabulary'

Tier 2 vocab: high-frequency words that are found in a variety of contexts and domains. These words often have multiple meanings; also known as 'descriptive vocabulary'

Tier 3 vocab: low-frequency, subject-specific words and phrases; also known as 'precision vocabulary'

Trigraph: three letters that represent one sound; examples include igh (like in light) and tch (like in watch)

Unvoiced: a consonant sound in which vocal cords are apart while air flows freely through them

Vocabulary comprehension: the ability to understand the idea(s) that a word represents.

Voiced: a consonant sound in which vocal cords vibrate as air flows, causing the air to impart a buzzing sound

Vowel: a speech sound produced without stricture or obstructing the flow of air from the lungs

Vowel length: the duration of time it takes to produce a particular vowel sound. Vowels that are longer and produced with greater narrowization are tense. Vowels pronounced with shorter duration and a widened mouth are lax

Whole language: a teaching philosophy in which emerging and early readers are exposed to whole text and are encouraged to make meaning by analyzing graphophonic, semantic, and syntactic aspects of language

Word: the smallest element in language that is able to convey complete meaning on its own

Word recognition: the ability of a reader to recognize written words correctly and virtually effortlessly

Word study: an instructional approach to spelling centered on teaching how the layers of English orthography influence word spellings and meanings. The goal is to help students develop phonemic awareness, phonics, and vocabulary skills through word analysis rather than memorization

Chapter 1: All About Words

__Rule 1 Practice 1__ phonology (3), renew (6), of (7), and schism (9) are words. un (1), re (2), f (4), and ism (8) are nonwords. In (5) and less (10) are both words and morphemes.

Rule 1 Practice 2

1. Phonology: noun
2. Renew: verb
3. Of: preposition
4. Schism: noun
5. In: preposition
6. Spa: noun
7. Relax: verb
8. Enjoyable: adjective
9. Energize: verb
10. With: preposition

Rule 2 Practice

1. 3 /f/ /ă/ /n/
2. 4 /p/ /l/ /ă/ /n/
3. 3 /ch/ /ŭ/ /m/
4. 5 /r/ /ē/ /l/ /ī/ /z/
5. 7 /r/ /ē/ /l/ /ī/ /ə/ /b/ /l/

Rule 3 Part 1 Practice 1

1. Long a /ā/
2. Short o /o/
3. Long i /i/
4. Long e /ē/
5. Short u /ŭ/
6. Diphthong /oy/
7. Schwa /ə/
8. R-influenced /er/
9. Diphthong /aw/
10. Long i /ī/

Rule 3 Part 1 Practice 2

1. Re- long e; fresh- short e
2. Bo- long o; nus- short u
3. Scar- r-influenced; let- short e
4. Ball- schwa; loon- long oo
5. Cir- r-influenced; cum- short u; fer- r-influenced; ence- short e

Rule 3 Part II Practice 1

1. G (soft)- dental
2. T- dental
3. C (hard)- guttural
4. D (soft)- dental
5. F- labiodental
6. S (/zh/)- dental
7. Ch-labiodental/dental
8. G (hard)- guttural
9. R (beginning r)- dental
10. R (final r)- guttural

Rule 3 Part 2 Practice 2

1. Feet: f is a labiodental; ee (/ē/) represents the long vowel; t is a dental
2. South: s and th are dentals; ou (/ow/) represents a vowel digraph
3. Like: l is a dental; k is a guttural; i /ī/ represents a long i sound
4. Clip: l is a dental; c (/k/) represents a guttural; p is a labial; and i /ī/ represents the short vowel
5. Flip: l is a dental; f is a labiodental; p is a labial; and i /ī/ represents the short vowel

6. Stream: s and t are dentals; m is a nasal labial; ee (/ē/) represents the long e sound vowel sound
7. Fabric: c (/k/) and r are gutturals; a /ă/ and i /ī/ are short vowels; b is a labial; f is a labiodental
8. Coffee: c (/k/) is a guttural; f and f are labiodentals; o /ŏ/ is a short vowel; ee ee (/ē/) represents the long e
9. Measure: s (/zh/) is a dental; r is a guttural; m is a labial; ea /ĕ/ represents a short vowel; ur represents an r-influenced vowel
10. Critique: c and que (/k/) are plosive gutturals; the first i (/ĭ/) represents a short vowel; the second i /ē/ represents a long e sound

Rule 4 Practice 1 answers will vary

Rule 4 Practice 2

1. Soft
2. Soft
3. Hard
4. Cy (soft); cl (soft)
5. Both c's are hard
6. Soft
7. Hard
8. Gi (soft); ga (hard)
9. Ga (hard); ge (soft)
10. Hard c; soft g

Rule 4 Practice 3

1. /ks/
2. /z/
3. /ks/
4. /ks/
5. Beginning x: /z/; final x: /ks/

Rule 4 Practice 4

1. /k/
2. /kw/
3. /k/
4. /k/
5. /kw/

Rule 4 Practice 5

1. Long e /ē/
2. ambiguous vowel/diphthong
3. Short i /ĭ/
4. Short o /ŏ/
5. Long u /ū/
6. ambiguous vowel/diphthong
7. Long o /ō/
8. Short a /ă/
9. Short e /ĕ/
10. Long /ō/
11. Ambiguous vowel
12. Long i /ī/
13. Short u /ŭ/
14. Long a /ā/
15. Ambiguous vowel

Rule 4 Practice 6

1. Hard
2. Soft
3. Soft
4. Hard
5. Soft

Rule 4 Practice 7 answers will vary

Rule 4 Practice 8

1. Digraph
2. Blend
3. Blend
4. Digraph
5. Blend

Rule 4 Practice 9

1. sc: blend; ff: digraph
2. th: digraph; gh: silent

digraph

3. tr: blend   4. tr: blend; ct: blend

5. fl: blend; sh: digraph

Rule 5 Practice 1

1. mag: closed (CVC)   2. bate: silent e (CVCe)

3. ship: closed (CCVC)   4. bri: open (V)

5. tern: r-influenced (CVr)   6. ceil: vowel team (VV)

7. stir: r-influenced (CVr)   8. cle: consonant + le (Cle)

9. phoid: diphthong (VV)   10. fi: open (V)

Rule 5 Practice 2

1. 1   2. 2 (pen-ny)

3. 1 or 2 (fi-re)   4. 2 (di-gest)

5. 1   6. 2 (knit-ted)

7. 6 (auth-or-it-ar-i-an)

8. 3 (me-an-der)   9. 3 (pi-et-y)

10. 8 (in-tel-lec-tu-al-i-za-tion)

Rule 5 Practice 3

1. 2 (awe-struck)   2. 4 (re-tract-a-ble)

3. 2 (goal-ie)   4. 2 (dis-tract)

5. 1   6. 2 (di-vide)

7. 3 (triv-i-al)   8. 3 (rack-et-eer)

9. 4 (com-tem-pla-tive)   10. 5 (dis-en-gen-u-ous)

Rule 6 Practice 1

1. mag-   short a (/ă/)   2. -take   long a (/ā/)

3. pre-   long e (/ē/)   4. lem-   short e (/ĕ/)

5. pi-   long i (/ī/)   6. -lite   long i (/ī/)

7. mu-   long u (/ū/)   8. tun-   short u (/ŭ/)

9. -void   diphthong (/oy/)

10. vow-   diphthong (/ow/)

11. pen- short e (/ĕ/)   12. le- long e (/ē/)

13. ea- long e (/ē/)   14. -pect short e (/ĕ/)

15. sus- short u (/ŭ/)

Rule 6 Practice 2

1st syllable	2nd syllable	3rd syllable
GRAND-father	Example: re-FIN-ish	10. def-in-I-tion
U-ni-form		8. re-in-VIG-or-ate
IN-val-id (noun)	1. De-MAND-ing	
	2. va-CA-tion	
	4. a-WARE-ness	
	6. in-VAL-id (adjective)	
	8. in-FLA-ted	
	9. in-FLEX-i-ble	

Extension

1. demanding   2. vacation

3. grandfather   4. awareness

5. uniform

6. invalid (adjective: not true; not to be recognized by law.

7. invalid (noun: a person that is not able to move)

8. reinvigorate   9. inflexible

10. definition

Rule 6 Practice 3

Nouns	Verbs
a- PRES-ent	b- pre-SENT
1: IN-sult	2: in-SULT
3: PRO-duce	4: pro-DUCE
5: PER-mit	6: per-MIT
8: CON-tract	7: con-TRACT
9: UP-set	10: up-SET

Rule 6 Practice 4

NORM-əl	TAR-gət	BĔT-tər	CĂP-tən
1. MĂP-əl	2. ĔX-ət	7. DŎL-lər	8. HŪ-mən
3. KOWN-səl	10. BĂS-kət		11. PER-sən
6. TRĂV-əl	13. PĬ-rət		15. DOL-Fən
14. VĬ-təl			

8. HŪN-ee (no category)   9. CHAIR-ee (no category)

Rule 7 Practice

1. PĬC-chər   2. RĀ-dē-ō

3. ĕks CLĂM   4. PŌ lər

5. THĬS-əl*   6. MAR-vəl

*The second t is silent

7. HŌM-less   8. /good/

9. MĂT-t ər   10. SŬN-sĕt

Rule 8 Practice

1. knew, new   2. mail, male   3. poll, pole

4. seller, cellar   5. mane, main   6. fur, fir

7. side, sighed   8. steal, steel   9. foul, fowl

10. mall, maul

Rule 9 Practice 1

play, stretch and internal are free morphemes.

Rule 9 Practice 2

1. slowly (slow) ly

2. bookstore (play) (store)

3. rewind (wind) re

4. interested (interest) interest

5. signature (sign) ature

Rule 9 Practice 3

door: 1 (door)

doors: 2 (door, s)

view: 1 (view)

review: 2 (re, view)

basket: 1 (basket)

interruptions: 4 (inter, rupt, (t)ion, s)

polyamorous: 4 (poly, amor, ous)

psalm: 1

irresistibility: 5 (ir, re, sist, ible, ity)

another: 2 (an, other)

<u>Rule 10 Practice 1</u>
See chart on p. 237

<u>Rule 10 Practice 2*</u>
1. symbolize: symbolic, symbology, symbolism
2. hypnotize: hypnotic, hypnotist
3. vegetation: vegetable, vegetate
4. terror: terrorize, terrify, terrible
5. personality: personal, person, personify, personage, impersonate

*This is not an exhaustive list

<u>Chapter 1 Summary and Review</u>
Summary: a thought/idea/meaning; phonemes; vowels; consonants; labials; dentals; gutturals; long; short; grapheme; syllables; morphemes/word parts; roots/base words; free morphemes/base words; bound morphemes/root words

A. Defining Key Terms
  1. word: e   2. phoneme: c
  3. grapheme: f   4. morpheme: b
  5. syllable: g   6. vowel: d
  7. consonant: i   8. labial: a
  9. dental: h   10. guttural: j

B. Count the Phonemes
  1. 6   2. 4   3. 4   4. 3   5. 5

C. Lexical Classifications *See chart on p. 237*

D. Count the Graphemes
  1. 4   2. 2   3. 1   4. 11   5. 8

E. Classify the Consonants (initial)
  1. /l/: liquid dental
  2. /d/: vibrating plosive dental
  3. /r../: liquid dental
  4. /p/: non-vibrating plosive labial
  5. /m/: nasal labiodental (or nasal labial)

F. Classify the Consonants (final)
  1. /k/: non-vibrating plosive guttural
  2. /ch/: non-vibrating fricative dental
  3. /f/: non-vibrating fricative labiodental
  4. /...r/: liquid guttural
  5. /th/: vibrating fricative dental

G. Consonant Clusters
  1. B (pl) 2. B (nk) 3. D (sh) 4. D (ck)
  5. B (str)

H. Vowel Types
  1. L (ow)   2. S (i)   3. R (ar)
  4. D (au)   5. schwa (a) 6. L (e); S (e)
  7. L (o); S (u)   8. R (ar); S (e)
  9. R (er); D (oo)
  10. R (ir); S (u); R (er); S (e)

I. Syllabification
  1. N/A (tea is a monosyllablic word)
  2. base-ball   3. bet-ter
  4. bun-dle   5. vou-cher
  6. re-flec-tion   7. pho-neme
  8. stri-dent   9. in-flam-ma-tor-y
  10. cham-pi-on

J. Stress
  1. RE (long e)   6. dle
  2. HIND (short i)   7. ble
  3. SERVE (r-influenced)   8. sel
  4. SERV (r-influenced)   9. tain
  5. noun- COM (short o);   10. tion
  adjective- PLEX (short e)

K. Homographs and Homophones
  I. Homographs
      1. suite; sweet   2. chord; cord
      3. mane; main   4. waste; waist
      5. prays; praise
  II. Homophones
      1. noun; verb   2. noun; verb
      3. verb, noun   4. noun; verb
      5. verb, noun

L. Morphemes*
1. bound; verify; clarify   2. free
3. bound; biology   4. free
5. bound; introduction

*word examples will vary

<u>Chapter 2: All About Prefixes</u>

Practice #1
1. anti   2. sub   3. un   4. con   5. re
6. trans   7. inter 8. fore   9. a   10. dis
11. a   12. fore 13. inter 14. anti   15. sub
16. con   17. un   18.trans 19. dis   20. re

Practice #2: answers will vary

Practice #3:
1. forward or forth   2. back; again
3. in   4. out
5. toward   6. back
7. between   8. forward
9. into   10. out

Practice #4: Answers will vary

Practice #5:

1. 4	2. 100	3. 8	4. 10	5. 1,000
6. half	7. many	8. 7	9. 1	10. 9
11. half	12. 6	13. twice	14. equal	15. 5
16. 5	17. 4	18. 1	19. 3	20. 1,000
21. many	22. 7			

Practice #6

1. octo (octagon)
2. 1,000 (millimeter)
3. mono (montone)
4. poly (polyglot)
5. multi (multimedia)
6. uni (unicorn)
7. du (duel)
8. tri (trisect)
9. multi or poly (multisyllabic, polysyllabic)
10. equi (equinox)
11. hemi (hemisphere)
12. semi (semicolon)
13. bi (binomial)
14. tri (trivium)
15. tetra (tetragrammaton)
16. hex (hexalogy)

Extension Activity
Practice #7

1. N	2. R	3. N	4. R	5. R
6. N	7. N	8. R	9. N	10. R

Practice #8

1. dis	2. mis	3. un	4. a	5. non
6. anti	7. il	8. ir	9. pseudo	10. contra

Practice #9: check dictionary for definitions
• Words with intensifying prefixes: resolute; comfortable; persuade; desolate

Practice #10

a. con firmation : non-intensifier
b. re plete : intensifier
c. re actionary : non-intensifier
d. com mentary : intensifier
e. convocation: non-intensifier
f. exclude: non-intensifier
g. elucidate: intensifier
h. persist: non-intensifier
i. perimeter: non-intensifier
j. declare: intensifier
k. demolish: non-intensifier

1. (b) replete	2. (c) reactionary
3. (d) commentary	4. (j) decclare
5. (e) convocation	6. (f) exclude
7. (g) elucidate	8. (i) perimeter
9. (h) persist	10. (k) demolish

Rule 1 Practice 1
• Member: dismember; remember
• Locate: dislocate; relocate
• Pose: dispose; repose; depose
• Take: mistake; retake
• Appoint: disappoint; reappoint
• Tract: subtract; protract; extract
• Stitute: substitute; prostitute; institute
• Ject: subject; project; inject; eject
• Vert: invert; will accept in(tro)vert and ex(tro)vert
• Spect: prospect; inspect; expect (ex + spect = exspect → expect)

Rule 2 Practice 1
1. re again; intro
2. dis (against/part)
3. in (not); ac
4. de (away/apart); com
5. mis (wrongly); in
6. de (away/apart); con
7. mis (wrongly); re; pre
8. ir (not); re
9. in (intensifier); sur
10. dis (not); re

Rule 2 Practice 2
1. disengage; en (into)
2. reinstate; in (into)
3. misunderstand; under (beneath or among)
4. incompatible; com (with)
5. preconception; con (with)
6. inefficient; ef (out)
7. indefinite; in (not)
8. reconvene; re (again)
9. miscommunicate; mis (wrongly)
10. inexplicable; in (not)

Rule 2 Practice 3
1. Nonconformist: one that does <u>not</u> conform to accepted beliefs, customs or practices
2. Irresponsible: <u>lacking</u> a sense of responsibility
3. Indistinguishable: <u>not</u> distinguishable; impossible to differentiate or tell apart
4. Reinstate: to bring <u>back</u> to a previous condition or position
5. Imperfect: <u>not</u> perfect
6. Decompose: to <u>reverse</u> composition (to decay or break <u>down</u>)
7. reconfigure: to arrange or shape <u>again</u>
8. Misinform: to give someone <u>wrong</u> informaton
9. Disinvite: to <u>cancel</u> or withdraw an invitation to someone
10. Represent: to present again; to stand for or symbolize something

Rule 3: Parts of Speech and their functions

Part of Speech	Function	Example	Answers The Question
noun	A word that names a person, place, thing, or idea	Brother; school; football; respect	who, what, where
pronoun	A word that used in place of a noun	He, it, she	who, what, where
adjective	A word that modifies or describes a noun or pronoun	Beautiful; red; many; few; enjoyable	what type, kind, shape, color, etc., ... how much? whose?
verb	A word that expresses action or state of being	Run; jump; am; was; were	what did he/she/it do? what is his state of being?
adverb	A word that describes or modifies a verb, an adjective, or another verb	Quickly; respectfully; surprisingly	how did he/she/it do something?
preposition	A word placed before a noun or a pronoun to form a phrase that modifies another word in a sentence	to (the store); on the way; through the storm	where, when, how, why
conjunction	A word that joins words, clauses, or phrases	And, but, because	
interjection	A word that is used to express emotion	Wow! Oh! Oops!	

Rule 3 Practice 1

1. befriend   2. throne   3. enrich
4. wake, awake   5. aback, back

Rule 4 Practice 1: answers below are for column 1; answers for columns 2 and 3 will vary.

Word	Prefix + Meaning	Word Example 1	Word Example 2	Word Example 3
synonym	syn: together	symmetry	syllable	syncopate
eject	e: out	excellent	efficient	eccentric
invite	in: in, into	encourage	embark	import
obtain	ob: against or toward	occur	opportunity	offensive
except	ex: out	eloquent	eclipse	effect
illegitimate	il: not	irresponsible	immature	inactive
suffice	suf: below; under	substandard	surreal	succor
sympathy	sym: together	syndicate	syllogistc	symbol
oppose	op: against or toward	obliterate	occult	offer
accept	ac: toward	adverse	arrange	affect

Rule 4 Practice 2

1. supplant   2. compassion   3. accustom
4. attempt   5. ascertain

Rule 4 Practice 3

1. Immeasurable; not able to be measured
2. Allocate; to place toward
3. Implausible; not plausible or possible
4. Eccentric; out of the center or norm
5. Symmetalism; putting two or more metals together
6. Irresponsible; not responsible
7. Indescribable; not able to be described
8. Suppress; to press down or below; to hold back
9. Illogical; not logical
10. Immobile; not able to be mobile or moved

Chapter 2 Summary and Review

Summary: Number; preposition; negation; intensifier; three; beginning or initial; assimilated

Review:
1. a   2. a, b, c   3. F
4. T   5. intensifier

Identifying, Classifying, and Defining Prefix(es) in a Word

Column 1	Column 2	Column 3	Column 4
delete	le	———	away
trigonometry	ri	#	three
antidote	..nti	———	against
biceps	bi	#	two
deplete	le	———	away
preponderance	pre	p	before
quadrant	uad	#	four
innovation	in	i	in, into
misinterpret	-----, inter	___, P	wrongly, between
convert	con	p	with
polyglot	poly	#	many
subconscious	sub, con	P,P	below; under
reexamine	re	p	back; again
transliterate	trans	p	across
disavow	dis	-----	against
unilateral	uni	#	one
centennial	cent	#	one hundred
duodecimal	duo	#	two
intermediary	inter	p	between
pentameter	penta	#	five
septennial	sept	#	seven

Words in Context: Fill-in-the-Blank

1. five (quint) 2. non/not (a)
3. to (af) 4. many (multi)
5. one (mon, mono) 6. after (post)
7. over/on top (super) 8. before (fore)
9. not (non) 10. equal (equi)
11. half (semi) 12. four (tetra)
13. six (hexa) 14. nine (nona)
15. eight (octa) 16. not (un)
17. ten (deca) 18. between (inter)
19. across (trans) 20. below (under)

Prefix Derivations

Tract: contract, retract; detract; attract; extract
1. detracts 2. extract 3. retract

Flect, flex: reflect; deflect; inflect; inflexible; biflect
1. deflect 2. inflections 3. biflex

Vert: invert; subvert; divert; advert; revert
1. divert 2. reverted 3. subvert

Sect: trisect; bisect; intersect; dissect; transect
1. transects 2. trisected 3. intersects

Gress: congress; digress; progress; regress; egress
1. egress 2. congress 3. progress

Spelling Practice

1. suspend (sub → sus) 2. support (sub → sup)
3. collusion (con → col)
4. corroborate (con → cor)
5. illicit (in → il) 6. ignore (in → i)
7. allusion (ad → al) 8. aggrandize (ad → ag)
9. evoke (ex → e) 10. effulgent (ex → ef)

Intensifier

1. re fine 2. com posure
3. con script 4. de finite
5. cor rect 6. per plex
7. e spouse 8. ob tain
9. occasion 10. con sideration

Chapter 3: All About Roots

Root	Meaning	Example 1	Example 2	Example 3
act, ag. igu	drive, go, move	action, agitate, ambiguous	transact	agenda
anim	breath, mind	animation	examine	unanimous animosity
anthrop(o)	human	anthropology	misanthrope	anthropopithecus
aqu, aqua	water	aquatic	aquarium	subaqueous
astro/aster	star	astronomy, asterisk	astrology	astronaut
audi	hear	auditory	audit	aquamarine audience
bio	life	biology	biography	antibiotic
cap, capt, cept	take, seize, get	capture; intercept	captivate	caption
chron(o)	time	chronology	chronicle	synchronize
clude, clus	shut, close	exclusive	recluse	seclude
corp	body	corporation	corpse	incorporate
cred	trust, believe	incredible	credulous	credit
dict	to speak or say	dictionary	dictate	indicate
duc, duce, duct	draw	reduce	abduct	introduce
fac(t), fec(t)	to make, to do	factory, affect	manufacture	facile
flect, flex	to bend	reflect, flexible	inflection	deflect
gen, gener	kind, type or produce (birth)	genealogy; generation	gender	gene
geo, gee	earth	geography	geology	geography geometry
graph	write	autograph	paragraph	biography geography
ject	to throw	rejection	inject	projectile
leg, lex	law, to bind	legal	lexicon	legislature

Rule 1 Practice 1

1. bene dict ion 2. ag itator 3. privi leg e
4. im port ant 5. in duc ement 6. per miss ion
7. dis sent 8. path o log y* 9. con tend er
10. circum scribe 11. magn anim ous
12. ana chron istic 13. theo cracy* or theo crac y
14. sent iment 15. di vis ion 16. apo gee
17. act uary 18. pro gen y 19. eu log y
20. dis aster

Rule 1 Practice 2

Words	Roots
indigenous-	gen
audition-	audi
inclusive-	clus
credential-	cred
indictment-	dict
affectionate-	fect
synchronize-	chron
transmission-	miss
animosity-	anim
antibiotics-	bio

Rule 2 Practice 1

1. ~~anthro~~pomorph~~ic~~
morph, form or anthropo, human
2. ~~sus~~ (s)pect spect, see
3. aqu ~~eous~~ aqu, water
4. ~~ad~~ ject ~~ive~~ ject, throw
5. ~~habeas~~ corp ~~us~~ corp, body
6. flex ~~or~~ flex, bend
7. cap ~~sule~~ cap(t), take or seize
8. ~~in~~ vis ~~ible~~ vis, look or see
9. graph~~olog~~ ~~y~~ graph, write; log, word
10. ~~mono~~ the ~~istic~~ the(o), deity

Rule 2 Practice 2

1. <u>bio</u> logy, <u>anthropo</u> logy　　2. mono <u>logue</u>
3. pro <u>duc</u> tion　　　　　4. de <u>flect</u> ed
5. sym <u>path</u> y　　6. <u>corp</u> oration
7. re <u>tent</u> ion　　8. re <u>clus</u> ive
9. <u>specul</u> ate　　10. juris <u>dict</u> ion

Rule 3 Practice 1

Word	Root	Example 1	Example 2	Example 3
defective	fect	*fiction*	*faction*	artificial
station	stat	re<u>sist</u>	Constitution	
reporter	port	<u>port</u>folio	<u>eupho</u>ria	
urgent	urg	<u>emerg</u>ency	dis<u>org</u>anized	
specify	spec	micro<u>scop</u>ic	incon<u>spic</u>uous	
generation	gener	<u>nativ</u>ity	<u>kind</u>ergarten	
provide	vid	ad<u>vis</u>or	e<u>vid</u>ence	
captor	capt	de<u>ceiv</u>e	in<u>cept</u>ion	

~~fiction, faction~~	portfolio	inception
nativity	euphoria	microscopic
resist	evidence	advisor
deceive	emergency	kindergarten
disorganized	Constitution	inconspicuous

Rule 3 Practice 2

1. vide (provide)　　2. vise (revise)
3. gene (genealogy)　　4. nat (international)
5. spic (inconspicuous)　　6. spec (circumspect)
7. scop (helioscope)　　8. fac (factitious)
9. fic (efficient)　　10. fy (magni)

Rule 3 Practice 3

Word	Root	Root Meaning	Definition
nativity	nat	birth	*
concept	cept	take or seize	g
unstable	sta	stand	f
introspection	spect	see	j
liquefaction	fact	make or do	h
miscegenation	gen	birth, kind, or produce	i
capstan	capt	take or seize	c
prefecture	fect	make or do	b
stethoscope	scope	see	a
desist	sist	stand	d
renascence	nasc	birth	e

Chapter 3 Summary and Review

Summary: basic; one; forms; to hold

Identify the Root

animadvert	anim: breath or mind
conscription	script: to write
lexicographer	graph: to write
tenacious	ten: to hold
provisional	vis: to see

Fill-in-the-Blank 1

geology: the earth (geo)　biopsy: living (bio)
genuflect: bend (flect)　portly: carry (port)
insensate: feeling (sens)

Match the Definition

Word	Root	Definition
counteract	act; move or go	*
equanimity	anim; breath or mind	a
relegate	leg; law or bind (by word)	f
anthropomorphic	anthropo; man morph; shape or form	e
disport	port; carry	g
retention	tent; hold or stretch	h
inflection	flect; bend	c
envisage	vis; see	j
sentient	sent; feeling	i
biotic	bio; life	d
circumscribe	scribe; write	b

Complete the Sentence

1. equanimity　　2. disport
3. circumscribe　　4. inflection
5. biotic　　6. retention
7. anthropomorphic　　8. relegate
9. sentient　　10. envisage

Chapter 4: All About Suffixes

Rule 1 Practice Identify the suffixes of the following words

Word	Suffix	Example
goodness	ness	happiness, mildness, openness
lovable	able	huggable, reliable, notable
hopeful	ful	joyful, baleful,
hopeless	less	penniless, harmful, spoonful*
selfish	ish	bluish, babyish, british**
selfless	less	see above*
friendly	ly	readily, happily, joyfully
friendship	ship	kinship, relationship, workmanship
childish	ish	see above**
childhood	hood	neighborhood, likelihood, priesthood
instruction	(t)ion	constitution, vacation, indication
instructor	or	realtor, monitor, doctor
empathetic	etic	phonetic, magnetic, athletic
empathize	ize	energize, realize, fossilize

Rule 2 Practice

1. rhetorical　　2. unlawfully
3. kindness　　4. mangnify

5. lovable
6. empathizes
7. quality
8. childlike; childish
9. nationality, nationalism
10. friendship, friendliness

Rule 3 Practice 1

Word	Suffix(es)	Part of Speech
internationally	ion, al, ly	adverb
responsibility	ible, ity / ible	noun
nationalism	al, ism	noun
friendliness	ly, ness	noun
respectfully	ful, ly	adverb
creativity	tiv(e), ity	noun
truthfulness	ful, ness	noun
peacefully	ful, ly	adverb
victoriously	ous, ly	adverb
instantaneously	an, eous, ly	adverb
regulatory	at(e), or, y	noun

Rule 4 Practice

Word + Suffix	New Word	Rule
Run + er	Runner	C
Beg + ar	Beggar	C
Cat + y	Catty	C
Execute + ive	Executive	B
Preside + ent	President	B
Pole + ar	Polar	B
Muse + ic	Music	B
Pure + ify	Purify	B
Hope + ing	Hoping	B
Office + er	Officer	B
Hop + ing	Hopping	C
Rectify + able	Rectify	A
Lug + age	Luggage	C
Convene + tion	Convention	B
Likely + hood	Likelihood	A
Glory + ous	Glorious	A
Busy + est	Busiest	A
Commit + ee	Committee	D
Delegate + (t)ion	Delegation	B
Fancy + ly	fancily	A
Note + ify	notify	B
Rate + ify	ratify	B
Artifice + ial	artificial	B
Simply + city	simplicity	A
Lyre + ist	lyricist	B
Seize +ure	seizure	B
Multiple + y + cation	multiplication	A, B
Haste +y + ly	hastily	A, B
Wit + y + ly	wittily	C, A

Rule 4 Practice 2

1. artificial (artificial ly)
2. artificially (artifice + al + ly)
3. inspired (inspir ation + e)
4. inspiration (inspir e + ation)
5. motionless (motion + less)
6. beauty (beaut ifulness + y)
7. restless (restless ness)

8. baggage (bag +[g]age)
9. patiently (patient + ly)
10. atone (atone ment)

Rule 5 Practice 1

A. Nouns: *oid, let, ling, ette, cule/cle/ule*
- grumbling (grumbl e + ling)
- tabloid (tabl et +oid)
- cubicle (cube + cle)
- rosette (ros e + ette)
- springlet (spring + let)

B. Nouns: *cion/sion/tion, ancy/ency/cy, ness, ism, ment*
- gentleness (gentl e + ness)
- altruism (altrui st + ism)
- agency (ag enct + cy)
- convention (convene + tion)
- movement (mov e + ment)

C. Nouns: *ar/er/or, ician, ist, ee*
- Metaphysician (metaphys ics + ician)
- conductor (conduct + or)
- botanist (botan y + ist)
- inductee (induct + ee)
- aesthetician (aesthet ics + ician)

D. Adjectives: *ic/itic, ive, ful, less, ar/ular*
- hopeful (hope + ful)
- spectacular (spectac le + ular)
- conducive (conduct +ive)
- spineless (spine + less)
- harmonic (harmon y + ic)

E. adjectives: *esque, able/ible, ory, al/ical/eal*
- predictable (predict + able)
- fluorescent (fluor ide + escent)
- picturesque (picture +esque)
- mandatory (mandat e + ory)
- magical (magic + al)

F. Verbs: *ate, fy/ify, ize/ise*
- Realize (real + ize)
- Qualify (quali ty + ify)
- Validate (valid + ate)
- Equalize (equal + ize)
  or equate (equ al + ate)
- Liquify (liqu id + ify)
  or liquidate (liqu id + ate)

Rule 5 Practice 2

percept
- perceptual
- perception
- perceive
- perceptible
- perceptive

vivid
- vivacity or vivaciousness
- vivacious
- vividly
- vivaciousness or vivacity

· vivaciously

prescript

· prescriptibility
· prescribe
· prescriptibile
· prescription
· prescriptive

tension

· tenable
· tenant
· tenacity
· tenacious
· tentative

substance

· substantial
· substandard
· substantiate
· substantive
· substantially

Rule 6 Practice 1:

1. similar + ity= similarity (BS)
2. refer + ee= referee (SS)
3. general + ize= generalize (NC)
4. astronomy + ical= astronomical (BS)
5. fulfill + ment= fulfillment (NC)

Rule 6 Practice 2:

1: No Change	2: Move Stress-Before Suffix	3: Move Stress-Onto Suffix
national beautiful	indication	revelation Chinese racketeer

Chapter 4 Summary and Review

Summary: end; part of speech; verb; noun; three; one who; the state of

Review:

Suffix Rules: Multiple Choice and True/False

1. C   2. B   3. F   4. T   5. Stress

Identifying, Classifying and Defining Suffix(es) in a Word

Word(4)	Suffix(es) (2)	Type of Suffix/Part of Speech (3)	Suffix Meaning (4)
anim**ate**	ate	V	to make
belligerency	ency	N	the quality of being
conversationalist	ation, al, ist	N	one who
anthropomorphize	ize	V	to make
religiously	ious, ly	ADV	in the manner (of)
strategic	ic	ADJ	dealing with
grotesque	esque	ADJ	-styled
solarium	arium	N	place
diversify	ify	V	to make
accommodate	ate	V	to cause or make
ineluctable	able	ADJ	capable of
native	ive	ADJ	having a tendency
miraculously	ous, ly	ADV	in the manner of
nationalize	al, ize	V	to make
boorish	ish	ADJ	like
knowledgeably	abl(e), ly	ADV	in the manner of
suffragette	ette	N	small thing
respectfully	ful, ly	ADV	in the manner of
inculpate	ate	V	to make or cause
nationally	tion, al, ly	ADV	in the manner of
cubicle	icle	N	like

Words in Context: Fill-in-the-Blank

1. belief in
2. to make
3. to make; to make
4. without
5. full of/having
6. makes
7. to make; to make
8. a person/one who
9. state of being (ity)
10. becoming
11. able to/capable of
12. the state of
13. an expert
14. full of
15. to make

Spelling Practice

Nouns: *ment, mony, ness, ship, ure*
- government (govern + ment)
- scholarship (scholar + ship)
- holiness (hol y + i + ness)
- acridness (acrid + ity)
- culture (cult + ure)

Adjectives: *al, esque, ic, ish, ory*
- majestic (majest y + ic)
- digital (digit + al)
- sensory (sens e + ory)
- statuesque (statu e + esque)
- knavish (knav e + ish)

Verbs: *ate, fy/ify, ize/ise*
- Codify (cod e + ify)
- Fabricate (fabric + ate)
- Digitize (digit + ize)
- Vivify (vivi d + fy)
- Invalidate (invalid + ate)

Adverbs: *ly, ically*
- maturely (mature + ly)
- Probably (probabl + l y)*
- Politically (political + ly)**
- Wholly (whol e + ly)
- civilly (civil + ly)

Suffix
Derivations

1. empath
    a. empathize   b. empathetically
    c. empathetic   d. empathy
    e. empathize
2. hydra
    a. hydrate   b. hydrated
    c. hydration   d. hydrant
    e. hydrator
3. litigate
    a. litigant   b. litigating
    c. litigator   d. litigatible
    e. litigation
4. respond
    a. responder   b. respondent
    c. responsive   d. responsible
    e. responsibility

Chapter 5: All About Word Parts - Putting It All Together

Prefix			Root	Suffix		
3P	2P	1P	0	1S	2S	3S
			sta	(a)ble		
		super	vise			
		post	script			
		re	ceiv(e)able			
	re	con	stit	ute		
	in	con	ceiv(e)able			
		aque	duct			
		re	anim	ate		
		en	vis	(s)ion		
		bene	dict	(t)ion		

Prefix			Root	Suffix		
3P	2P	1P	0	1S	2S	3S
		de	port	ment		
		sub	ject			
		sym	bio	sis		
		a	path	y		
		dis	ject	(t)ion		
		de	leg	ate		
		de	port	ee		
			port	age		
			leg	al	ity	
		ex	path	ic		
			leg	al	ize	
	auto	bio	graph	er		
		ab	ject			
		anti	bio	tic		
		psycho	path	ic		

Rule 1 Practice 1:
1. deportment (l)   2. subject (g)
3. symbiosis (h)   4. apathy (n)
5. disjection (a)   6. delegate (o)
7. deportee (m)   8. portage (j)
9. legality (i)   10. exopathic (b)
11. legalize (k)   12. autobiographer* (d)
13. abject (c)   14. antibiotic (f)
15. psychopathic (e)

Rule 1 Practice 2 *See on p. 237*

Rule 2 Practice

Word	Prefix(es)	ROOT (JUST ONE!)	Meaning
genealogy	gene- birth/kind/origin	log- word, study, science	a
thermometer	therm	meter	h
tensiometer	tensio	meter	c
vociferous	voci	fer	k
hydroscope	hydro	scope	g
thermostat	thermo	stat	j
theopathy	theo	path	d
philologist	philo	log	e
pathology	path	log	i
liquefaction	lique	fact	b
animadvert	anim, ad	vert	f

Rule 3 Practice
1. native (1)   2. postnatal (6)
3. inadmissible (9)   4. supervise (4)
5. interventionist (7)   6. nativity (2)
7. rationalize (3)   8. imperfect (5)
9. denationalize (8)   10. inconsistently (10)
11. illegalization (11)

Rule 4 Practice 1

Word	Denotation	Connotation
generous	a	l
speculate	e	q
spectacular	f	s
special	d	o
habeus corpus	g	v
portfolio	b	n
animosity	h	m
manumission	c	t
emotion	k	u
provisional	j	p
nationality	i	r

Rule 4 Practice 2 — Use the words above to complete the sentences below.
1. generous   2. animosity
3. nationality   4. manumission
5. speculate   6. portfolio
7. special   8. provisional

9. habeas corpus   10. spectacular
11. emotion

Chapter 4 Summary and Review

Summary : prefixes; roots; suffixes; define;
denotation; connotation

Roots Focus Set act/ag, anim, anthro, aqua

Definitions

1. g	2. i	3. h	4. c	5. j	6. d
7. l	8. e	9. k	10. a	11.f	12. b

Sentences

1. subaqueous   2. proactive
3. agile   4. misanthrope
5. philanthropic   6. nonaquatic
7. magnanimous   8. animalcule
9. aquastat   10.activate
11.reanimate   12.anthropoid

Roots Focus Set bio, aster/astr, aud, cap(t)/cept

Definitions

1. i	2. j	3. f	4. b	5. l	6. k
7. d	8. c	9. a	10.g	11.h	12.e

Sentences

1. captor   2. asterisk
3. atral   4. antibiotic
5. interception   6. audiology
7. astrology   8. audience
9. amphibious   10. biopsy
11.receptacle   12.inaudible

Roots Focus Set cred, chron, clud/clus, corp

Definitions

1. c	2. i	3. f	4. j	5. k	6. d
7. g	8. l	9. b	10. a	11. h	12. e

Sentences

1. corporeal   2. seclusion
3. corporation   4. credulous
5. incorporate   6. anachronism
7. credibility   8. discredit
9. exclusive; include   10. chronometer
11.chronology

Root Focus Set dic(t), duc(t), fac/fic/fec, flec(t)

Definitions

1. j	2. i	3. f	4. e	5. l	6. d

7. a	8. b	9. g	10. k	11. h	12. c

Sentences

1. deflect   2. biflex
3. verdict   4. abduction
5. reflective   6. inducement
7. fictitious   8. benefactor
9. contradiction   10. aqueduct
11. infectious   12. benediction

Root Focus Set graph, gee/geo, gen, ject

Definition

1. e	2. h	3. c	4. a	5. f	6. k
7. l	8. d	9. b	10. g	11. i	12. j

Sentences

1. geocentric   2. apogee
3. choreograph   4. interject, interjection
5. geocentric   6. photogenic
7. reject   8. monograph
9. heterogeneous   10. subject
11. genocide   12. graphology

Root Focus Set lex/leg/log, meter, miss/mit, opt

Definitions

1. f	2. i	3. e	4. h	5. c
6. j	7. g	8. b	9. d	10. l
11. k	12. a			

Sentences

1. eulogy   2. prologue
3. thermometer   4. optometry
5. remission   6. promissory
7. lexical   8. neologism
9. privilege   10. emit
11. legislation   12. perimeter

Roots Focus Set sta(t)/stas/stain, spec(t), ten(d), therm

1. e	2. g	3. i	4. j	5. l
6. d	7. c	8. a	9. b	10. k
11. h	12. f			

Sentences

1. scriptorium   2. sensible
3. deportee   4. consensus
5. transportation   6. apathy
7. circumscribe   8. portfolio
9. sympathy   10. sensitive
11. psychopathy   12. postscript

Roots Focus Set <u>path, port, scrib/scrip(t), sens</u>

Definitions

1. b 2. a 3. h 4. e 5. j
6. l 7. k 8. g 9. d 10. c
11. i 12. f

Sentences

1. tenacious
2. abstain
3. theologian
4. thermometer
5. pantheon
6. retrospective
7. thermostat
8. specimen
9. tension
10. monotheism
11. thermos
12. spectator

Chapter 6: All About Word Origins

Rule 1 Practice
E, A, C, D, B

Rule 3 Practice 1
1. C 2. B 3. A 4. C

Rule 3 Practice 2

Germanic	Greek	Latin
today	antithesis	contrary
king	baptize	identical
meal	pandemic	malefactor
hoof	philanthropic	tenacious
lady	cosmogony	conviction
	podium	contrary

Rule 4 Practice

Word	Origin	Original Word	Word Meaning
consider	Latin	considerare	to address the stars, lit "with the stars"
sophisticated	Greek	sophistikos	of or pertaining to a wise man
teach	Old English	tǣcan	to declare, show, demonstrate; point out

almanac*	Coptic; Greek; Latin	almenachiakon	calendar
hallelujah	Hebrew	*hallelūyāh*	to praise (*hēllsl*) Yaweh (*Yah*)
monolith	Greek	*monolithos*	consisting of a single stone
alkaline*	Arabic; Greek	*alkai + -ine*	Pertaining to (*-ine*) ashes (*alkai, al-qaliy*)
bagel*	Middle High German; Yiddish	*beygel*	Ring-shaped hard bread roll
moose	Natick	*moos*	hoofed mammal with large flat antlers
expulsion	Latin	*expel (expellere) + sion*	The act (*ion*) of driving (*ex*) out (*pel*)
quartz	West Slavic, German	*kwardy, quarz*	hard rock to grasp
avocado	Nahuatl	*Ahuacatl*	testicle (because of the shape of the fruit)
nice	Latin	*nescire*	not (*ne*) knowledgable (*scire*); ignorant
plunder	Middle Dutch or Frisian	*Plunderen* or *plunderje*	to rob of clothes and household goods
cider	Hebrew	*shēkār*	a strong drink
subterranean	Latin	*subterraneus*	Under (*sub-*) ground (*terraneus*)
odd	Old Norse	*oddi*	literally "point of land, angle", referring to pointy, unleveled things; additional number
hurricane	Carib (Kar'nja), Spanish, Portuguese	*huaracan, furacan*	wind
sofa	Hebrew, Arabic	*sapāh, suffah*	carpet, divan

Rule 5 Practice 1
1. key/board 2. fire/fly 3. make/up 4. note/book
5. day/dream 6. head/line 7. head/first 8. stomach/ache
9. view/point 10. whirl/wind

Rule 5 Practice 2
1. milestone: a stone set up on the side of the road to mark a mile; event marking an important stage in development
2. icebreaker: a ship designed to break ice in a channel; something that services to relieve tension between two people or start a conversation
3. drawback: a disadvantage or a problem; something that holds back access
4. wallpaper: vertical strips of paper pasted on the wall to provide a decorative or textured surface
5. pigeonhole: a small recess or hole where pigeons nest; to be placed in an overly restrictive category

Rule 5 Practice 3
1. brunch 2. motel 3. spork
4. blog 5. skort 6. vitamin
7. emoticon 8. malware 9. hazmat
10. Pokémon

Rule 5 Practice 4
1. *alphanumerics*= alpha + numerics
2. paratrooper= parachute + trooper
3. infomercial= information + commercial
4. multiplex= multiple + complex
5. Eurasia= Europe + Asia
6. mathlete= mathematics + athlete
7. sitcom= situational + comedy
8. redox= reduction + oxidation
9. Comcast= Communication + Broadcast
10. sheeple= sheep + people
11. telemarket= telephone + market

Rule 5 Practice 5

Basic Compound Words
backpack
football
layman
forklift
sharecropper
hindsight

Portmanteau/Blended Words
moped (motor + pedal)
bash (bang + dash)
webinar (website + seminar)
podcast (iPod + broadcast)
televangelist (television + evangelist)
camcorder (camera + recorder)

Chapter 6 Summary and Review

Summary- Germanic; Greek and Latin; exploration and colonization; compound; portmanteau; blended

Review

A. Which is a word?

1. (meter)
2. ex
3. (ball)
4. (I)
5. b

B. Germanic, Latin and Greek Sort

Germanic	Latin	Greek
tomorrow	maternity	biography
mother	legal	myriad
law	cow	microcosm
beef	vitality	orthodox

C. Origin of Words

safari	Arabic
savanna	Taino
pet	Old English
jubilee	Hebrew
ebony	Egyptian
caucus	Algonquin (indigenous American)
cashier	Old French
magazine	Arabic
tycoon	Mandarin
guru	Sanskrit

D. Building Compound Words

1. earthquake
2. drawbridge
3. crosswalk
4. timeline
5. cardboard
6. longhouse
7. passport
8. turnkey
9. bedspread
10. snowbank
11. foothill

E. Defining Compound Words

1. lifeguard: an expert swimmer that attends to a body of a water and saves swimmers in danger; someone that guards the life of another
2. pancake: a thin cake of batter fried on a pan or a griddle in oil or butter
3. ballroom: a large room used for dances or balls
4. watermelon: a large melon -like* fruit with a hard green rind red, sweet, watery pulp
5. scapegoat: a person blamed for the wrongdoings of others; derived from the Jewish custom of symbolically laying the sins of the people on a goat and sending it out into the wilderness to escape (free oneself) from the sin

*Note: watermelon is not a melon at all, it is a part of the gourd family with squash and cucumber

F. Portmanteau Words: Creating Portmanteau Words

1. internet
2. Velcro
3. cyborg
4. Brexit
5. botox
6. Gerrymander
7. Tanzania
8. Beetles
9. ethanol
10. endorphins

G. Dividing Portmanteau Words

1. Jazzercise= jazz + exercise
2. urinalysis= urine + analysis
3. workaholic= work + alcoholic
4. affluenza= affluent + ~~in~~fluenza
5. docudrama= documentary + drama
6. biopic= biographical + picture
7. newscast= news + broadcast
8. electrocute = electrical + execute
9. blog (short for weblog) = ~~web~~ + blog
10. Microsoft= microcomputer + software

Rule 10 Practice 1

Word	Inflected Ending	Derivational Ending*
sun	suns, sun's, suns'	Sunset, sunrise, sunglasses, sunflower, sundress, sunbathe, sunburn, sunlight
carry	carries, carried, carrying, carries	carrier
trust (n.)	trust's, trusts', trusts	trustee, trustor, trustworth, distrust, trusty, mistrust, antitrust, rustless, entrust
trust (v.)	trusts, trusted, trusting	See above
front		forefront, frontrunner, frontal, confront, affront, effrontery, frontier, frontage, frontman, frontlet, storefront, riverfront, frontwards, lakefront, breakfront, beachfront, housefront, upfront, refront
tract	tracts, tract's, tracts'	Distract, retract, tractor, subtract, contract, attract, attractive, contract, contraction, intractable, protracted, abstract, abstraction
insist	insists, insisted, instisting	insistence, insistent, insistently
organ	organs, organ's, organs'	organic, organize, reorganize, organelle, organism, disorganized, organization, organizable, inorganic
calculate	calculates, calculated, calculating	miscalculate, recalculate, calculator
repay	repays, repaid, repaying	repayment

C. Lexical Classifications

Word	Lemma	Lexical Unit
impeaching	impeach	-ing
reacted	react	-ed
shape's	shape	-'s
tallest	tall	-est
roasts	roast	-s

Rule 1 Practice 2

1. deportment
2. subject
3. apathy
4. disjection
5. delegate
6. portage
7. deportee
8. legality
9. exopathic
10. psychopathic
11. legalized
12. autobiograph (remove the su??x -y)
13. abject
14. antibiotic
15. symbiosis

Pre-Test

1. b
2. c
3. d
4. a
5. a
6. **Lexemes**: do, trace, pen
   Lexical units: doesn't, does, redo, did; tracing; pen pa, pen name, penknife, penned
7. **Free morphemes**: class, ??ip, try, mount, recent
   Bound morphemes: gener, un, ??d, pro
8. True
9.

Word	Vowels	Consonants	Phonemes	Graphemes	Morphemes	Syllables
mislead	2	4	6	7	2	2
scale	1	3	4	5	1	1
graphic	2	4	6	7	2	2

10. b
11. d
12. a
13. c
14. diaper: d, r
    gargle: g, r, l
    chop: none
15. vapor: p
    teach: t
    shake: k
16. tiger: open
    bishop: closed
    little: consonant + le
17. wife: Old English
    solar: Latin
    psychopath: Greek
18.

Word	Prefix + meaning	Root + meaning	Suffix + POS
interdict	inter- between	inter- between	N/A
repair	re- back	fract- pull	N/A
malefactor	mal- bad	fract- do, make	or- one who
verify	N/A	vert- truth	ify- to make
asteroid	N/A	aster- star	oid- a little

Post-Test

1. b
2. c
3. d
4. a
5. a
6. **Lexemes**: sprinkle; access
   Lexical units: sprinkled, sprinkling, sprinkler, sprinkles; accessorize, accessed, accessory, accessing
7. **Free morphemes**: mint, tract, cry, ??ne, trine, in
   Bound morphemes: ment, fract, ly, in (like inactive or inside)
8. True
9. Latin

10.

Word	Vowels	Consonants	Phonemes	Graphemes	Morphemes	Syllables
sleep	1	3	4	5	1	1
shell	1	2	3	5	1	1
mash	1	2	3	4	1	1
test	1	3	4	4	1	1
refraction	3	6	9	10	3	3

11. b

12. a

13. b

14. c

15. bin: b, n
    melt: m, l
    ring: r, n, g

16. jump: p
    castle: c (/k/)
    flee: none

17. dip**per**: r-influenced
    sni**per**: open
    bub**ble**: consonant + le

18. testify: Latin
    umbrella: Latin
    admiral: Arabic

19.

Word	Prefix + meaning	Root + meaning	Suffix + POS
interdict	*inter-* between	*inter-* between	N/A
repair	*re-* back	*fract-* pull	N/A
malefactor	*mal-* bad	*fract-* do, make	*or-* one who
verify	N/A	*vert-* truth	*ify-* to make
asteroid	N/A	*aster-* star	*oid-* a little
ingenious	*in-* intensifier	*gen-* kind, race	*ious-* adjective ending
inclusion	*in-* inside	*clus-* to close	*ion-* noun ending
untenable	*un-* not	*ten-* to hold or stretch	*ify-* able to
important	*in-* intensifier	*port-* to carry	*ant-* adjective ending
intercontinental	*inter-* between *con-* with	*ten-* to hold or stretch	*ent, al-* adjective ending

Made in the USA
Middletown, DE
07 January 2023

19682139R00135